Bull Session

Other Books By Terry Pluto:

Tark with Jerry Tarkanian
You Could Argue, But You'd Be Wrong with Pete Franklin
Forty-Eight Minutes: A Night in the Life of the NBA with
    Bob Ryan
Sixty-One with Tony Kubek
Baseball Winter with Jeff Neuman
Weaver On Strategy with Earl Weaver
The Earl of Baltimore
The Greatest Summer

Bull Session

An up-close look
at MICHAEL JORDAN
and courtside stories
about the Chicago Bulls

Johnny Kerr
Terry Pluto

Bonus Books, Inc., Chicago

93   92   91   90   89   5   4   3   2   1

International Standard Book Number: 0-929387-01-5
Library of Congress 89-61556

Bonus Books, Inc.
160 East Illinois Street
Chicago, Illinois 60611

Printed in the United States of America

This book is dedicated to my Number 1 draft choice, Betsy, who has a no cut contract and the six players in the deal who were to be named later, John, Ed, Matt, Bill, Essie and Jim.

—Johnny Kerr

To Susan Gorsky.

—Terry Pluto

Contents

The Best Job In The World

I have the best job in basketball because I get to watch Michael Jordan for free at least 82 times a year. I have to admit that Michael brings out the fan in me when he takes off and does one of those dunks that only he could have imagined, much less pulled off.

There has been a point in every game Michael Jordan has played where I find myself leaping out of my seat. Remember, I'm sitting there at the press table, wearing headphones and I'm wired up, almost as if I'm connected to a switchboard. One false move and my brains will be fried zucchini.

So it's the players who are supposed to be jumping around, not the announcer at the table. Then Michael takes the ball, sticks out his tongue and just soars. It seems like he'll never come down and then *boom!*, he's slamming it over a couple of 7-footers.

That's when I lose it. I'm yelling, I'm on my feet, I'm almost crazy.

And the thing is that I've seen great players all my life. I played against guys who are in the Hall of Fame—Jerry West, Elgin Baylor, Oscar Robertson, just about everyone. I was with

the Virginia Squires when Julius Erving came into pro basketball and he was jumping and dunking like no one ever had before.

But no one I've ever seen affects me like Michael Jordan.

I find myself acting like the guys on the NBA's Fan-tastic
commercials. I want to touch someone, slap hands or give them
a friendly punch in the arm. Michael does that to everybody. I
don't care if you're a Bulls fan or a Bulls hater, you are destined
to like Michael Jordan. I remember when we were playing the
Clippers in Los Angeles and Michael stole the ball. He had about
60 feet of open court in front of him when one of the Clippers
players grabbed him from behind. The 11,000 fans went nuts.
They were booing their own player because they wanted to see
Michael dunk. It is that way in every arena in the NBA. The
fans may want their own team to win, but they want Michael
to have a great game and to give them at least one move that
they can spend the next day telling their friends about.

Everybody gets a kick out of watching Michael play. No one
talks about the fact that he signed a new $25 million contract
and that he makes who knows if its another $25 million in com-
mercial endorsements off the court. The guy is a corporation, but
that doesn't matter to the fans. That is because on the court,
Michael is their dream. He plays the way we think we would
if we had his extraordinary talent—he plays hard all the time,
he loves the game, and I'm talking about every game, every
night. What Michael Jordan conveys to us is the sheer joy I've
always felt from watching and playing basketball. That's why
when Michael slams one, we want to touch the guy next to us
and say, "Look at him. . . ain't he something?" We love to see
Michael Jordan because he loves basketball as much as we do.

One day Michael and I were sitting in the dressing room and
he said to me, "I try to enjoy every game I play. I don't think
it's right to look at this as a job. To me, basketball has never
been a job. At a job, you don't have fans cheering for you, waiting for you to do something on the court. Just because you're
getting paid doesn't make it a job."

Often it seems like Michael and Magic Johnson are the only
two guys who really relish playing in the NBA. Too many guys
talk about "doing my job," and I think they lose something when
they think like that. For the players, these are the greatest
moments of their lives. Some people find it amazing that Michael

will stop at a playground and get into a game with some guys off the street or just maybe just shoot around. But that doesn't surprise me or anyone who knows Michael. He lives for the game. He plays it for millions of dollars with the Bulls and he plays it for nothing back home in North Carolina. That part of Michael's personality really turns on the fans and it gets me going.

Basketball is show-biz and Michael is a headliner. The Bulls games are his concerts. No one says "I saw Horace Grant" or "I saw Dave Corzine." It's "I saw Michael." He appeals to fans of Michael Jackson, Bruce Springsteen, Willie Nelson and U2. Did you know that Willie Nelson's sister plays the piano at his concerts? Do you care? I mean, she may be a great piano player, but it doesn't matter. Willie is the show. For the casual basketball fan, Michael is the show and the other guys are his band. When Michael comes on the floor and Chicago Stadium is packed and they turn off the lights for the introduction and turn up the music, my blood starts pumping and I begin to sweat a little. I've seen every one of Michael's games with the Bulls, but I can't wait to see the next one.

Bulls play-by-play man Jim Durham and I have a promotional tape where for about 30 seconds you see Michael doing his stuff. Durham says things like, "Michael down the side, takes a jumper and scores. . . Michael in the lane, to the basket, he jams it."

After about three of those plays, I'm yelling over Jimmy.

What am I saying?

"Oh. . . Oh. . . Oh!"

That's it.

Real insightful commentary from the former coach and player.

Other times, I'll give you, "I just can't believe Michael. . . "

Suddenly I don't know what to say.

Can't believe what?

I'm not sure. I guess I just can't believe that Michael was being Michael again. He has literally taken my breath away with one of his moves. I'm so excited that I don't know what's coming out of my mouth. It's just sounds.

When Michael hit a shot at the buzzer to beat Cleveland in the playoffs, all I could do was scream "Bulls win!" over and over.

Sometimes, I say, "If you're watching this game on television with us, then you know what Michael just did. If you're listening on the radio, then just take my word for it, that was a great play."

Even when you see what Michael does, you're not always sure what he did because it happened so fast.

There was a game in New York where Chicago's point guard Sam Vincent lobbed a pass to Michael. The second Vincent released the ball, I said, "Oh no!" I thought the pass was going over the backboard. But Michael hit the afterburners and he did his rocket-man act as he caught the pass and slammed it through the rim. As he was coming down, the Knicks' Mark Jackson whacked Michael, which knocked Michael off balance. Michael grabbed the rim so he wouldn't come down wrong, but his feet were swinging all over the place and he kicked 7-footer New York center Pat Ewing in the mouth.

It wasn't intentional and Ewing didn't get mad. But I was just wondering what Ewing would have said if his mother asked him where he got that bruise on his chin. Would he say, "Well, Mom, I got kicked in the mouth by Michael Jordan, who was hanging on the rim."

Like Ewing, a lot of NBA players can give you a very detailed description of the bottom of Michael's Nikes.

Michael is the most electrifying player I have ever seen, and he also is one of the most fascinating people I've known, because of his unique background and lifestyle. Not only has no basketball player ever played the game quite like Michael Jordan, no basketball player has had a life quite like Michael.

————————●

You know there is something special about Michael when you see his family. He is the only one over 5-foot-9.

I mean, there's Michael at 6-foot-6 and everyone else is smaller than the average guy. When I mentioned this to Michael's father, James Jordan laughed.

"I can't explain it," said James Jordan.

When I looked at James, I saw a miniature version of his son. His lean build is almost identical to Michael's. One look at James' face and you know he's Michael's father. The smiles are the same. James is bald, Michael is getting there.

But James Jordan is 5-foot-8 . . . maybe . . . and he's the big man in Michael's family.

One night I was sitting next to James Jordan on an Air-West charter flight out of Boston's Logan Airport. The Bulls had just lost to the Celtics in Boston Garden and we were taking a flight back to Chicago because we had a home game with Cleveland the next day.

James sometimes travels with his son. That is unusual in the NBA, but Michael and his father are very close. Michael has a real need to be near people he knows and trusts because he has reached such a star status that he is constantly being approached by strangers. His fans just want to meet him, but others are after his money, wanting him to go into business with them and who knows what else.

When I see Michael with his father, I can tell that Michael feels comfortable just knowing that his dad is near. It's not like they walk hand-in-hand through the airport or anything. Sometimes, James slips so far into the background that you don't even know he's there. James knows that Michael's friends are his teammates and other people his age. There is a difference in the generations. Michael doesn't talk that much about his father. But the fact that James Jordan sometimes travels with Michael really does say a lot about their relationship. If Michael didn't want him around, I know James wouldn't be there.

On that night we were just a couple of fathers talking about our children. He reminded me of how I feel about all my children—proud of them, proud that these wonderful people actually somehow came from me. James spent a lot of time talking about their life in Wilmington, a coastal North Carolina town of 50,000 people. Unlike a lot of NBA players, Michael didn't come from the ghetto. He didn't come from a broken home. His parents were determined people. They believed in the American Dream. They worked hard, they made sure their kids stayed straight and they taught their kids values. Maybe all that sounds like a cliche, but look at Michael and look at the family. Somebody did something right.

James told me that he was 25 when Michael was born. Michael was their third of what would become five children.

"The family was from Wilmington, but Michael was born in Brooklyn [N.Y.]," said James.

He and his wife, Delores, had left North Carolina so James

could attend night school in Brooklyn. He studied hydraulics so he could become a mechanic specializing in automatic transmissions. During the day, James paid the bills by driving a truck. After he finished school, the family went back to Wilmington. Because the world has changed so much, especially in the South during the last 30 years, I find it hard to imagine what it must have been like for James Jordan raising a family in the 1950s and 1960s. He and Delores were children of sharecroppers. This was before Martin Luther King, back when the South was a place that was separate and unequal for blacks.

In many ways, the Jordan family is the American Dream. James went from being a mechanic to a fork-lift driver to a dispatcher to a supervisor at General Electric; blue collar to white collar, a guy on the line to a guy in charge. Delores went from a drive-in bank teller at a branch of the United Carolina bank to the head of the customer relations department at the bank's main office; just another face in a crowd to the one face that the bank wanted the public to see.

The Jordans also built their own house virtually from scratch, James doing most of the work. Their home is south of Wilmington, not far from the Intracoastal Waterway. It's a brick split-level with a small porch, a two-car garage and a nice backyard shaded with tall Carolina pines. Wilmington is a historic town, but the Jordan's home is in the newer suburbs. If you walk through downtown Wilmington, you can go blind from reading all of the historical markers. The only sign near the Jordan home is in front of the Arab Shrine Club, about a half-mile away. It says, "STATE SALT WORKS: The state of North Carolina, to relieve a wartime scarcity, operated a salt works from here to Myrtle Grove Sound in 1861–64." In other words, this was the site of a salt mine during the Civil War. Big deal. The point I'm making is that Michael's neighborhood is middle America. It really is a two-car garage and a chicken in every pot because his parents worked hard to make it that way.

What James really wanted to tell me about wasn't his struggles, but his children.

"When each of my children were old enough, I got them a car," said James. "Michael was the most mischievous of the kids. He was a daredevil so he probably got a car later than any of the five kids. His first car was a 1977 Pontiac Grand Prix and he was a sophomore in college when I bought it for him. The reason was that Michael had a problem with a motorcycle that we bought him when he was 13. We gave him the bike and told him all the rules for riding it safely. In our yard was a big drainage ditch and I told him not to ride the motorcycle near the ditch. Probably telling Michael that was just asking for trouble, but I was worried he'd ride the thing into the trench and get hurt.

"One day I came home from work and the kids were out back with the motorcycle. They would race the bike right up to the ditch, then slam on the brakes and kick dirt all over the place near the bank. I watched for about 20 minutes and made sure that they weren't going to do something stupid like try to jump the ditch with the bike. I went and changed my clothes and then sat down in front of the television set. I sat down and started to watch the news and then it dawned on me that I hadn't heard the motorcycle for a while. A few minutes later, I heard some real heavy footsteps on the steps outside—bam, bam, bam. I called for Michael, but he was gone or something. Then I called Larry, Michael's older brother.

"Larry stuck his head around the corner.

"I asked, 'What's wrong?'

" 'Nothing,' said Larry.

" 'Then how come you're hiding your arm behind your back?' I asked.

" 'It's nothing,' said Larry.

" 'Come here and let me see,' I said.

"Larry came around and showed me his arm. His hand was all bloody.

" 'I'm not hurt,' said Larry.

" 'Then what's that?' I asked, pointing at his arm.

" 'Michael tried to jump that ditch on the motorcycle and it tipped over on him and he got all skinned up. I had to help him out of the ditch,' said Larry.

"So it was Michael's blood on Larry's arm. It turned out that Michael was okay, just cut and bruised. The next day, the boys came to me and said, 'Daddy, maybe you should sell that motorcycle.' Michael was really scared by what happened. So I sold it and bought the boys ten-speed bikes.

"I guess I should have known that there would be an accident in the ditch. Michael was always like that—always testing us, his parents. If we told him the stove was hot, don't touch. He'd touch it. If there was a Wet Paint sign, he'd touch the paint to see if it really was wet. All the kids had chores and sometimes Michael would get into one of his moods and purposely mess them up. That used to drive us crazy. He'd end up spending more time listening to us telling him what he did wrong and how to do it right. . .you see, he knew how to do it and he would have been better off just getting it done so he could go out in the yard and play ball. One time I found out that he was taking his allowance money and paying other kids to do his chores. That really got to me."

Michael's brothers and sisters all had part-time jobs cutting and chopping tobacco, but Michael went one day to do it and strained his back. He refused to go to the tobacco fields again and his parents let it pass because they could see that this just wasn't going to work for Michael.

James Jordan told me how he built his sons a basketball court in the backyard.

"At first, it was just a half-court but we kept having more kids over to the house so we made it a full-court," he said. "I liked having the kids around the house so I knew what they were doing. Since we had a big yard, it was easy for me to make them a court. Instead of having just our three boys playing, soon we'd have 15–20 kids from the neighborhood at our house. Michael first started playing against Larry, who was only 5-foot-7. Back then, Larry was a little taller and much stronger than Michael, who was still in grade school. Anyway, Larry would beat Michael unmercifully. As Michael got older, he got bigger and the games became much closer. That's when the fights started. As long as Larry would beat Michael, everything was okay. Larry would brag about it and while Michael didn't like it, he let it pass. Michael just kept practicing. Then Michael started beating Larry, and they'd end up rolling on the ground and one of us would have to go out there and break it up. The next day, they'd be on the court again, playing like nothing happened.

"Now Larry was a very good player. Like I said, he was 5-foot-7, but he could dunk. Actually, Michael was able to dunk before Larry because Michael was taller, but Larry kept working at it and working at it and then he could dunk, too."

So Michael isn't the only Jordan who can jump.

"I'm very serious when I say that Larry might be the best basketball player in the family," said James Jordan. "He just doesn't have the size, but he can shoot and really handle the ball. Another difference is that the game seemed to come more naturally to Michael, but both boys were dedicated. It was fun to watch them play on the same team in the pick-up games. They were fiercely loyal to each other. A couple of hours before, they would have been almost killing each other in 1-on-1, now they were ready to take on the world. I guess it's like that in most tight families.

"An interesting thing about Michael is that he always was very strict about the rules. He didn't make up his own rules, he wanted to 'play by the book.' That's what he'd say. The kids would be playing stick baseball in the yard and maybe they'd have only four on a side, so they'd want to make up special rules about where you could hit the ball and all that. Michael would say, 'Wait a minute, the book says . . .' and he always knew the rules. If you were playing a game to 21 points with Michael and got tired and wanted to quit, Michael would make you play to 21 because that was the rule."

James Jordan talked about his neighborhood, "about a dozen families and everyone had kids. Most of the kids were playing little league or something with sports. The parents took turns driving the kids to and from games and practices. It was really special, everyone seemed to look after everyone else's kids."

That was when the Jordan family first began traveling to Michael's games. It continued at Laney High in Wilmington, where Larry was a very fine player. Larry wore number 45. When it came time for Michael to pick a number, he took 23 because it was about half his brother's number. Michael was 5-foot-9 when he was a freshman.

"He was maybe a better baseball player than basketball player," said James Jordan. "He was a good pitcher in little league and threw a number of no-hitters. When Michael was 12, his little league team won the North Carolina state championship. He was always pushing himself. We thought it would be better for him to play with kids his own age, but about every time I looked in the yard he was playing ball against bigger, older kids. He told me that he didn't like to play kids he knew he could beat, so he wanted to face the older guys."

Listening to James Jordan talk about his son, it was clear that he never imagined that Michael Jordan would become *Michael Jordan*. The family went to Larry and Michael's games because that's what families did.

The sign in front of Michael's high school reads: EMSLEY A. LANEY HIGH, Home Port of the Buccaneers. It is on Route 132, a little north of Wilmington and about ten miles from Michael's home. The gym is small—14 rows of bleacher seats on each side meaning it probably seats about 700. The main baskets have glass backboards, but the four side backboards are wooden and a couple of the rims are bent. Could those be the survivors of some early Jordan dunks? Even if that's not the case, it's nice to think so. Against one wall of the gym is a 30-foot picture—not of Michael Jordan, but of a huge buccaneer.

In fact, there are very few signs that Michael Jordan attended Laney. Most of the trophies on display aren't for basketball, but for cheerleading. There is a small picture of Michael in a North Carolina uniform and above it is his Laney blue and yellow No. 23 jersey folded up in about a one-foot by one-foot square, but nowhere does it identify the jersey or the picture as Michael. Guess you're just supposed to know who it is. Michael's name appears in only one place—on a plaque that says "E.A. Laney H.S. Division II Champs, 1980–81." His name is among the names of all the other players on the team and it is simply, "MIKE JORDAN."

When Michael was a sophomore in high school, he tried out for the varsity and was cut. He was 5-foot-11 at the time. Some people have made it sound as if Michael didn't play at all that year, but he was on the junior varsity team and averaged about 25 points a game. He wanted to be called up to the varsity at the end of the season, but that didn't happen. He did go to the regional tournament with the varsity, but that was because Michael filled in for the team manager who was sick. Michael also remembers that his parents were in the stands for this state playoff game and all they got to see was him hand out towels.

It was strange. It was Leroy Smith who was promoted to varsity instead of Michael. Michael will never forget the name because Leroy Smith has come to symbolize Michael's one basketball failure. Occasionally, people will say, "I know who you are, but I can't think of your name." Michael will smile at them and say, "Leroy Smith."

Then he laughs as people scratch their heads.

"Michael was very determined after his sophomore year," said James Jordan. "He kept working and he kept growing. He was about 6-foot-3 as a junior and that's when he really started to play well."

Sometimes, Michael spent too much time in the gym and not enough in the classroom. James and Delores were told that their son was cutting class to practice his jumper. A word from James and a paddle to the butt from Delores put an end to Michael as a truant. But it didn't put an end to Michael's extra practice. During his senior year, he was at the gym at six in the morning where he would practice with his high school coach. In the evenings, he would play Larry, who once played with the Chicago franchise in the under 6-foot-5 World Basketball League.

"Parents always worry that their kids might get in trouble," said James Jordan. "I knew for a fact that in Michael's last two years of high school, a couple kids on the team were smoking marijuana. But Michael and our other children weren't interested. A couple of kids in our neighborhood had gotten messed up on drugs and I think that made an impact on our children. They stayed away from the stuff. Now I know that Michael would sometimes sneak a beer here and there, but it was nothing serious. We were there—at the practices, at the games—and the kids stayed close to the house. We knew what was going on and we could head off trouble that way."

One of the courses Michael took in high school was home economics.

"I wanted to learn how to cook and clean and sew and all that," said Michael. "I figured no girl would ever want to marry me and I didn't know if I'd have enough money to eat out."

Guess what?

Michael Jordan can afford to eat out. He even can find a date if he wants one, although he is still single. My wife, Betsy, saw a segment on television about Michael at his Chicago home and it showed him ironing his clothes and dusting his furniture. The only thing missing was an apron and he could have been Felix in "The Odd Couple."

"All the mothers should tape this and show it to their sons

who want to grow up to be like Michael Jordan," Betsy told me.

So maybe that home economics class did come in handy, but my guess was that one of the reasons he took home economics in the first place was to get dates. You had to like the boy-girl ratio in a class like that if you happened to be Michael.

As his senior year began, Michael was nearly 6-foot-6. He had been outstanding at several high-profile summer basketball camps and every major college coach in the country knew about Michael Jordan.

"I was a North Carolina State fan as a kid," Michael once told me. "David Thompson was my idol."

Thompson was N.C. State's 6-foot-5 guard in the middle 1970s who led the Wolfpack to a national title in 1975. He was a raw Michael Jordan, a guy who could run and really jump. But Thompson was an inconsistent player and eventually had drug problems. Of course, when Michael was a David Thompson fan, Thompson was dunking as no one in college had ever dunked before.

"I wanted to stay close to home to be near my family," said Michael. "I visited both N.C. State and North Carolina [at Chapel Hill]. Once I saw the campus at Chapel Hill, I just fell in love with the place. It was really something with all those pine trees. I went there on a recruiting trip and another time on my own, just so I could see the place as a regular student would. No one knew I was coming and I liked it even better the second time."

In fact, Michael would also say that his friends in Wilmington expected him to go away to Chapel Hill and sort of slip into a black hole, become lost on the bench and no one would ever hear of him again. Michael liked the idea of proving them wrong. It was a Leroy Smith situation all over again. This told me a lot about Michael. He didn't just become an astute businessman after college; he always had a practical streak I'm convinced he picked up from his family and the competitive streak you find in any great athlete.

James and Delores Jordan missed only one game in Michael's three years at North Carolina.

"My parents and my brothers and sisters went everywhere with our North Carolina team," Michael said. "Even when we played in Greece and Hawaii, my father went. I was glad that they made enough money so they could travel with me. It meant a lot to everyone for them to be there."

James Jordan told me: "I was just happy that Michael went to school in the Carolinas. He was very impressed by (N.C. State coach) Jim Valvano. Also, Michael did try to emulate David Thompson, especially how David used to leap. I remember seeing Michael in the yard, practicing the kind of dunks he saw Thompson do on television. But there was something he felt about North Carolina . . . he never exactly said what it was. I do think it had something to do with the players they had. Michael once said that guys like James Worthy, Sam Perkins and Buzz Peterson were a lot like the people in our family. He said they all felt like brothers."

I think that the University of North Carolina was the perfect place for Michael. It put him in a winning system and a team system. When a team is coached by Dean Smith, no individual— no matter how great the player—dominates the offense. Michael likes to tell people that during his freshman year his job was to carry the film projector to and from team meetings. It didn't matter that Michael had gone out and scored 30 points the night before against Duke, the next day he hauled around the projector and took orders from the seniors, and I mean all the seniors, even the guys on the end of the bench. That's how Dean Smith does it.

North Carolina is one of those unique situations, almost like John Wooden's UCLA program in the 1960s and 1970s. Nevada-Las Vegas Coach Jerry Tarkanian once said that "schools like North Carolina don't recruit, they draft." Every year about ten high school All-Americans try to get in. North Carolina doesn't have to gamble on kids. They don't have to take chances on kids who are the wrong size or head cases or have single-digit SAT scores. If a five-star camp is the highest level a high school kid can reach in the summer, then North Carolina is like a ten-star camp. Rather than the kid looking over the school on a recruiting trip, it's the North Carolina coaches who are judging the kid, deciding if he will fit into the program.

Just consider some of the guys who have come out of there— Billy Cunningham, James Worthy, Sam Perkins, Walter Davis, Brad Daugherty, Kenny Smith and Michael Jordan.

When a pro coach gets a kid from North Carolina, you don't

hear him complain that the kid lacks fundamentals. You won't hear a coach call a North Carolina kid, "a project." When Dean Smith sends a player to the pros, he's a finished product, both on and off the court. North Carolina kids have paid their dues when they get to the NBA. So when Michael went to North Carolina, he wasn't going to be bigger than the program. Dean Smith's job wasn't going to depend upon how Michael played. North Carolina was already established as a great program and Smith was already known as a great coach. If Michael took a dumb shot or loafed on defense, Dean Smith had the option of putting Michael's butt on the bench and then bringing another high school All-American into the game. Michael couldn't get away with just trying to score his 25 points and coasting. In fact, Dean Smith made Michael into a complete player. He made him pass to the big guys, he made Michael dig in and play defense and he made him really think about what he was doing on the floor.

It may sound elementary, but so many college players are lost in their first pro camps. They don't know the terminology. The NBA coach says, "watch the backscreen . . . double down and then rotate."

The college kid nods but he's really thinking, "What language is this guy talking? The only back screen I know about is on my porch."

That wasn't the case with Michael or anyone else from North Carolina. It was like Michael took a Ph.D. course in basketball taught by Dr. Dean Smith. One of the jokes told by NBA scouts is that only one man held Michael under 20 points, and that man was Dean Smith. The implication is that Dean didn't let Michael loose, didn't let him be *Michael Jordan.* In his three years at North Carolina, Michael averaged 17.7 points and only took 13 shots a game. That took real discipline. Remember that Michael Jordan hit the shot at the end of the Georgetown game to win a national title for North Carolina, and that happened in Michael's freshman year. In his next two seasons, he was the College Player of the Year. Yet he played within the system and his ego stayed under control. That is a tribute to both Michael and North Carolina.

Dean Smith tells a revealing story about Michael. Smith told Michael that Michael had received an invitation to try out for the 1983 United States Pan American team. Smith thought that Michael would be excited, but he seemed a bit quiet and sort of confused.

"I don't know if I'm good enough," said Michael.

Smith and Jordan talked about some of the other premier college players that year, and Michael continued to say that he thought a number of those guys were better players than him. Finally, Smith told Michael, "Believe me, you're good enough. You should go."

This wasn't false modesty at work. At this juncture in his career, Michael needed Dean Smith to reassure him that he belonged among the elite. It also may have been the last time his confidence required a boost.

Michael played under one of the greatest coaches ever to draw up a play. He learned the hard part of basketball and was forced to do the things coaches love but players hate, such as defense and not forcing shots. For Michael, the most entertaining games were in the summer when the North Carolina alumni returned to Chapel Hill and played pick-up with the current North Carolina players. That's what Michael does now during the summer, he goes back to school and plays ball. During the season, you'll see the Lakers and Bulls playing and James Worthy and Michael will be talking about some game they had last August in Chapel Hill. I don't know of any other group of athletes closer to their college coach than the North Carolina guys are to Dean Smith. In those pick-up games, the alumni take the court first. Then the current players are used, ranking from the seniors down to the freshman. In other words, a North Carolina freshman might have to sit for two hours in hope of getting into a 45-minute game. Then if he loses, he sits for two more hours.

Michael sat. James Worthy sat. They all did. Now when they return to Chapel Hill, they play while the latest group of phenoms sits.

The other reason I like North Carolina's program is that they work with their kids in the classroom. Virtually all of them graduate. They take speech courses so they can deal with the media. They are made to wear suits and ties on the road. On Sundays, they go to church. They come out of that place with an education and a sense of public relations.

Michael was on track to graduate with a B average in his

major of geography when he declared for the 1984 NBA draft. Really, there wasn't anything left for him to accomplish at North Carolina after three years. He was one of the few cases where coming out of school early wasn't going to be a mistake.

Michael
Hits
Chicago

The 1983–84 season was just another long day at the office for everyone associated with the Bulls. The team had a 27–55 record. The starting lineup was Ennis Whatley and Quintin Dailey in the back court, Dave Corzine at center and David Greenwood and Orlando Woolridge as forwards. A player I always liked—Reggie Theus—also was on that team for much of the year, but it didn't matter what I thought about Reggie since Coach Kevin Loughery didn't like him. More importantly, Loughery kept Theus and his 20 point average on the bench until the 6-foot-7 guard was traded to Kansas City for Steve Johnson.

This was the condition of the Bulls as the 1984 college draft approached. Chicago had the third selection. No. 1 belonged to Houston and the second pick was property of Portland.

From the Bulls' perspective, handicapping this draft was easy. Everyone knew that Houston would take Akeem Olajuwon, a 7-foot center from the University of Houston. Akeem was the best center in college basketball, and you always, always, always take a guy who has a chance to become a great pivot man in the NBA. That's exactly what Portland was thinking when it came time for the Blazers to make the second pick. The Blazers thought they had to choose either Kentucky's 7-foot Sam Bowie or Michael. Bowie had tremendous skills in the middle. But he also missed about half of his college career because of stress fractures in his legs. That was scary. But the Blazers already had Clyde Drexler, a guy they thought was a Jordan-like guard. Portland's center was Mychal Thompson, 6-foot-9 and better suited to be a power forward. Like about every other team in basketball, Portland wanted a big guy. Bowie was a big guy and a very good one when he wasn't hobbling around on crutches so Portland took him. Unfortunately, he has spent even more time in the NBA on crutches than he did at Kentucky.

That made it easy for Bulls general manager Rod Thorn, who used the third pick on Michael.

It is interesting to look back and ask a couple of what-ifs:

• What if Portland had known that Bowie's leg wouldn't hold up and drafted Michael?

• What if the Bulls then took Bowie and ended up with all his medical bills?

• What if the Bulls had decided that since Michael was a guard and no guard had ever turned around a franchise, maybe they should draft big. In the NBA, the thinking is that a team would rather make a mistake on a big guy than on a guard. So what if the Bulls decided to draft the next available big guy instead of Michael? Well, the fourth player taken was Sam Perkins, Jordan's North Carolina teammate. But the lanky 6-foot-9 Perkins was never viewed as a center. Let's say the Bulls wanted a center in 1984. Then their pick would have been Melvin Turpin, also from Kentucky. Could you imagine where the Bulls would be today if they had Dinner Bell Mel instead of Michael? I don't want to think about it, especially since Turpin was a 300-pound back-up center in Utah and now plays in Spain.

There are a lot of ifs. In 1979, the Bulls lost the coin flip for the No. 1 choice in the draft to the Los Angeles Lakers. The Lakers took Magic Johnson, the Bulls went for David Greenwood. It was like a repeat of the Kareem Abdul-Jabbar—Neal Walk situation in the 1969 draft.

I do wonder what the Bulls would have done with the second pick in 1984. Suppose Olajuwon went first, then it was the Bulls' turn to pick. The choice would have been Bowie or Jordan. As always, the Bulls needed a center. Bowie came from a high-profile program at Kentucky. He had the stress fractures earlier in his career that had cost him two full college seasons. But Bowie did play in every game during his senior year and *appeared* healthy. There also was no question that Bowie was a terrific talent. Also, Michael was an underclassman. Various surveys have shown that 70 percent of the players who leave college early for the pros don't last more than two seasons. So you might ask if maybe Michael could use another year of seasoning.

Anyway, that is just a hypothetical situation, one the Bulls never faced, because Bulls' general manager Rod Thorn was sold on Michael.

Right after Michael was drafted, Thorn told us, "Michael is a very good offensive player, but not an overpowering one. He is not the kind of guy who will single-handedly turn around the franchise and I'd never ask him to do that."

Looking back at the draft, here's how Thorn sized up the situation:

"From the moment Michael indicated he was going into the draft after his junior season, we were very, very interested. To us, the key wasn't Houston. The Rockets had the first pick and all along they said they would take Akeem. In fact, Akeem was the only player we had rated ahead of Michael. If he slipped to third, we would draft Akeem. But otherwise, if Michael was there, we would take him. The only other player we gave just a cursory thought to drafting was Michael's teammate at North Carolina, Sam Perkins. Sam was 6-foot-9 and he had quite a bit of ability, but we didn't think about him seriously. I can say that we never would have taken Sam Bowie. I was very concerned about Sam's legs. Frankly, I was afraid to gamble on an injured player because I got burned in 1980 when I took Ronnie Lester. I loved Ronnie as a player and thought he was a terrific kid, but he suffered a serious knee injury at Iowa and no matter how hard he rehabilitated, he could never get back to his old form. So I was afraid of Bowie's legs, I never did give any real thought to Charles Barkley (who went fifth to Philadelphia) or to Turpin (sixth to Cleveland via a trade with Washington). So from a psychological standpoint, I couldn't take another chance on an injured player. For me to take that risk again, I'd have had to thought Bowie was a super-superstar. I thought Bowie would be good, but not so great that it was worth gambling on his legs.

"What I was doing was sweating out Portland. The Blazers really liked Michael and I worried that they would take him with the second pick. From the start, I loved Michael. I won't claim to think that he'd become what he is now—a player with his greatness. I had watched Michael at North Carolina and with the Olympic team and I thought he was extraordinary. We were intent on drafting him. It's strange, we never even had a formal interview with Michael. I felt I knew Michael from just watching him play. I have a good relationship with Coach Smith, and he was extremely high on Michael, not just as a player, but as a person. Hey, at North Carolina Michael was 6-foot-6, could jump over the moon and he was a pretty good shooter. Not as good as he is now, but he could hit from the outside. After the Olympics, Bobby Knight proclaimed Michael a 'great, great player,' and we know that Bobby doesn't throw around praise like that. The coach from Italy said Michael was the greatest player he had ever seen."

As for Michael, he was somewhat surprised that he was drafted by the Bulls.

"I thought I was going to Philadelphia (which had the fifth pick)," Michael told me. "I knew that Chicago was coming off a losing season and about the only players on the team whom I really was familiar with were Corzine and Quintin Dailey. My basic impression of the Bulls was that it was a team in the dumps."

There was nothing basic about Michael's impression, it was a bull's-eye.

While Thorn was trying to take the pressure off Michael and talking about Michael working his way in and how the fans shouldn't expect too much, too soon, the Bulls' marketing department was giving off a different signal.

There was an advertising campaign with the Bulls claiming to be a "Whole New Breed." There also were television and newspaper advertisements featuring shots of Michael under the heading, "Here Comes Mr. Jordan. . .His first starring role since the Olympics." The advertisement said that Jordan would be playing in Chicago for "41 nights only."

Despite Thorn's words, the expectations for Michael were high. As a freshman, he made the shot that won a national title for North Carolina. He was a two-time College Player of the Year. In 1984, he led the U.S. Olympic team to a gold medal. Now he was supposed to make the Bulls a whole new breed and he had yet to arrive in town.

I remember going to training camp on Michael's third day and I asked (Coach) Kevin Loughery what he thought.

"I believed that Michael was really good when we drafted him and now I know he's better," Loughery said. "If I put him with the starters, they win. If I put him with the second team, they win. If I put him on the offensive team, it seems that his team always scores. When I put him on the defensive team, they about always stop the offensive team. No matter what I do with Michael, his team wins."

The Bulls knew they had something, but none of us exactly knew what. There was no talk about Michael being Rookie of the Year, averaging close to 30 points or anything like that. All we could be sure of was that the Bulls had drafted a very good player. Only the marketing department was building Michael up as being great.

In the back of my mind, I was asking myself if Michael could make a big difference. As I mentioned, I was a Reggie Theus fan and Reggie was a fine pro guard, but we couldn't win with Reggie. It was the old thing about guards not being the answer when it comes to making a loser into a winner. Even by the end of training camp when the coaches and players were first starting to put the word "unbelievable" next to Michael's name, no one ever dreamed he would become *Michael Jordan* as we know him now.

———●

"They should have hung a halo atop Chicago Stadium Friday night because this was no basketball game. It was a revival meeting. Step aside Elmer Gantry. Shut down Billy Sunday. The Bulls have been saved."

That was the lead of a game story written by Jim O'Donnell in the Arlington Heights (Illinois) Herald.

This was Michael Jordan's first game with the Bulls, a game where he had 16 points, a game where he shot only 5-for-16 from the field and had six rebounds and five turnovers.

In other words, it was a typical rookie game, but O'Donnell's story reflected the public's expectations of Michael.

The Bulls beat Washington 109–93 on October 26, 1984. Their leading scorers were Orlando Woolridge (28 points) and Quintin Dailey (25). But it was Jordan who dominated the story we were told:

• Exactly 21 seconds went by before Jordan took his first shot, an 18-footer that banged against the back of the rim.

• Exactly 54 seconds elapsed before he made his first NBA steal, taking the ball away from the Bullets' Frank Johnson.

• It was at 7:27 of the first quarter when Jordan made his first NBA field goal, a 12-foot banker from the right side.

No mention was made of when Michael took his first sip of water as a pro, but you get the idea. As O'Donnell wrote, "No one was denying the fact that the celestial Mr. Jordan had alleviated the spiritual malaise plaguing the team for much of the past three seasons."

What immediately impressed me about Michael was how he attacked the basket. Michael and Atlanta's Dominique Wilkins are the most vicious offensive players in NBA history. By that, I mean that they don't just drive to the basket, or even jump, they *explode*. Everything, even their double-pump moves where they drive under the basket for a reverse lay-up, is still a power move because it is executed with such authority. Vicious is a term reserved for defensive players who try to make you into a piece of tile when they block your shot. Michael showed me that he could go to the basket with a vengeance that is almost frightening.

I'd watch Michael get the ball around the free throw line, his tongue would come out of his mouth and I knew what was going to happen. He'd look at the rim like it was a guy who had just killed his mother. His stare was almost like he was threatening the basket. Then Michael would go to the rim and *pow*, it was like it was a punching bag and he wanted to knock it over. And Michael didn't just dunk, he dunked over people as if they weren't there. It was the intensity Michael showed that told me he would be something special.

Michael had 37 points in his third pro game and 45 in his eighth. In 10 of his first 15 starts, Michael scored at least 25. The Bulls had averaged 6,365 fans before Michael and attendance had doubled. On the road, sellouts were common and Michael was constantly being interviewed.

But Michael was not a complete player. About all he did was drive. Teams played off of him and he had a hard time making that wide open 18-footer. Sometimes, he lacked confidence and passed up the open outside shot. If any defender tried to play up on Michael, he was dead meat. Michael could drive around anyone, any time. But his lack of an outside game bothered me.

One of the problems was that Michael had very little help. His point guard was Ennis Whatley, whom I considered a crummy carpenter. By that, I mean he was one of those guys who always had all the tools but for some reason, he just didn't work out. He was a player who would tease you. He looked like a point guard, but he didn't play like one. The back-up point guard was Wes Matthews and he was lucky to be that. The other shooting guard was Quintin Dailey with all his personal problems. Orlando Woolridge could score from the small forward spot, Dave Corzine worked hard in the middle and the power forward was a revolving door.

Michael led this team in rebounding, and that tells you all you need to know. When a guard is the leading rebounder, the team is in trouble.

Kevin Loughery was not the ideal coach for Michael. I like Kevin, but I don't have much respect for him as a coach. I didn't think he prepared the team well for games. His style was to scream a lot, and that gets old, especially on the pro level. I remember a game at Golden State where Kevin took Michael out early and then didn't use him again. After the game, Kevin said something like, "Well, I got caught up in a situation and time just flew and I didn't get Michael back in."

So people also accused Kevin of doing some strange coaching things (such as keeping Michael on the bench for too long) near the end of the season so that the Bulls would play Milwaukee instead of Boston in the first round of the playoffs. One of the writers did a story saying "The Bulls are taking a two-lane highway to the playoffs," only he spelled two-lane as Tulane, for the college team that fixed games. As it turned out, the Bulls did play Milwaukee in the first round and got knocked off anyway. Whether Kevin actually did this or not, there was a black mark next to his name because it was being talked about.

Also, the Bulls had some problem guys on the team. When Michael gives his anti-drug speeches, one of the things he sometimes mentions was that early in his rookie year, he went to a team party but when he walked in, a number of the guys were either drunk, high on cocaine or both. He looked at them and had no idea what to say because this wasn't how basketball players acted, not at North Carolina. Finally, he mumbled something like, "Hey, guys, take it easy," and he left. All of this had to be a dramatic change for Michael. Hey, no one ever confused Kevin Loughery with Dean Smith. Dean was a father-figure to his players. They trusted him, talked about their personal problems with him. When you played for Dean Smith, you weren't away from home, you had another home and guys weren't stoned. That's why his former players go back to Chapel Hill in the summer. It is home to them, and they are an extended family.

To top all this off, the Bulls were still losing. It's true that their record improved from 25–57 without Michael to 38–44 in his rookie year, but 44 losses to Michael was like 444. He didn't lose 44 games in his high school and college career combined. Michael didn't complain about Loughery, but you could see that the losing got to him.

The controversy surrounding Loughery did not involve Michael, but what happened during the 1985 All-Star weekend at the Slam Dunk Contest did. It was the now famous "freeze out" of Michael. Rumor has that it was organized by Detroit's Isiah Thomas. I also heard that George Gervin may have been involved, but who knows? What I do know is that there was a real odor of sour grapes all around the 1985 All-Star Game and that still bothers me.

It began at the Slam Dunk Contest where Michael wore his Nike warmups and gold chains around his neck. Some of the other players had on their team uniforms. Supposedly they were upset by what they considered Michael's arrogance. They thought since Michael was a rookie that he shouldn't have had all that gold around his neck and he shouldn't have been a walking commerical for Nike. As it turned out, Michael finished second in the competition to Dominique Wilkens, but the ramifications weren't known until the next day.

I worked the 1985 All-Star Game on CBS radio with Jerry Gross. Michael just wasn't *Michael Jordan* in the game. A couple of times he was wide open on the wing in a fast break situation. I mean, there's Michael going to the basket, you give him the ball and *wham!* you've got two points. It's a no-brainer. But the pass always went the other way. Sometimes, Michael cut across the key and was open, his hand up. The guy with the ball would look right at Michael and then throw the ball to someone else. Sometimes, guys took jump shots instead of passing the ball to Michael who was in position for a dunk. There were just too many instances like these for them to be coincidences. I didn't like the looks of it.

In 22 minutes, Michael was 2-for-9 from the field and 3-for-4 at the foul line for seven points.

After the game, Michael didn't blame anyone but himself. He talked about being "tentative" in his first All-Star game. He talked about "not being in the flow" and "not having good rhythm."

In other words, he let them off the hook. But Michael had to know what was happening.

I played in three All-Star games and they were great experiences. Sure they were run-and-gun games and sure there were times when I wondered why the ball didn't come my way more often. But I also know that when you put that much talent on the floor at once, guys are going to look to shoot first, shoot second and maybe pass third. I loved being in the dressing room with all the great players, feeling part of a special fraternity. I remember how excited I was when I was picked for the first time. It was like being named to the Dream Team or something. A lot of these guys were my heroes and now I was going to be on the same team with them.

It may sound corny, but I was honored. I imagine that Michael felt exactly like that before his first All-Star game.

Okay, maybe it wasn't the smartest thing for Michael to be a walking billboard for Nike during the Slam Dunk Contest, but I don't put that on a level with what happened the next day.

Michael's actions were perhaps self-serving, but they didn't hurt anyone. The players who froze out Michael were small and vindictive. It would have been better for one of the veterans to take Michael aside and say, "Hey, kid, we don't do this kind of stuff." But not saying a word to him off the court and then freezing him out on the court was inexcusable.

Supposedly, Dr. Charles Tucker, who was a friend of such players as Isiah and Magic Johnson, spread the word to reporters that the players were snubbing Michael. Tucker supposedly said that some of the all-stars wanted to give Michael a lesson in humility. Tucker, Isiah and Gervin were later seen at the airport laughing about having taught Michael "a lesson." Supposedly, it was Isiah's idea, and that wouldn't surprise me because he could control the ball during the game from his guard position. I understand that some players were jealous of all the attention and more importantly, all the commerical endorsements Michael was receiving as a rookie. Michael Jordan was not in with those guys. His friends are the former North Carolina players. So maybe since Michael didn't bow down to Isiah and the rest, they wanted to get back at him.

Michael tried not to make an issue of it. We were talking about it again in the spring of 1988, and Michael told me, "I think all the rumors have been put to rest and that's how I want it. I never knew if all the speculation about what happened at the first All-Star game was true or not. Obviously, I never dreamed that anything like that would happen, but I didn't feel very comfortable there. I'm just glad it is over."

It is ironic that Isiah Thomas plays for the Detroit Pistons, the most hated team in the NBA. Are they maligned as they claim or are they "Pond Scum" as Chicago sportswriter Terry Boers calls them?

Now, there is a difference between the hate the Boston Celtics have earned over the years and the hate for the Pistons. People are sick of the Celtics because they win all the time and they're cocky.

But the Pistons—they try to bully you. If you were in a boxing ring with them, they would always be trying to hit you below the belt when the referee was looking the other way. On the court, they always seem to be involved in a fight with someone.

I was there in 1987 when Detroit's Rick Mahorn almost decapitated Michael when Michael drove to the basket. And I was there when Mahorn grabbed Chicago coach Doug Collins by the throat and threw him into the scorers' table. I've seen Detroit center Bill Laimbeer throw a lot of guys, not just Michael, down to the floor when they drive to the basket. Why is it that almost every team in the league has problems with Detroit? Why do the Pistons always seem to be in the middle of controversy? Detroit is a very fine basketball team and they don't need to do a lot of the garbage they use on the court to win.

I'm hardly alone in this opinion, it is shared by most of the NBA.

"I can't prove it, but I have a feeling that the Pistons pay the fines for Mahorn, Bill Laimbeer and Dennis Rodman," said Washington Bullets Coach Wes Unseld. "Those guys think they are tough, but they're not. They're just cheap shot artists."

"Everyone around the league knows about the Pistons, specifically Laimbeer and Mahorn," said Cleveland Cavaliers General Manager Wayne Embry. "Those guys deliberately try to hurt people. That's a fact as far as I'm concerned. Why are they allowed to market themselves as the Bad Boys? Why do they have a skull and cross-bones for a logo? You can talk to basketball people anywhere and they'll tell you that they can't stand Laimbeer."

That is just a small sample of the tirades the Pistons inspire in basketball people from about anywhere but Detroit. So put me down as a guy who doesn't like the Pistons and I'm leery of some of their players.

That's why I was so happy that two days after the 1985 All-Star Game, the Bulls played Detroit. Michael had nothing to say to Isiah before the game. They even shook hands and made up. But on the court, Michael ripped the Pistons for 49 points and his actions spoke much louder than Isiah's had at the All-Star Game.

———●

At the end of Michael's first year, Loughery had been fired and replaced by Stan Albeck as coach. Rod Thorn was out as general manager and Jerry Krause was in. The city of Chicago has started to fall in love with Michael, but the fans really only showed up in big numbers for the good teams—Boston, Los Angeles and so on. When New Jersey or San Antonio was in town, the usual 7,000 showed up.

My impression of Michael after the first year was that he had great natural talent. He average 28 points, was Rookie of the Year and showed he was the most exciting player this franchise had ever seen.

But would he make the Bulls a contender?

I didn't know that he would grow into the kind of superstar that could turn a team around from the guard position. I was thinking that Reggie Theus had some great years for the Bulls. He could score 25 a night, but we still were at the bottom of the standings. I kept thinking that Oscar Robertson was a great guard, but he never won big until he played with Kareem Abdul-Jabbar. Jerry West was a great guard, but he needed Wilt Chamberlain in the middle before he won a championship.

I started to ask myself—didn't we read this script before with Reggie Theus? At first; they loved Theus and two years later they said he was too selfish and shot too much and the Bulls couldn't win with him. I didn't believe that Michael would go the way of Theus, but there were some similarities. Would we see headlines, "Michael scores 60, Bulls lose"?

All I could say was I hoped that didn't happen, but I was worried because the players around him weren't very good. A team just isn't heading anywhere with Ennis Whatley, Quintin Dailey and some of those other guys playing important minutes.

Another factor was that Michael led the team in rebounding at 6.5 per game. The only other Bulls guard to do that was Jerry Sloan when he played for me in 1966–67. But again, when a guard is getting all the rebounds, a team is in trouble.

To the credit of Jerry Krause, he drafted Charles Oakley from Virginia Union. Oakley could be a 6-foot-9 Charles Atlas poster. He has mountains for biceps and a chest wider than Montana. The first thing Charles said after he was drafted was, "Michael will never be the Bulls' top rebounder as long as I am here."

As a fellow big man, I liked hearing those words.

There were no tears shed when Loughery was fired. Stan Albeck came to Chicago for the 1985–86 season with the track record of a guy who liked to run. He had George Gervin in San Antonio, and Gervin set team scoring records for Albeck. Michael felt good about Albeck because Albeck would design an offense around him. Albeck also was a far better bench coach and a more even-tempered guy than Loughery. With Albeck, we knew that the days of ranting, raving, screaming and throwing tantrums were over. Albeck never would have buried a guy as Loughery did Reggie Theus.

At the start of training camp, the mood was very upbeat. The players were glad that Loughery was gone and off their backs. Michael had a strong exhibition season and the Bulls won the first three regular season games. In the opener, Michael had 29 points as the Bulls beat Cleveland in overtime. The second game was against Detroit and there was trouble as usual. Michael drove to the basket and was flattened by Bill Laimbeer. Michael ended up in a shoving match with Isiah Thomas. Albeck and Detroit Coach Chuck Daly were out on the floor screaming at each other. It was the usual ugly scene you have when you play the Pistons and they start cheap shotting people. Anyway, Michael had 33 points and the Bulls won again.

Victory number three was at Golden State, but with 45 seconds left in the second quarter, Michael went down. It appeared that he had hurt his left ankle. The crazy thing was that it happened in the open floor, it wasn't like he was dumped or as if he jumped and landed on another guy's foot when he came down. He was helped off the court by Oakley and back-up center Mike Smrek.

The next day, the Bulls were in first place at 3–0 and Michael was on crutches. Reportedly, the X-rays showed no break, just a "severely jammed ankle." Without Jordan, the Bulls had the dubious distinction of losing to the Clippers.

Michael's foot was X-rayed again by team doctor John Hefferon and this time a break in the navicular tarsal bone was discovered. He went on the injured list and the future that was so promising a week earlier was really bleak.

Someone asked me what I missed the most about Michael, and I said, "Replays."

When you watch Michael every day, you can never see some of his moves often enough. I'd see them live on the court, then I'd look down and catch them a couple of more times on the television monitor. We'd have them in slow motion, stop-action and at the regular pace. With Michael out, it was like someone pulled the plug on the Bulls. The electricity was gone.

I felt very bad for Albeck. He was 3–0, armed and ready for

war. Now someone took his bullets away. He had to tear up his entire offensive game plan. Hey, it was time to abort the mission and bring the ship home. Except for one fact—the Bulls had 79 games left.

Some people said that since Michael was out, the ball would be distributed more and the Bulls would be a better all-around team. Okay, the ball was moving around. So what? The other guys weren't going to do much with it.

I was asked if Michael ever left me speechless. I said, "No, but his teammates have." They were doing things on the floor that were better left unsaid. This was a crazy-quilt of a team, a bunch of older guys and a few kids and none of it matched. Michael was the one thread that held it together. The Bulls had picked up veteran point guard Kyle Macy. They also got another experienced guard, John Paxson. Both of those guys were solid outside shooters, but they needed to be set. That means they needed picks or they needed to feed off a creative player. For example, when Michael played with Macy or Paxson, it was a good situation for everyone. Michael would take the ball and drive to the basket. The other guard (Macy or Paxson) would run to his favorite spot on the floor. When the defense collapsed on Michael, he would pass to the other guard for an open shot.

Only without Michael, there was no one to penetrate, no one to set up the other guard.

The Bulls then traded for George Gervin, who was a big-time scorer for Albeck in San Antonio. But Gervin was 34. He had lost his starting job in San Antonio to Alvin Robertson. He just wasn't the same guy who used to step on the court and put 25 points on the board night after night.

Now Gervin wasn't the Iceman, he was just plain cold.

Once in a while, Ice would throw in 30, but his speed and defense had slipped to the point where Albeck just couldn't play him at the end of the game. Guys drove around Ice as if he were frozen in place. In one game, we went down to San Antonio and won when Albeck started five players who used to be with the Spurs. That's all he had left—gimmicks. In the NBA, gimmicks last about as long as one of those exploding cigars. You give it to a friend, he lights it and it blows up in his face. In two minutes, the gag is over and everyone asks, "Now what?"

Meanwhile, Michael was going crazy. He would see the lights

come up and he'd look out at Chicago Stadium, which was *his* arena in his mind, and he couldn't go out there and play. Michael had never been seriously injured before, never been sentenced to walking around on crutches and spending his life in doctors' offices. After a while, he stopped going to games because he just couldn't watch anymore. The losing was eating him up and you could see it in his face. He was tense and edgy. Eventually, he had to just get away from it so he went home to North Carolina to start his own conditioning program. He used to drill himself jumping and dunking off his healthy right foot, which was at least something he could do.

The frustrations continued. There would be reports that Michael was coming back. Then the doctors would say he couldn't. Michael was holding his own impromptu press conferences, saying he was physically ready to play. Management would cite doctors' opinions that the broken bone in Michael's foot had not fully healed.

It reached the point where the Bulls were telling Michael not to play. The doctors were telling Michael not to play. Even his agent, David Falk, was telling Michael to sit out the season. Michael was demanding to play. He was questioning the team's motives, wondering if the Bulls wanted to keep him out so they would lose enough games to miss the playoffs and earn a spot in the 1986 college draft lottery with a chance to get the No. 1 pick in the country, which turned out to be Jordan's old North Carolina teammate Brad Daugherty, a center currently with Cleveland. Were the Bulls trying to keep Michael out to make the lottery? I'd like to think not. I'd like to believe that they were just being cautious with a player who was the franchise. Why have Michael risk another foot injury, especially when a second break could end his career?

But honestly, I can't read people's minds so I don't know all the motives. I do know that the easiest thing would have been for Michael to bag it. There would have been no questions asked. The guy broke his foot, how was he supposed to play? But Michael kept insisting that he must play. He said if the Bulls didn't want him to play, he didn't want to play for the Bulls. Eventually a compromise was made and Michael was allowed to return, but he could only play something like seven minutes a half. It kept increasing until he finally reached 15 minutes a half.

After missing 64 games (the Bulls were 24–43), Michael came back and he looked like a guy who had sat out 64 games. He'd drive to the basket and miss easy shots. His timing was off and he shot 34 percent in his first five games back. His first game was memorable because he entered in the middle of the second quarter against Milwaukee to a standing ovation. The first time he touched the ball, he took off and dunked on 7-foot-3 Randy Breuer.

It took about two weeks for Michael to find his legs, then he was scoring 20 a night while not being allowed to play more than 30 minutes. The situation was ridiculous. I don't think any coach ever had to operate under the same restrictions as Albeck. As if he didn't have enough to worry about in the normal course of coaching a game, now he had to keep track of Michael's minutes.

Suppose Michael was allowed to play nine minutes a half. Should Michael start, play four minutes, sit down and then play the last five minutes of the half? Or should he sit until there was nine minutes left in the second quarter and then play out the period? Or should it be divided up another way?

The second half was even more mind-boggling. How do you use Michael's nine minutes? When will those nine minutes help the team the most?

Just getting Michael into the game was an ordeal. Suppose he had five minutes left and there was six minutes remaining in the game. Albeck would send Michael to the scorer's table, figuring about a minute will go by before the game will be stopped and substitutes will be allowed in. But what happens if there is a break in the action right after Michael gets to the table? Then he'd be on the floor for the last six minutes, but he'd only be allowed to play five, meaning Albeck had to get him out of the game for another minute.

Something like that happened in a game. Albeck just said the hell with it, and he let Michael play the extra minute. The next day I saw Albeck in a hotel lobby and he told me, "Jeez, they (management) called me in and gave me hell for playing Michael one minute too long. They told me that if I do it again, I'll really be in trouble."

The implication was clear—Albeck had better follow the game plan or find another job.

There was one game in Milwaukee where former Bucks coach Don Nelson yelled to Michael, "Hey, that's it. Your seven minutes are up."

Michael was making the most of the minutes, doing things like scoring 28 points in 26 minutes. But this changed his game. He thought he had to shoot more because he had only so many minutes on the court and he couldn't waste a second. This caused him to force shots he normally wouldn't take. There was a game in Indiana that showed how ludicrous the situation had become. Michael was up to 30 minutes a game but his time ran out with 31 seconds left. The Bulls were down by a point and Albeck had no choice—he yanked Michael. After all, Albeck remembered his meeting. The Bulls did win that game 109–108 on a John Paxson jumper, but Michael exploded after the game. He felt he was being harnessed. It was like everyone was in a race and Michael had one foot in a 20-pound cement block.

Michael said, "I'm no piece of meat. Their system is ridiculous. Why can't I play when the team needs me? All I want to do is get back to basketball. That's my first love."

Management was unhappy with Albeck for making a farce out of the rule, so no matter what he did, he couldn't win.

I had never seen anything like this situation. Either a guy can play or he can't. He's healthy or he's not. Or you can tell a player to test his foot in the first half and see how it feels and then make a decision from that time on the court.

The Bulls did make the playoffs that year and the timetable was tossed out. In three games against Boston (all losses), Michael averaged 44 points and shot 50 percent. The most famous game was a 135–131 loss in double-overtime at Boston Garden where Michael scored 63 points and was 22-for-41 from the field. At the end of the first overtime, the Bulls were down by two points and Kevin McHale fouled Michael. There was no time on the clock and Michael went to the line for two shots. The crowd was screaming, but Michael made them both to force another overtime. Larry Bird talked about Michael for about an hour after the game, and ended by saying, "God came to the game tonight and played under the name of Michael Jordan."

What always amuses me about that game is that Michael played 53 of the 58 minutes. So the guy went from not being allowed to play more than seven minutes in a half to playing

53 minutes about six weeks later. If anything showed how dumb those restrictions on Michael were, it was this playoff game.

My respect for Michael just grew during his second season. Everyone from the team owner to the general manager to his agent was telling Michael to sit out. No championship was on the line and he was under absolutely no public pressure to come back, but Michael demanded his time on the court.

I remember him telling me, "I know my own body. I'm ready to play."

The doctors told him to rest and he was playing in pick-up games with his friends in North Carolina. And Michael doesn't play just to play, he plays to win. He hates to lose, he hates it when people don't play by the rules and he hates it when people don't play hard. I don't know of another NBA player who would have acted the same way Michael did. Most guys would say, "What the hell, I'm getting paid big bucks. They tell me not to play, I won't play. I'll come back strong next year."

I love the way Michael just stood up to everyone.

When he was back, I don't think he worried about reinjuring his foot while he was on the court. I'm sure he had to think about it, maybe when he was lying in bed at night. But on the court, he was fearless. He doesn't think, he reacts. Michael is like most kids. He doesn't think he'll ever get hurt. He doesn't think he'll ever die. Nothing can touch him. I do think it was fortunate that Michael was injured just running down the floor rather than being knocked out of the sky on one of his dunks. After you've been knocked down once, there is a moment's hesitation, a hint of doubt. In one game I caught an elbow in the nose and my nose broke. The next game, I was playing in a protective mask, but I couldn't see a damn thing. I threw the mask away, but when I got my first rebound I instinctively put a hand in front of my face to protect my nose. It took a few games for me to get over that.

Michael never showed any of that fear. I think I was more nervous watching him in those first few games than he was. He's taken the hardest spills I've ever seen on the court because he plays higher off the ground than anyone ever has, but he just gets up and does it again. It is like Michael enters a fantasy world. He goes out there and acts like he is in a pinball machine. He bounces off people and ring-ring-ring, the points go up on the board. Lights flash, he is hit with flippers. . . I don't know. . . it's just that nothing on the court scares him or really upsets him.

One thing Michael has going for him is that when he hits the floor, he knows how to roll. Just as he plans his moves as he soars, he plans his falls. He probably doesn't know how he does it, he just does it. I don't know how many times I find myself saying on the air, "I know Michael is down, but it isn't as bad as it looks because he landed all right."

The guy who suffered the most from all of this was Albeck. It bothered me when he was fired because the guy didn't have Jordan for 64 games, then when Michael came back Albeck had to spend so much of his attention determining when and how to use Michael. I do believe that one of the reasons he was fired was that he didn't keep the management's timetable for Michael. The official reason was that management didn't like Albeck's offense. He ran a lot of isolation plays with Michael and another player on one side of the court while three guys stood on the other side and watched. The owners said they wanted more passing and movement like the great New York teams of Bill Bradley, Walt Frazier and Willis Reed, and I agreed with that concept.

So Albeck was out and Doug Collins came in for Michael's third year. That wound up being a terrific change because Collins is an enthusiastic, young coach. He relates to the players better than any coach Chicago has ever had. But at the time he was hired, Collins had never even been an assistant on the NBA level. He was only 34 and had been an assistant at Arizona State. He also was an analyst for CBS television. Michael matured as a player under Collins and the Bulls went from a 30–52 record in 1985–86 to 40–42 in 1986–87 as Michael won the NBA scoring title with a 37.1 average.

———●

Michael Jordan is the only player in the league who can't go on the floor about an hour before the game to shoot around. If Michael wants to practice, he does it a couple of hours before the game when the gates haven't opened and there are no fans in the stands.

Michael and I talked about this one night when all his teammates were on the floor and he and I were the only ones left in the dressing room. It was about 50 minutes before game time.

"I used to go out there before the game, but I found out that I really couldn't concentrate," Michael told me. "The fans were always coming up to me and asking for autographs or to pose for pictures. I hate to say no to kids and I found myself spending time meeting the fans instead of practicing, and that's not good about an hour before the game."

When Michael comes on the court to shoot around, kids start begging him for his autograph. He smiles and says he can't do it now. Then the kids' fathers show up and start yelling, "Hey big shot, ain't you got a minute to sign a little kid's program?" Or Michael hears, "Hey, buddy, they're paying you a million bucks and now you're too big to sign for the kids. What's the matter with you?"

The joke my announcing partner Jim Durham and I make at the press table is that you can always tell what end of the court Michael is shooting at. That side looks like it should tip over because all the people are there and no one is by the other basket.

"I spend a lot of time during our morning shoot-arounds getting ready for games," said Michael. "It's just me and my teammates. Then I find that I can get focused on the game. I do the same thing in the dressing room. I think about what I have to do."

Michael does join the team for lay-ups about 20 minutes before the game. It's an organized drill with all the players taking part and the fans seem to accept that it is part of the actual game and leave Michael alone.

So what about not even being able to shoot around before a game like a normal player?

"It's just something that has evolved," Michael told me. "What can I say? I'm glad the fans like me. It isn't just at the arena, but everywhere I've had to make adjustments. If I want to go to a movie, I go to the late show. If I want to get my hair cut, I go to a place where the barber closes at night and then opens up again so he can take me. If I want to go to a restaurant, I call ahead and see if they have a booth or a table in the back. Autographs and fans are a fact of life for me. When I'm trying to practice or even eat a meal, I try to keep the contact to a minimum just so I can do it."

"A legend before you're 30?" I asked Michael.

"A legend? I never thought about it in those terms," he said. "A legend is someone like Doctor J (Julius Erving), someone who has played a long time or is retired. I'm not a legend now. I'm just waiting my turn. I think the reason the fans like me is a credit to how I've been marketed and the endorsements I've had. I like to think that I've crossed some racial barriers, that when people look at Michael Jordan they don't see him as black or white, but as a basketball player, a guy who when they see him play, he makes them feel good."

At first I wasn't sure if I had never seen anyone quite like Michael Jordon on the court, but I immediately knew there was never a basketball player quite like Michael off the court.

In Michael's rookie year, we were in New York and there was a pack of kids by the Bulls' bus waiting for Michael. Orlando Woolridge looked at me and said, "It's not like we're the Chicago Bulls. We're Michael Jordan and the brothers."

That comparison was perfect. It's like the Jackson-Five. We all know Michael Jackson, but who can name the other four Jacksons? It's like there's Michael, now name the other four Bulls. Only the hard-core fans can do that.

Michael came into the league with the most incredible following I've ever seen for a basketball player and it's just gotten bigger. At a game in Seattle our bus was surrounded by about a thousand people, all wanting Michael. There were fans everywhere, on all sides of the bus. When the security department knows there will be that kind of a crowd, they slip him out the back door and he walks about two blocks to a designated corner. We'll be on the bus and the fans will be screaming for Michael. One of us will tell the fans that Michael already left, then we'll pull out of the parking lot and pick up Michael on the corner.

Sound crazy?

It's either do that or Michael will need a police escort to get on the bus. I'm not talking about a couple of overweight rent-a-cops with billy clubs. I'm talking secret service types are best suited for the job. It's not that anyone wants to hurt Michael, it's just that too many people want him. They want to stand by him, shake his hand and maybe hear him talk.

In another instance in Seattle, Michael was scheduled to appear at a shopping mall. Earlier, Magic Johnson had made a similar appearance at the same place and attracted about 1,000 people. Police estimated Michael's crowd at 5,000 and they had to call out reinforcements because fans were breaking things and stepping over each other to get to Michael.

If we're in an airport, word inevitably gets out that Michael is there. People know if the Bulls are taking a flight, then that means Michael is around and they look for him. Eventually, you'll see a line or a pack of people by one of the waiting areas. You won't see Michael, but you'll know that he's in the middle of it. Michael may not want to sign autographs, but he signs. He has a sense of responsibility and I believe it comes from his family. That's why he hasn't gone the way of Bill Russell or some of the other players who just refuse to sign autographs.

James Jordan told me, "When I see Michael with a crowd, it is very strange. It's almost like he's not my son. He has become such a huge celebrity. People act like he's some kind of god. I'm just happy that he takes time and is polite with them."

It is almost a form of adulation and magnetism that I've never seen for or from an athlete. Maybe Babe Ruth was like this, I don't know. But there is no one else I can compare him to and Michael has been getting this since he was a freshman at North Carolina. That's why for Michael, everything is different.

After the game, he is the last one out of the dressing room because he is the most interviewed player in the league. As Brad Sellers told me, "One of the first things I learned about being on the Bulls is not to get a locker next to Michael's or else you'll end up with writers standing all over your clothes and sitting on your chair."

It's not Michael's nature to give one-word answers or hide in Mark Pfeil's training room. You ask him a question, you get an answer. Ask Michael a follow-up question, he doesn't get mad—he elaborates. That's why he has been voted to the Basketball Writers' All-Interview team every year he has been in the league. During his rookie year, Michael was magnificent. He went from city to city answering the same questions over and over. He had more than just canned answers because the stories came out with a variety of angles. Michael knows that writers have to do their stories so he takes time to think before he answers.

When Kareem Abdul-Jabbar came into the league, about all

he'd do was mumble at the press if he talked at all. The same
with Pat Ewing. Neither of those players faced the press
onslaught that was waiting for Michael because they turned
everyone off. It's not right to say that Michael welcomed the
constant interviews, but he handled it. To Michael, this was as
much a part of being a basketball player as developing his jumper
or keeping in shape.

————●

Michael's limousine driver is George Koehler.

Yes, Michael has a limo driver. I told you he wasn't like any
other basketball player.

George Koehler is a bulky guy, about 30, with a beard. Everyone from the Bulls knows who he is and what he does, but I never
bothered to really talk to him about it until one day late in
Michael's fourth season. I had heard the stories about women
who lie down under the tires of Michael's limo to get his
attention—all true stories, according to Koehler. And I had heard
that Michael likes to take the limo to McDonald's.

True again.

"Michael's favorite is a quarter-pounder with cheese, a large
fry and an orange drink," said Koehler. "We sometimes play a
little game. We'll go to the drive-in lane and I'll place the order.
When we get to the window, I'll pay for the food and when the
girl hands us the order, Michael will pop his head out of the back
and take it. The girl usually yells, 'My God, that's Michael
Jordan.' Then all the other employees will rush to the window
and we'll drive off. It's almost like one of those 'Who was that
masked man?' stories. It's just something we do once in a while.
McDonald's is one of Michael's favorite places to eat."

Koehler has known Michael from the day he first reported
to training camp with the Bulls.

"I was working for a limo company and had been sent to the
airport on a pick-up," said Koehler. "I was standing there with
a sign with the client's name on it, but the guy wasn't getting
off. You could tell the plane was about empty because even the
pilot got off. I asked the pilot if there was anyone else on the
plane and he said one more person. I assumed it was the guy
I was waiting for, but it turned out to be Michael. I was also

a high school basketball coach at the time and I got so excited
seeing him that I said, 'Oh my God, it's Larry Jordan.' Actually,
I had played ball with a kid named Larry Jordan and that was
the first thing that came out of my mouth. I got my composure
back and I asked Michael if he was going downstairs for a taxi
and he said he was. I told him about the brand new limo I had
and how my client wasn't there and asked him if he needed a
ride. So he said that sounded good to him and I drove Michael
to the Lincolnwood Hyatt House, where the Bulls were putting
him up. I gave him a business card, shook his hand and told him
I was available if he ever needed me. I was just getting started
in the limo business and I was ready to do about anything for
anyone, but I never figured I'd hear from Michael again.

"About two weeks later, I got a call and someone said, 'George
my boy.'

"I said, 'Who's this?'

"He said, 'It's M.J.'

"I said, 'Who?'

"He was quiet for a minute and said, 'Michael Jordan.'

"I got all fired up and asked Michael what I could do. He
said his mom and dad were coming to Chicago and could I pick
them up at the airport. I told Michael that I'd drive to North
Carolina to get them. Michael was bringing them to town so they
could help him pick out an apartment and decorate it. I knew
he thought that his parents would get a kick out of being picked
up by a limo. But that's how it started. Then Michael and I made
a verbal agreement where I'd pick him up at the airport after
road trips and then it branched out into public appearances and
everything else."

Michael does own a Corvette and a Blazer. He does like to
drive, but he believes that a limo is almost a necessity.

"ProServ (Michael's agents) give me an itinerary for Michael
and I know when and where he has to be and it's my job to get
him there," said Koehler. "That can be tricky. The first year was
really a zoo because no plans were made to get him out of the
arena. It used to take about an hour for Michael just to get out
of the building, into the limo and for us to make it out of the
parking lot. There were just people all over him. Now the security is better, but it still takes us about 20 minutes to make it
out of the lot. Sometimes we can't get the door of the limo open

because there are so many people around the car. Now there is a fenced-in area where we can keep the car so at least we can open the doors without a hassle. We still have problems getting out of the lot because people don't move. I have to inch along because I don't want to run over the fans.

"I'm amazed at how Michael has dealt with all this. The fans won't hurt him, but he gets recognized everywhere. Michael likes to do his own grocery shopping and we go to the stores late at night right before closing. Someone will spot him and start screaming that Michael is in the store. The next thing you know, people come running, knocking over displays and things like that and Michael signs the autographs. He's used to it. Michael can't shop like a regular guy, but he likes to go out.

"Michael also likes movies, but what we have to do is go to the late show in the middle of the week. We try to time it so that when we arrive at the theatre it's dark and the movie is just starting with the credits on the screen. What often happens is that an usher spots him and starts shining a flashlight in his face. Then the people look up and see what's going on and they see Michael's face in the light and the next thing you know, no one is watching the movie and everyone is lined up for Michael's autograph. It's a tough thing because Michael is always wrestling with where his obligation to the fans ends and his right to a private life begins. But more and more, Michael is finding that he has to stay at home with his old friends from North Carolina. His best friend on the Bulls used to be Rod Higgins and they still get together when Rod is in town. It's becoming such an ordeal for him to go out. For the most part, Michael is a quiet guy. He doesn't paint the town. I have friends ask me where I drove Michael today and they don't believe it when I say we went to the game and on the way home we stopped off at McDonald's. If his parents are in town, Michael will call from the car phone and ask his mother to make him some pancakes and eggs. He loves pancakes and eggs. But that's it, a regular night for Michael."

————●

Michael is a corporation—JUMP—Jordan Universal Marketing and Promotion. Since he signed with the Bulls, Michael has set his parents up in a sporting goods store in Charlotte. Michael is a chameleon and I mean that in the best sense. He can walk through the corporate world or hang around with the guys on the playground and feel at home in both places. Maybe that's because there are two sides to him, but the reason he is respected both places is his sincerity.

Who can question Michael's dedication to basketball, especially after his second season when he forced the Bulls to play him? On the court, who can doubt that the guy plays hard all the time, that he is totally dedicated to winning and doesn't hold anything back?

Doug Collins put it best when he said, "Michael leaves his heart and soul out there every night. He plays when he's bruised and banged up, he never wants to come out of the game for a rest. He's from the old, hard-nosed school of basketball."

But he's also from the new school of economics. When he attends a corporate meeting, he wears a sharp three-piece suit, carries a briefcase and has a very good idea what issues are on the table. He understands that appearance is important in business.

Michael also can work a crowd, he is a convincing public speaker and he has credibility. You see him using the products he endorses. He does commercials for Chevy, and he drives his Blazer and Corvette when he's home in North Carolina. Some of those spots are interesting because they seem unrehearsed. Michael is sitting on top of a Corvette in a casual shirt and jeans and he's just talking about growing up in North Carolina. There is no set script. He is just staring at the camera, telling you how he was cut from his high school varsity team, what his parents have meant to him...there are several different commercials with Michael talking about various aspects of his life. The theme is the making of a legend. You can imagine an actor doing this, but a 26-year-old basketball player?

We've already talked about how Michael goes to McDonald's. That's why he has no problems selling Big Macs.

Finally, there's Nike.

The tennis-shoe company signed Michael to a $2.5 million deal for five years when he came out of North Carolina. He also receives royalties and other fringe benefits. At the time, Nike was in trouble. Their big money-maker had been running shoes, but the jogging craze was starting to end and all the companies were producing those same running shoes. In terms of basketball, Converse had the two marquee names in Larry Bird and Magic Johnson.

But Michael put Nike on the map and he did it with a very ugly red and black high-topped shoe that looks like something a guy wears when he's trying to climb a telephone pole. The kids loved it, even at 65 bucks a pair. Then Michael put out other models of shoes and clothing. Nike reportedly sold more than two million pairs of Michael's shoes from 1985 to 1987, worth well over $100 million to Nike. The Air Jordan line of shoes and clothes has meant at least $250 million to Nike. Michael wears his Nike stuff everywhere. He'll score 50 points one night wearing a pair of white Nikes and the next night he'll wear a different colored pair. He is a tennis-shoe freak, wearing new and different models every day.

The Nike commercials are very creative. Here's a shoe company showing us Michael as he soars and asking, "Who says man was never meant to fly?" The message is clear—Air Jordans get you off the ground. Every kid who ever wore his wrist band up on his forearm as Michael does and every kid who ever wore shorts with extra-long pants legs as Michael also does, wants Air Jordans. On every playground in the country, there is some kid in those red and black shoes, wearing a Bulls No. 23 jersey pretending he is Michael Jordan. Everywhere I go, people have the same question—what's Michael Jordan like? I can't think of any basketball player who has captivated basketball fans as he has.

3 •————————————————————

Michael Jordan, the One-Man Team

When the Bulls opened the 1988 Eastern Conference Semi-final playoffs in Detroit, a newspaper printed: "Coming Soon to an arena near you: Michael Jordan the most exciting act in the NBA. The Chicago Bull is a ONE MAN SHOW."

This wasn't an advertisement, it was the headline over a story about Michael. It also is the kind of publicity that would tear most teams apart. By its nature, basketball is a team game. It is a delicate balance of egos and talents.

It is the opposite of baseball, where the players can absolutely loathe each other and then forget it all when they step on the field. In baseball, they have the sacrifice bunt and sacrifice fly, but few sacrifices are made. Even when they do "sacrifice," it doesn't count against a player's batting average. In fact, special statistics of sacrifice flies and bunts are kept to show that a guy is a team player. Also in baseball, the individual nature of the game means that a guy can play for himself and still be a great team player. Pete Rose's mind worked like an adding machine. Rose would line a single to center and he'd be figuring out his batting average as he ran to first base. That was fine. It helped his team. Players are paid to hit, pitchers are paid to get them out. I'm convinced that baseball is far more of a 1-on-1 sport than basketball.

That's because no statistics are kept for how many times Dave Corzine or Horace Grant sets a pick to free Michael for a shot. No one keeps track of how often any member of the Bulls passes the ball to Michael, thereby passing up an open shot. Sure basketball does count assists, but that only happens after a pass leads directly to a basket. But suppose Grant gets the ball about eight feet from the basket. He has the choice of making a move to the hoop or throwing the ball back out to Michael, who is 25 feet away. Textbook basketball logic would tell Grant to take the shot. But Bulls' logic is get the ball to Michael. So Grant passes out to Michael, and it may take Michael several dribbles to create his own shot. Grant may even go outside and set a pick for Michael. Grant has sacrificed. His pass led to a basket but he didn't get an assist according to the rules.

That's why Michael and Bulls coach Doug Collins become outraged when they read stories about Michael being a one-man team and the Bulls being called "The Chicago Bull, a bicycle built for one." Hey, even *Michael Jordan* couldn't beat anyone 1-on-5. He needs four other guys.

Baseball history is full of teams that detested each other yet won big. The Oakland A's of the middle 1970s and the New York Yankees of the late 1970s are two recent examples. But the basketball teams that win championships are teams where the players at least get along, and often really like each other as friends would. There is an undercurrent of respect that binds them together and a minimum of the jealousy that often destroys a team.

What has made the Bulls a success is more than Michael Jordan The Basketball Player. It's what Michael has done to the team, how his personality has become the Bulls' attitude.

I'm still not convinced teams can play for an NBA title until they get a dominating rebounder and shot-blocker in the middle. Maybe I say this because I'm 6-foot-9 and I just happen to like big guys. Maybe I also can page through the NBA guide and see that no matter how great the guard, a team goes home early in the playoffs without a good center.

For example, Oscar Robertson is the only player in NBA history to average a triple-double—30.7 points, 12.5 rebounds and

11.4 assists. He did that for the Cincinnati Royals in 1961–62, yet the Royals' record was 43–37. They were a decent team but were eliminated in the first round of the playoffs.

The only player to lead the NBA in scoring (34.0) and assists (11.4) in the same season was Nate Archibald. The 6-foot point guard did that with Kansas City in 1972–73, yet the Kings were 36–46.

A strong case can be made that those seasons by Robertson and Archibald were the finest individual performances ever recorded by a guard...at least until Michael's explosion in 1987–88, a year where he made NBA history by winning the Most Valuable Player award, the scoring title, the Defensive Player of the Year award, the steals championship, Most Valuable Player in the All-Star game and the Slam Dunk championship. If they gave a trophy for it, Michael won it.

Here's a statistical look at Michael with the Bulls:

YEAR	AVERAGE POINTS	FG%	AVERAGE SHOTS	RECORD
1984–85	28.2	.515	19.8	38–44
1986–87	37.1	.482	27.7	40–42
1987–88	35.0	.535	24.3	50–32
1988–89	32.5	.538	22.1	47–35

There are several things to consider from these numbers:

- Before Michael came to the Bulls, they were 27–55. When he was a rookie and still finding himself as a pro, the Bulls record went to 38–44 in 1984–85, an eight-game improvement.
- The 1985–86 season was left off the graph since Michael sat out 64 games with a broken foot. In the 18 games in which he did play, the Bulls were 9–9 compared to 21–43 without him.
- In his third full season (1986–87), the Bulls were 13 games better than before Michael.
- In 1987–88, the Bulls won 50 games for the first time in 14 seasons. The remarkable thing is that Michael's shooting percentage rose dramatically to almost 54 percent. The fact that he sees so much double-teaming and that there are moments when you and the whole Western

world know Michael is going to take the shot and he takes it anyway. . .to hit 54 percent is amazing.

I don't want to dwell on statistics because most of them are meaningless. I will say that Michael has meant more to the Bulls than any other guard has meant to his respective team. That isn't a statement you can totally support with numbers. It is an opinion based on the one set of numbers that mean the most— the team's record.

The reason the Bulls have improved so much is that his team- mates have accepted Michael controlling the offense. The Bulls averaged 85 shots a game in 1987–88 and 24 of them belonged to Michael. That means he was taking 28 percent of the shots, leaving 72 percent for the other 11 guys. Most coaches would tell you that this is a dangerous distribution. One guy is just shooting too much.

I know a little about the psychology of the players who pass for a living. When I played, I wanted to call my autobiography 12 Years In The Pivot Without The Ball. That's about how I felt. I did like to pass and my job was to rebound, but what the hell, there isn't a basketball player who ever touched a ball who didn't *love* to shoot.

The bottom line is winning. If a guy on your team is going to shoot 20 times, you'd better win. Pete Maravich was a tremen- dous talent and he was usually on awful teams. Pete had to fire it up there at least 20 times for his team to be in the game at the start of the fourth quarter, but his teammates didn't like Pete shooting because they lost.

What's the difference between a scorer and a gunner?

A scorer is a guy who shoots a lot on a winning team. A gunner is a guy who shoots a lot on a loser. And both guys may be taking the same number, even the same kind of shots.

Vinnie Johnson is Detroit's third guard and here's a guy who needs to ice down his arm after the game. Vinnie comes off the bench taking 20-footers and he goes down taking 20-footers. If you pass the ball to Vinnie, you may as well hit the boards because you aren't going to get it back. Despite his 45 percent mark from the field, Vinnie Johnson is considered a scorer because the Pistons win. His streak-shooting often is just the spark they need to get them out of those lulls that are a part of every game. The Pistons also have the luxury of depth. When Vinnie's jumper is knocking the paint off the rim, they can sit him down.

When World B. Free played for such teams as Cleveland, the San Diego Clippers and Golden State, he was a gunner. Free shot no more than Vinnie Johnson, but his teams got beat. Also, Free's coaches didn't have the talent that Detroit's Chuck Daly has to work with. So when Free was taking shots for which he deserved to be shot, his coaches had no choice but to stick with him and pray he'd shoot his way out of it since there was no help on the bench.

When Wilt Chamberlain first came into the NBA with Philadelphia in 1959, a lot of guys didn't like to play with him. Wilt got his points, but Philadelphia didn't win. After a while, players started to say, "Hey, this ain't much fun watching Wilt shoot while we're getting our asses kicked."

Here's at look at some of Wilt's numbers:

YEAR	AVERAGE POINTS	FG%	AVERAGE SHOTS	RECORD
1959–60	37.6	.461	32.1	49–26
1960–61	38.4	.509	31.1	46–33
1961–62	50.4	.506	39.4	49–31
1962–63	44.8	.528	34.6	31–49
1966–67	24.1	.595	14.1	68–13

With Wilt shooting 30 times a game, his teams were good, not great. In 1961–62, he set a league record that probably will never be broken by averaging 50 points. He also led the NBA with 25.7 rebounds a night but Philadelphia didn't win 50 games. In Wilt's defense, it should be noted that his teammates were respectable—Paul Arzin, Tom Meschery, Al Attles and Guy Rodgers—but that was not overwhelming talent.

Chamberlain didn't win his first NBA title until 1966–67. By then, his scoring had dropped from a high of 50 to 24 points and his shots went from 39 to 14. He was still a dominating force, but he was learning the lesson many of us already knew, namely how to survive in the pivot without the ball.

That's why I was fascinated by the success of the 1987–88 Bulls. The 50 games they won is a tremendous accomplishment given the fact that it was a team with a journeyman center in

Dave Corzine. It also was a team where John Paxson began the year as the starting point guard and then lost the job to Sam Vincent, who couldn't get off the bench in Boston. Oakley was a force at power forward, but small forward went between Brad Sellers and Scottie Pippen. The fact that two rookies, Horace Grant and Pippen, were called upon to play major roles also would seem to indicate that the team might be in trouble. In the NBA, when rookies play, you lose. But the Bulls won and the reason was Michael. Not Michael as a one-man team, but the Chicago Bulls as Michael's team.

————●

In many ways, the Bulls were like an expansion team when Michael was drafted. You look back to Michael's rookie year (1984–85) and the only other guy still with Chicago is Dave Corzine.

Having coached two expansion teams, I've always believed that if you are doing a good job after three seasons you should have only one or two of your original players left. The other guys should be replaced with better talent, and that's what Bulls general manager Jerry Krause has done. Even though Krause didn't draft Michael, he recognized what he had in Michael and Krause said, "Let's build a team around him." That's what Krause has done.

Suppose Michael had come to a veteran, winning team. He certainly couldn't take 25 shots a game. And once all the commercial endorsements and the publicity came his way, it probably would have upset some of the other players. But with the Bulls, Michael was about all they had. It was a team without an identity and he gave it one. Who were the stars on Michael's first Bulls team—Quintin Dailey? Orlando Woolridge? Ennis Whatley? The Bulls didn't have a player with anything approaching Michael's talent or leadership ability.

From his first year, Michael tried to be a presence in the dressing room. He told Woolridge, "I bet you $100 that I'll get more rebounds than you do."

Woolridge is 6-foot-8 and can jump and change the lights on the ceiling, but he just isn't a good rebounder. I don't know if it is a lack of effort or if he just can't figure out how the ball comes off the rim. In his five years with the Bulls, he barely averaged five rebounds a game from the small forward spot. Michael is a great leaper, but he should not get more rebounds than Woolridge. Nonetheless, Michael did and he won that bet. Michael's idea wasn't to take $100 off Woolridge, but to get Orlando on the boards. As it turns out, that 1984–85 season was Woolridge's best rebounding performance of his seven-year NBA career, but it still wasn't good enough to beat Michael. Woolridge eventually was traded.

At 25, Michael was clearly in charge of the Bulls by the 1987–88 season. Even when older players with more experience came to the team, they had to sit back and see how Michael ran things. I say this in a very positive way. Just as Larry Bird controls the Celtics and Magic Johnson is in charge of the Lakers, Michael sets the tone for the Bulls. None of these stars overrule the coach, but their attitude and approach to the game rubs off on the rest of the team.

I consider Michael the first vocal leader the Bulls have ever had. Jerry Sloan was the Bulls first real captain, but he led by example. Sloan didn't say much, he just played relentless defense and went to the floor for every loose ball. At one point, Norm Van Lier sort of tried to lead but he was always mad at his coach, mad at his agent, mad at the writers. . . he was mad at the world. That style wasn't going to work.

Michael speaks out and he backs up those words with his actions. He can see the bigger picture. He isn't a guy coming from total poverty and a dirt-floor house who is just happy to be making the big bucks and seeing his name in the newspaper. Several times, Michael has looked me right in the eye and said, "What I want is a ring." It's the same thing you hear from Larry Bird, Magic Johnson and the other truly great players. Those guys already have their money. Sure they want more, everybody wants more money, but dollar signs aren't what drives them. A championship does.

And Michael knows that he needs the other guys to win a championship. Nothing is openly said about this unless some-one charges the Bulls with being a one-man team. Then Michael and coach Doug Collins circle the wagons. Collins asks how the (1987–88) team could lead the league in defense if all the Bulls had was Michael? How could the Bulls lead the league in rebounding if all they had was Michael? On and on Collins talks, building up the other 11 guys. He'll talk for 15 minutes and barely mention Michael, except to say that there is far more to the team than Michael Jordan.

As for Michael, he'll praise Grant's rebounding, Sam Vincent's passing, Dave Corzine's experience, you name it. He really does like to talk about the other players, and that's because Michael likes his teammates. Collins and Michael are on the same wavelength. That's why their quotes often are almost identical after a game. This isn't rehearsed, they both just happen to know that it's a team that will win a championship, not Michael Jordan.

This is something that comes from his parents and from playing under Dean Smith at North Carolina. Michael might have been with even better players at North Carolina than he has played with in Chicago. Certainly that's true of front-court players—James Worthy, Sam Perkins and Brad Daugherty all would look good in a Bulls uniform.

Michael won a national championship in college, he won a gold medal in the Olympics and now he wants an NBA title. He knows he needs to help to get there and he wants the other guys on the team to realize that he appreciates them.

When Michael won the Slam Dunk Contest, he brought the $12,500 in prize money into the dressing room and said, "Okay, guys, let's divide it up."

All right, you can say that everybody on the Bulls is making six figures, what do they care about picking up another grand? Remember this about basketball players—they usually are very tight. They don't like to spend 35 cents for a newspaper. They don't tip well and they like people to buy them lunch. Believe me, this gesture went over real well in the dressing room.

Three of the players drive Chevy Blazers. I don't know exactly what the deal was, but I do know that Michael played a part in these guys getting a bargain.

Not long after Sam Vincent joined the Bulls, the team was in Portland. Michael had a limo pick up him and Vincent and take them to the Nike plant where Sam could pick out all the shoes and clothes he wanted.

Another story is from when Michael was in his second season and was voted by the fans as a starter in the 1986 All-Star Game.

He couldn't play because of his broken foot, but Michael still had a free trip for two to the game. So Michael came up to Charles Oakley and said, "Hey, Charles, what are you doing next weekend?"

Oakley was a rookie and he had no plans.

Michael invited Charles to the All-Star Game—all expenses paid.

"I like Charles," said Michael. "I wanted him to see the All-Stars. It's an experience to be there and I thought it might motivate Charles to work a little harder so he can get to the game. We can both get there as teammates one year. I call Charles my bodyguard. He takes care of me on the floor, I'll take care of him off the floor."

That has been the relationship between the two players. Oakley was also one of the Bulls who drives a Blazer. On the floor, if anyone touched Michael, Oakley was there to make sure that no one went after Michael again.

Being on the same team with Michael is like following around a banker. Everywhere he goes, $100 bills fall out of his pockets. The other guys can just pick them up. Michael appears at his teammates' basketball camps, he gets them commercial work and things like that. There are a lot of stories of Michael and the other players, but here is one that's a little different.

During Michael's rookie year, the Bulls were having a Christmas party at the Marriott in Los Angeles. The guys were all dressed in t-shirts, cut-offs and tennis shoes. It was very informal. Jim Durham and I put on a little skit, we made up poems that took some shots at the guys and had a good time. We were drinking beer and soft drinks, and I saw Michael take a waiter aside.

"Do you have anything better than beer?" he asked.

The waiter looked at Michael as if Michael should be the guy taking the order.

"Like what?" asked the waiter. The guy was very arrogant.

"Do you have a wine list?" asked Michael.

"We have champagne," said the waiter. He mentioned a brand. "It's $99 a bottle."

"I'll take two for my teammates," said Michael.

"I said it was $99 a bottle," said the waiter.

"And I said I'll take two," said Michael.

Then we toasted the end of our Christmas party with

champagne.

There is a generous side to Michael. No one said he had to take Oakley to the All-Star game or give away his Slam Dunk money. I don't think Larry Bird, Magic Johnson or any of the other superstars in the league go out of their way to do as much for their teammates as Michael. Michael has almost a paternal instinct about his teammates and it shows.

That's why his teammates are patient with Michael.

Michael is always the last guy out of the dressing room, and on the road he holds up the bus. That's because he has to talk to the writers, and then the fans mob him. The Bulls often send Public Relations Director Tim Hallam on their road trips to handle the media crunch for Michael. Traditionally, the P.R. man seldom travels with an NBA team, but the Bulls made an exception because of Michael.

You also don't hear the other guys saying, "Jeez, will Michael get on the bus already?"

A few may think that, but then they also remember what Michael has meant to them and the team. He signs an eight-year, $25 million deal, then the Bulls rework Oakley's contract so that his salary almost triples and Charles gets $1 million a year for something like six years. Michael's salary trickles down to some of the other guys and I think they are smart enough to know that.

On the bus, Michael sits in the back with the guys, plays cards, calls people names and they get on him, too. Just as he is at home in a three-piece suit in the corporate boardroom, Michael is comfortable with the guys on the bus and in the dressing room. And just as he changes his clothes for each setting, his vocabulary is different. Which is the real Michael? I don't know. Having watched him since he was a rookie, it sometimes seems as if Michael is two people and both personalities seem genuine.

———●

If Michael weren't a great player, if he didn't play defense and push himself as hard as anyone on the team in practice, no one would care that he is a nice, good-hearted guy. For Michael Jordan, being merely good would hardly be good enough because there are a lot of very, very good basketball players in the NBA.

It begins on the court.

Michael has had to live with greater expectations than even Charles Dickens could have imagined.

He made the shot that won the national title as a *freshman* at North Carolina. Where does he go from there? After a sophomore named Magic Johnson led his Michigan State team to a national title, he went hardship. There was nothing else after the NCAA championship. The same was true of another sophomore, this one from Indiana named Isiah Thomas. He also was a pro by his 20th birthday.

But Michael played two more years at North Carolina after that national title. The Tar Heels never were NCAA champs again, but Michael won consecutive College Player of the Year awards. Then he led the United States to a gold medal in the 1980 Olympics.

He was NBA Rookie of the Year. Then he missed most of his second season with a broken foot and came back to score 63 points against Boston in the playoffs in a performance that inspired Larry Bird to talk about God being disguised as Michael Jordan. Bird also said: "I never would have believed that anyone could score 63 points against us, not in Boston Garden. But Michael is the best, one of a kind. I've never seen anyone like him. He's doing things early in his career that I could never do. They may be things that have never been done. You have to play the game to really understand how difficult some of Michael's moves are. I've never seen a player have the impact on a team that Michael has had on the Bulls."

Remember that this testimony from Bird came after Michael's second pro season.

In his third pro year, Michael was the NBA scoring champ averaging 37 points a night. No one under 7-foot had scored like that before.

In his fourth year, Michael won every conceivable individual award.

That's why I say that good would never have been good enough for Michael. Greatness is a given and Michael knows it.

"I realize what people expect from me and I know that those expectations are there all the time, on and off the court," Michael told me. "I've set a standard. It has gotten to the point where some people don't think I've had a good game unless I've scored 50. I don't think that's right, but I can deal with it."

Kids pack the stands wearing Chicago jerseys with Michael's No. 23. The Bulls games are one of the most popular offerings on the satellite dish because fans across the country love to watch Michael night after night. The mail Jim Durham and I receive about Michael and the Bulls comes from about every state. People see Michael play once and they're hooked, turned on by his presence on the court.

Michael also is aware of this.

So when he gets the ball on a breakaway and has an open shot, he can't just lay it in. He can't even do a normal one-handed dunk. Michael has to *slam*. He has to try the sensational. The fans expect a dunk that they've never seen before and Michael usually gives them just that.

"I get excited when I get the ball in those situations," Michael told me. "I know if I can get a good dunk, it brings the crowd into the game. It gets them behind me and the whole team."

I have never seen a player attack the basket as Michael does. Early in his career, we went on a West Coast trip. In Houston, Michael slammed on 7-footer Akeem Olajuwon. In San Antonio, he slammed on 7-foot-2 Artis Gilmore. In Utah, he slammed on 7-foot-5 Mark Eaton. In Los Angeles, he drove around 7-foot-2 Kareem Abdul-Jabbar and then turned right back and slammed the ball in Jabbar's face. I know that Michael didn't set out to dunk on every center, but that's what was happening. It was like he was marching through the West, putting another notch in his gun handle each night.

In another game in Utah, Michael took 6-foot John Stockton under the basket, posted him up and scored. A Utah fan yelled, "Hey, Michael, why don't you pick on someone your own size."

A few minutes later, Scottie Pippen stole the ball and gave it to Michael, who drove the middle and hammered one home over 6-foot-10 Mel Turpin. It was a super dunk, a *wham-bam* sonic job that about tore down the backboard, a 5.6 on the Richter Scale that they had to feel in San Francisco. As Michael was running down the floor, he turned to that same fan and said, "Was that guy big enough?"

Another aspect of Michael's game that impresses me is his passing.

There are two basic categories of passers:
1. The creative passer.
2. The bailout passer.

The bailout passer often is a scorer. He gets the ball, makes his move and only gives it up when there are two players in his face and he can't get off a shot. Jerry West was a great player, but I consider him a bailout passer. When Jerry West passed, it usually was because he couldn't take his shot, not because he was thinking about getting a teammate involved.

Players such as Magic Johnson, Isiah Thomas and John Stockton are creative passers. They like to drive to the basket with the idea of drawing defensive attention and then giving the ball to a teammate for an easy basket. These guys are point guards, and they have a passing mentality.

Michael is somewhere between these two areas. If he sees a man open under the basket, Michael will get him the ball, and Michael will do that even if he has an open shot himself. Michael's main job on offense is to score, but he does look for the other guys. With Michael, passing isn't a last resort. If he was surrounded with enough talent, I also think that Michael could play as Magic does, moving the ball around and only shooting when the other guys are cold. Michael has averaged almost six assists per game in his career, which is very high for a player with his scoring average, and he nearly doubled that total when he switched to point guard this season.

————●

I've always said that if they make a movie of my life, I want Michael to portray Johnny Kerr as a player. Forget how he plays, I wouldn't mind having his build. At 6-foot-6 and 200 pounds, he has almost the perfect frame for a pro guard. His body is like a missile. He doesn't seem to have that many muscles, but he is so firm that you can see every vein.

As for fat?

Forget it, he has none.

Okay, they say that Michael has a body fat count of something like 3.3. That's about what most of us have in our left pinky finger.

He has incredible quickness. When Michael was a freshman

at North Carolina, he was continually called for traveling just as he made his move.

"Coach Smith put together a videotape of my moves in slow-motion," said Michael. "He sent it to the NCAA and it showed that I wasn't traveling. My first step was just faster than what the officials were used to seeing."

That's what I used to tell the officials, too. But when they ran a tape of me in slow-motion it looked like I was standing still.

Anyway, no one is used to watching what Michael does. In one of my all-time favorite quotes, Delores Jordan said, "Some of the things Michael does on the court just shock me. But I do know he is human since I was there when he was born."

Obviously, Michael can jump but he says that his vertical leap has never been measured. That's fine with me. I'm sick of reading about guys who can jump 38 inches or 42 inches and then I see them play and they can't get a rebound. There are some guys in the NBA who'd win a high jump contest, but who wants them on their team? They don't know when to jump, they don't even know how to jump. By that, I mean they need a running start before they can get up.

Michael seems to levitate. He is standing there one second and then going up the next. It's called being able to leap from a standing position and that's how you get most rebounds. You establish position under the basket as you block out, and to do that you must be standing. The shot is taken and then you jump, and you're jumping from a standstill. Michael is great at that. Offensively, Michael can control his body in midair—he changes directions to weave between defenders not as he's driving to the basket, but as he's flying. I've never seen anyone do it quite like Michael, and that includes Julius Erving.

"I don't plan these things," Michael told me. "I just know that I'm going up for the shot. Then instinct takes over."

So Michael takes off with the ball in his right hand, switches it to his left, pump fakes and then nicely touches it off the glass and into the basket without even knowing exactly what he did?

"That's right," said Michael, then he laughed.

Another aspect of jumping is hang time. Michael doesn't just go up and then come down, he hovers for a while. It seems like he jumps, then the defender jumps, then the defender comes down and Michael is still in the air. That's his amazing body control.

He just stays in the air.

When he coached in Milwaukee, Don Nelson had his players hit Michael with a very hard double-team, "But the thing was, Michael just jumped over it," said Nelson. "If he was close to the basket, it didn't matter that we had two guys on him, he just soared and then scored."

Sometimes, I don't even know how he dunked. There have been several occasions where there was a loose ball under the basket; guys are bending over, diving, and the ball is scooting through them like a greased pig. Then Michael seems to scoop it up with one hand and—*wham!*—it's a dunk. It happens so fast that the only way to begin to appreciate what he did is to see the play on a slow-motion replay.

The jumping is God-given. A player can't go into his driveway and practice leaping like Michael Jordan. But Michael does more than rely on his natural gifts, and that's why he is a team leader.

When he first came into the NBA, Michael wasn't a good jump shooter. Everyone played off of him, waiting for Michael to drive and daring him to take the 15-footer. His jumper didn't seem very smooth, it didn't go in that often and he lacked confidence in the shot. Even in his third year, Michael's jumper was shaky. He averaged 37 points and didn't like to shoot from the outside.

But Michael kept working. And there is only one way to develop a jump shot, and that's to get in the gym and practice. It's not much fun. You take 25 shots from this spot, 25 shots from that spot, 25 shots over there and 25 shots over here. You spend hours, alone, just shooting. There are no short cuts. Either you put the time in at the gym or you don't.

Guys like Michael love the game. More to the point, they love to play the game, any kind of game—full-court, half-court, even 1-on-1. But practicing your jumper is one-on-none. It is almost like golf where you're competing against yourself.

All I know is that Michael did it. Early in his fourth season, I remember telling Jim Durham, "He's got it."

"Got what?" asked Durham.

"The jumper," I said. "Michael's got that jumper down."

And he did. The 18-footer had become automatic. Suddenly, the defense had no idea how to guard him and that's why

Michael's field goal percentage went from 48 percent in 1987 to almost 54 percent in 1988. That's a huge jump and it's a direct product of a summer in the gym. Shooters also get better from year to year. Larry Bird was far more deadly from the outside in his fourth season than his first. Dominique Wilkins had absolutely no outside shot when he entered the league. Four years later, he was respectable.

Another improved area of Michael's game that is a result of practice is his foul shooting. Michael makes 85 percent from the line. The only way to be a great foul shooter is to shoot thousands of foul shots. That's what Michael does. It also shows his concentration. Often Michael isn't just fouled, he's bludgeoned. He has to be picked up off the floor and trainer Mark Pfiel is out there asking Michael if he knows what day it is, or at least the license number of the truck that hit him.

When a player goes to the foul line, the tendency is to relax and catch your breath. After doing that, you take the foul shot. And often you miss, because you relaxed and caught your breath.

Don't get it?

By relaxing, a player drops his concentration a notch. When the concentration slips, so does the foul shooting. The next time you watch a basketball game, notice how often a player will miss the first foul shot and then make the second. That happens because the first miss serves as a slap in the face. It tells the shooter to wake up and pay attention. Then he makes the second.

Sometimes, the opposite happens. Suppose a team is behind by a point with two seconds left and a player is at the line. Often the player will make the first shot to tie the score—then he relaxes and takes a deep breath, thinking that he's got it licked. That leads to a miss of the second shot.

Michael is machine-like at the line because he is so strong mentally. He stays zoned in. He doesn't relax. He stands there, 15 feet away from the basket, and scores.

Players know how difficult it is to make 85 percent from the foul line, which puts Michael in the top ten percent of all foul shooters in the NBA. The players know how Michael has upgraded his outside shot. They know this guy has done more than rely on his legs. They also know that when Michael comes to a game, the odds are that he spent part of that morning watching tapes of himself against that particular opponent. I've coached and watched players who you could approach an hour before the game and ask who will guard them. These guys will look at you as if you demanded they explain the theory of relativity. It isn't because they are so dumb that they can't remember who guards them, it's that they're too lazy to pay attention. It's not important to them.

Everything about basketball is important to Michael. He can reach deep inside himself and find a little more intensity, a little stronger concentration in the key moment of a game.

"I guarded Michael in the playoffs," said Cleveland's Craig Ehlo. "He gets the ball on the wing and starts with the head fakes. You know that you're in trouble. Then he maybe gives you a shoulder fake and his tongue comes out. That's when you can just forget it. When Michael puts out his tongue, he's going to the rack."

And then he dunks.

Just as Michael isn't sure what he does on his dunks, he isn't aware that his tongue is out. The last great athlete to stick out his tongue was Babe Ruth, who supposedly did it early in his career when he was getting ready to throw a curveball. That was cured when Ruth was converted from a pitcher to an outfielder.

"My father sticks his tongue out when he's working on something," Michael told me. "So I guess that's where I got it from. It used to bother Coach (Dean) Smith. He was worried that I might bite it or something and he had me wear a mouth guard, but I didn't like it."

Michael has never bitten his tongue.

Body language is a big part of Michael's game.

In a crucial part of the game when his man has the ball, Michael will pull his pants up a little bit and then he gets very deep into a defensive crouch, his arms hanging down and loose. It's like he's preparing for war.

Michael's defense is the final reason why his teammates accept him.

A lot of guards just like to score points. Defense? Forget it. That's a rumor, something someone else does. Michael relishes his defense. He wants to stop the man he is guarding. He likes making steals and blocking shots. In 1988, he blocked more shots than 17 of the league's 23 starting centers.

Michael does more than just watch his own man. He will drop

down to double-team. He plays team defense. I've seen other players who figure, "If I stop my guy, I've done my job." So they won't switch off to stop a teammate's man who may have gotten free. But Michael is at his best in this situation. That's why he blocks so many shots from behind or makes steals. He likes to ambush his teammate's man. It goes back to his North Carolina basketball roots—Michael understands the concept of team defense.

I know that the Lakers' Michael Cooper has a reputation as a tremendous defender and he is very good, but Cooper doesn't have to give as much of himself as Michael. Cooper does 90 percent of his work at one end of the court—on defense. When his team has the ball, Cooper spends most of his time wandering around the 3-point line waiting to take a set shot. Michael is taking a pounding on offense, driving in the key, getting knocked over. Then he gets up and plays defense. Cooper doesn't take anything like the beating Michael absorbs, yet they play the same kind of defense.

Like a lot of stars, Michael could say that he uses so much energy to score that he has nothing left to play aggressive defense. He could say that he plays so many minutes during games that he needs to rest when the team practices. But I've seen Michael practice and he practices as if it were a game. The day after a game, Michael will wear out the guys on the bench who had plenty of rest the night before.

What I'm saying is that Michael transcends the guard position. He has all the guard skills—passing, shooting, quickness. But he also can guard bigger players and block their shots. I'm convinced that he could move to small forward and kill people at that position.

During the Olympics, Coach Bob Knight said it best, "Michael does everything. He's just a great basketball player, period."

Not only do I agree, but so do Michael's teammates.

4 •───────────────────────

Coaching
Michael Jordan

In his three years as the Bulls' coach, Doug Collins and I talked basketball during quiet mornings in hotel coffee shops and late at night on quiet airplanes. We've talked in empty arenas, in crowded banquet rooms and about any other time we ended up next to each other.

That's one of the things I'll miss about Doug Collins—he loves to talk basketball as much as I do. Doug was fired by the Bulls in July 1989 and replaced by assistant Phil Jackson, something I'll discuss in the last chapter of this book. But I will say now that I was generally impressed by what Doug did, especially how he coached Michael Jordan. The Bulls job is one of the toughest in the NBA because the Bulls are Michael Jordan's team, and they also have to be the coach's team; this year, they'll be Phil Jackson's team. That's a very long and thin tightrope for any coach to walk. In the case of Doug Collins, the coach had a very strong personality, perhaps too strong. But he also had credibility with Michael Jordan, which is why Doug won 55 percent of his games in his three seasons with the Bulls.

Chicago fans have been taken for a very long and jerky ride by the Bulls since 1966. There have been more ups than downs and never an NBA championship. When Doug Collins was hired in 1986, he was the Bulls' twelfth coach in 22 years and he was Michael's third coach in three years.

So when they talk about leadership from the coach, how can

there be any when you don't know who is the coach?

In Collins, the Bulls had a coach with a spine, a coach with the backing of the front office. Michael is a leader of the team, but not *the only* leader because Collins had many of the same leadership qualities. That's a crucial point, and my opinion hasn't changed because Doug was fired.

I'm convinced that coaching Michael would be a delight. That's not to say it's easy, but every coach has to want Michael Jordan on his team, and that's not true of all the superstars in the league.

First of all, the fans adore Michael. He has their respect, their love. He tells them Nike is a good tennis-shoe and the fans say, "Damn right it is." He tells them that one day the Bulls will win a championship and they say, "You better believe it."

Second, other teams fear Michael.

Michael loves to watch films of the opponents. He is always searching for an edge and pays special attention to the man he is guarding. But imagine being in the other dressing room, being the guy who has to guard Michael Jordan and you're watching a tape of Michael driving through three guys and dunking on a 7-footer. That's intimidating even before the game starts and it's a tremendous psychological weapon. As a coach, I'd want players who scare the hell out of the other team.

That's also why Michael can't be just another player. Anyone who coaches Michael and says that "I plan to treat him like the other 11 guys on this team," is asking for trouble. Michael Jordan is more than just the heart of the Bulls, he is the head and the soul. He has become the franchise.

That's why the relationship between Michael and his teammates and between Michael and his coach is fascinating. Listen to Michael talk about his relationship with the team. He says things such as, "The guys here think I'm the leader, so that's a role I've taken on. There are times when I have to step in and pick the team up."

The message is clear—the Bulls really need Michael and he knows it. Michael doesn't say, "Everyone knows who is the leader of this team," even though everyone does know.

Nor does Michael say, "Everyone knows I have been carrying this team for so long that I feel like the Hunchback of Notre Dame." Even though there are days when he has to feel exactly that way.

And when a reporter says, "You had 63 points and you were great tonight," Michael doesn't say, "Yeah, you got that right."

When the Bulls lose, Michael is the guy the reporters go to for an autopsy. I know there are times when Michael must want to say, "What do you want from me? I play hard. I'm a great player. They had three guys beating the hell out of me all night and I still scored 40 points. How can you dump on me because I missed a couple of shots down the stretch? We never would have been in the game without me."

But he doesn't.

He may say that the Bulls needed more of a team effort or that they made some bad plays at the end of the game. But he keeps the frustration in check. The responses Michael gives are honest, but not disruptive. On the court, he plays with tremendous heart. In the dressing room, he speaks with a very shrewd head. I respect him because he won't just mouth some cliche like, "Aw shucks, guys, all I want to do is help the ball club and what I did was really nothing." Michael walks that verbal tightrope between egotism and pride. He has to sound confident when he talks to the press because the fans and other players are listening to what he says. His mood often dictates their moods.

Michael is very careful in what he says and how he says it, and his coach has to do the same.

Obviously, I never coached a talent such as Michael. Few men have. But when I was with the Bulls, I was accused of favoritism toward Jerry Sloan, who was the greatest Bull until Michael came along.

My response was, "That's right, I really like Sloan. I do let him get away with a little more."

That's because Sloan gave me so much more than the other players. The guy would throw his body in front of a subway car to take a charge. His body was bloody and bruised after some games because he took such a pounding. So when Jerry Sloan forced a shot or two, I didn't complain. I wasn't happy about it, but I knew that Sloan didn't take that shot to pad his scoring average. He did it to help win the game. Guys who do so much for a time often try to do too much. No matter what anyone says, the most any player can give is 100 percent. All this 110 percent garbage is just that—it's garbage. When a player attempts more than he can do, he'll fail. It's that simple. But a coach also has to understand that there will be times when a great player will fall into this trap—the player so desperately wants to succeed and he hates losing so much that he pushes himself over the edge.

On the 1987–88 Bulls, I know that Doug Collins would feel like hanging Charles Oakley from the rafters when Oakley cut loose with a 20-footer that had no chance of going in. In the huddle, Collins would yell, "Charles, what the hell are you doing?"

But there were times when Michael would come down on a 3-on-2 fast break and maybe Michael should have passed the ball. Instead he forced the shot and missed.

Collins wouldn't scream at Michael for this. He might have pulled Michael aside just as Michael was leaving the huddle and whispered, "You forced that shot."

A coach doesn't let this pass, but in the case of players such as Michael Jordan and Magic Johnson, they know that they messed up the moment they did it. That's not true of most other players.

If the problem continues, the coach may talk to the star in private about it, explain that he saw what happened and that he knew why it happened.

I don't think you coach players such as Michael Jordan, you direct them. You rest him at the right times, you give him a little direction in regard to the game plan and you talk about situations.

But what the hell, Michael already knows what he's there to do. He doesn't need to be told. You see Michael get a rebound late in the fourth quarter and he's bringing the ball up the court, looking at the game clock, looking at the 24-second clock, looking over the floor to see who is open and what the match-ups are under the basket. His mind is like a computer sponging up data from everything he sees and doing it in about two seconds. That's what the great ones can do while most of the other guys are running around with no idea of what the score is or how much time is left on the clock.

What is there really to tell a guy like Michael Jordan?

But sometimes a coach has to tell him things anyway, just because that's a coach's job.

It's true that Michael isn't equal with the other guys on the team—it's almost like there are two teams. There's Michael Jordan and there's the 11 other guys. A coach has to make sure that the 11 other guys are equal—equal to each other, but not equal to Michael. In return, Michael has to back his coach.

Doug Collins pulled this off as well as any coach I've ever seen. That's why he should have a "Dr." in front of his name, because "Dr." Doug Collins has the makings of one super shrink.

But Doug told me that he relished the chance to coach Michael Jordan:

"Even before I knew Michael Jordan, I could see that he had a terrific love for the game. I knew that he had a tremendous enthusiasm and when Michael was on the court, he would paint his picture as no one else could paint it. That was one thing a coach could never take away from Michael—the artistic side of his game. I felt what needed to be done with Michael was to channel his talent so that Michael could best fit in with the rest of the team. The idea wasn't for Michael to score 60 points, but for the Bulls to win and Michael would be the first to tell you that."

Nonetheless, the first meeting between Michael and Collins was not what Collins had hoped:

"It was right at the end of his second season when Michael was still going through his problems with the broken foot. The season was over and he had played great in the playoffs, but X-rays showed that his foot still wasn't completely healed. I asked Michael not to play much during the summer, to let the foot rest. He got upset and said that I shouldn't tell him what to do, that he knew his own body better than anyone. I said, 'Michael, that's not the case. I'm not saying I know more about your foot than you do.'

"Then I took off my shoes and socks. I said, 'Michael, look at my feet. I broke them both when I played and it ended my career because I didn't let them heal properly. I had seven operations. I know what pain is and I know how frustrating it is to want to play and not be able to. All I'm saying is that you should rest your foot for three more months and it might save you ten years in the league. Nothing is worse than wanting to play and not being able to because you're hurt. That's real heartache and I faced that for a long time. I don't want you to go through the same thing.' "

———————●

To understand why the relationship between Michael and Doug worked, you have to know something about Doug Collins. He was named after Paul Douglas Collins, the late senator from Illinois. Doug was born in 1951 in Benton (population 7,748) which is in the southern part of Illinois, much closer to St. Louis and Paducah, Kentucky, than Chicago. This is Jerry Sloan country and it seems that everyone from this part of Illinois is long and lean with a mean streak. They also are incredibly determined.

When Doug was growing up, Benton was a town with one movie theater, no traffic signals and not much to do but throw a basketball at a hoop. His father was the Franklin County sheriff, his grandmother cooked for the prisoners and the family lived on the second floor above the jail. Doug remembers that he had an outdoor basket near the cells, and when one prisoner was around, which was a lot, he'd sing to Doug as Doug practiced.

"One of the biggest things that ever happened in Benton was when Rich Herrin became our high school's basketball coach. He made Benton, Ill., almost synonymous with the Benton High Rangers basketball team. His enthusiasm for the game spread from the high school, to the junior high, to the grade school level. My goal was to play for Benton High. I got caught up with it. When I was in the fifth grade, I used to work out with the junior high team. I was at the gym every morning at 6 and our practices were from 6:15 to 8:30 a.m. and then we'd be back for another two-hour workout after school. It was a passion with a lot of kids. Our goal wasn't to play in the NBA or even the Big Ten, but to play for Rich Herrin and the Benton High Rangers. We worshiped the kids on the high school team. I'm serious, it was almost like idolatry and Herrin had tremendous influence on the entire community.

"I'm very serious when I tell you that I don't remember a school day from the fifth grade on in which I didn't go to the gym about six in the morning to practice either with some other guys or on my own. In the summer, there were no basketball camps as there are today. Also, it was illegal for the coach to be present for off-season workouts. But he would give the keys to the gym to one of the seniors on the high school team, and that kid would open it up so we all could go in. The senior also had a set program that he wanted us to work on. In other words, even though Herrin wasn't coaching, we were still getting things done. You wouldn't believe it—early in the morning, there were kids lined up in front of the gym waiting for it to open so they could rush inside and get the basketballs that were in the best condition.

"My summers were spent from 7–10 a.m. in the gym, then I had several summer jobs over the years—bagging groceries at the IGA store, working on the highway cleanup crew and working in a hay field. At night, we'd play the older guys who used to attend Benton and were now in college or working. So we had double sessions of basketball sandwiched around a full-time job.

"My father was great to me because he never pushed me. I really respect him for his approach. I knew he was very proud of me and the fact that I did well for the high school team— remember how important the Benton Rangers were to the town— but my father always stayed in the background.

"He used to like to watch practice, but I didn't want him there. I guess I was self-conscious about it. Finally, I told him, 'Dad, please don't come to the practices because the coach won't yell and holler things at me with you sitting there. I'd just appreciate it if you didn't come anymore.'

"He did what I asked. There were times when he got to the gym early to pick me up while practice was still going on. He wouldn't go in the gym. He just would sit in the car in the lot and wait for me. Now that I have children, I realize how hard that had to be for him. A parent wants to be a part of his child's life and he knows those years go by so fast. But he did teach me a lesson and I hope I can follow it with my kids—there are times when you just have to back off."

Doug and Herrin were inseparable. They went to other teams' games together. Herrin put Collins on special programs and Doug followed them. He jumped rope. He ran steps while wearing a weighted vest and ankle weights.

"I never even started until I was a senior," Doug told me. "I was a late developer. As I was ready to start college, I was only 6-foot-2 and 155 pounds. That was not exactly a big-time body. I did have about one hundred scholarship offers, but I went to Illinois State because it was close to home and the coach was an old college teammate of Rich Herrin. So there was a bond there between Herrin—a man I loved and respected—and my new coach at Illinois State since they were friends."

Perhaps the man who had the biggest influence on Collins was Will Robinson, who became the basketball coach at Illinois State before Doug's sophomore year. Robinson didn't know Rich Herrin, had never been to Benton and he also was the first black NCAA Division I head basketball coach when he was hired in 1970. Robinson was a legend in Detroit, a man who coached great team after great team at Pershing High. He also was the coach who put the finishing touches on Collins, making him a pro-caliber player and person.

"Normally, you have a white coach and a black star," said Collins. "That's the relationship that most people are used to and comfortable with. But with me, it was different. Will Robinson was the coach at a major college and he was a black man. I was a white kid from Benton, where everyone else is white."

Despite the work-ethic instilled in him by Rich Herrin, nothing quite prepared Collins for Robinson.

In the corner of the gym, Robinson hung up a 25-foot rope and made his players climb it.

Before many practices, he had his players put on gloves and box against their teammates.

Also before every practice, he set up chairs in the four corners of the gym and he made his players run 50 laps around them. Robinson wouldn't watch. He'd sit in his office while the players did their running and then he'd come out and ask if any one had cut corners. The point was to test the players' integrity, in addition to making them cover about three miles. The message was clear—if you cut corners in practice, you'll cut them in life. According to Robinson, those who cut corners were "nothing but losers."

This sounds to be more like boot camp with a strong dose of practical philosophy than it does basketball practice.

"Will Robinson was far more than a basketball coach," said Doug. "He talked a lot about life. He'd say things such as if you let your opponent steal your heart, he'll steal your jump shot. If he steals your heart, he has you beat and you've got no backbone."

Doug would ask Robinson why he was boxing.

"What color are you?" asked Robinson.

"White."

"What color is about everyone else who was ever worth a damn in this game?" asked Robinson.

"Black."

Robinson then delivered a lecture about intimidation. There are those who push and those who are pushed. Those who are taking the pushing are those who end up on the floor.

"I had a lot of good work habits, but Will Robinson pushed me even harder," said Collins. "He would never let me be satisfied. In my first game as a junior, I had 40 points against Oral Roberts, but we lost in a tight game. The next day, I was the first one on the floor for practice. He saw me shooting and pulled me aside. He said, 'You're not working very hard. You're thinking about those 40 points last night. You keep this up and that kid who guarded you is going to kick your ass the next time we play.'

"I don't just like or respect Will Robinson. I love the man. He was instrumental in my becoming coach of the Bulls. When (Bulls general manager) Jerry Krause called Will about me, Will said, 'Doug will do the job for you.' "

Actually, Robinson told Krause not to worry about Collins' lack of NBA coaching experience. He told Krause that Collins would win and that Collins would become a major part of the Bulls franchise.

So just as Michael was molded by three years under Dean Smith at North Carolina, Collins is a product of three years with Will Robinson.

———•

Collins became the premier college guard in the country. He averaged 28.6 points as a sophomore and then 32.6 as a junior while shooting 50 percent. That's 32 points a night in the days when college basketball had no 3-point, nineteen-foot, nine-inch chip shot. Collins probably would have been near 40 a game with a 3-pointer because many of his field goals were from the 20-foot range.

Like Michael Jordan, Collins became a member of the U.S. Olympic team after his junior season.

Collins started in the back court under Coach Henry Iba. One assistant with that team was John Bach, who is now an assistant under Doug with the Bulls.

"To this day, the 1972 Olympic team is the most disappointing basketball memory for Doug and me," Bach told me. "The Russians were getting better and better. For about 15 years, I used to warn the other people in the Olympic program about them. But they'd say, 'Listen to John crying about the Russians again' and leave it at that. I was especially worried when Bill Walton turned down a chance to play for us.

"Doug came to the Olympic trials with a reputation as a scorer. He was from Illinois State, which was not a Top 20 college program. We knew that Doug racked up big numbers in college, but we wondered about the competition. One day early in the trials, Henry Iba told me, 'Collins couldn't guard an ice cream cone on a hot summer's day.' But three months later, Doug was one of our best defensive players. He also roomed with Eddie Ratleff, a black guard from Long Beach State, and that was when it was still unusual for a white kid to room with a black kid. Because he was from a small school, Doug wasn't immediately accepted by the other players. He had to prove that he belonged."

The finals of the 1972 Olympics became far more than a basketball game. It became a war—Communist Russia vs. Democracy and the U.S. It was almost as if two systems of government were on trial, or at least that's how the players felt.

"We hated the Russians," said Collins.

Russia won a highly-controversial 51–50 decision. The game was played in Munich and started at midnight so it would be televised in prime time in the U.S. It also was a game where Doug stole the ball with ten seconds left and was knocked flat and knocked out.

"I was just coming to but still pretty dazed when I saw that Henry Iba was on the court," Doug said. "(Assistants) Johnny Bach and Don Haskins were talking to Iba and they were figuring out who they wanted to shoot the free throws. Since I had been flattened, they had the option of putting me or anyone else at the line. The feeling among the assistants was that I was too groggy to shoot, but Coach Iba said, 'If Doug can walk, he's taking the shots.'

"I heard that and I felt a shot of adrenaline flow through my body. I was tingling and I had this tremendous feeling of confidence. I kept thinking, 'Here's a guy (Iba) who is one of the all-time greatest coaches and he wants me to take the shots, nobody else.'

"I went to the line and I just made them. Later, I saw a tape of those shots and it was as if I was in my backyard in Benton, practicing. I went through the same routine and had the same rhythm. I'm proud of that."

Collins' shots put the U.S. in front 50–49.

This was the infamous game where the final three seconds were replayed, after it appeared the Russians had not been able to get off a shot. But Dr. Williams Jones (president of the Federation of International Basketball Coaches) ruled that the Russians had not one, but two more chances with three seconds to go and the ball under their own basket. Finally, the Russians threw a length-of-the-floor pass that led to a basket at the buzzer.

"The game was over," said Collins. "There were people on the court. The Russians had panicked and we knew we had won. So many rules were broken in those last few seconds...I mean...it was a travesty. It hurts just to talk about it."

Even in defeat, Doug became an Olympic hero.

"I was a student broadcaster at Illinois State when Doug was there," said Jimmy Durham. "When Doug got back from the Olympics, he was on the Today Show and written up in all the national magazines. Before the Olympics, only the hardcore basketball people knew him. After, he was a national name. At Illinois State, they held a parade for him that culminated with a big rally on the football field. Thousands of people were there, not just students but people from the Bloomington-Normal area. It was such a major event that the radio station I worked for covered it live from the press box at the football stadium. It was as if Doug's shots had won the game for America."

After the Olympics, Pat Williams, the Bulls general manager, offered Collins a 3-year contract worth $150,000 annually to skip his senior season and go into the 1972 hardship draft.

"I didn't give turning pro after my junior year any serious thought," Doug told me. "I didn't like the idea that I had to declare myself a hardship case. I mean, I didn't need to quit school and make money. My father had worked his hind end off for all his life and my mother had worked her hind end off all of her life so I could grow up and go to college. It wouldn't have been right.

"Also, I was looking forward to my senior year at Illinois State. I thought we had a talented team, but it turned out to be one of the worst years of my life. We were riddled with dissension. That also was the first year that the freshmen eligibility rule was in place, and I think it ruined our whole team because there was a lot of resentment between the players."

Jimmy Durham broadcast the Illinois State games that season and he remembered what Doug was talking about: "That was the year Bubbles Hawkins came to Illinois State as a freshman and I think he was jealous of Doug. Bubbles wanted to be a star, and Doug already was one. In the last game he played at Illinois State, it was Doug Collins Night. There was a play when Bubbles had the ball on the fast break and his obvious play was to pass the ball to Doug for a wide open lay-up. But Bubbles took the ball in himself for the shot and missed it. Fortunately for Bubbles, Doug came along and tipped it in. The next day in the *Peoria Journal-Star,* someone wrote that Collins' tip-in had 'saved the freshman (Hawkins) from a lynching.' And that's about right."

Doug was a 29-point career scorer at Illinois State and the first pick in the 1973 NBA draft.

Doug told me:

"This time, I thought I was going to Chicago for sure. I was in the Bulls' office on draft day because there was supposed to be a trade. Philadelphia had the first pick, but the Sixers were going to trade that choice (Collins) to Chicago for Clifford Ray and Bobby Weiss. But Ray had knee problems and he failed the physical, so the deal was called off.

"So I went to Philadelphia where Gene Shue was the coach. I had a very good rookie camp and our first rookie league games were against Buffalo. I played poorly in the first one and we lost. The next game, I had 37 points and we won. I was really pumped up about the season. I could see that I was going to play a lot, even though I was a rookie. I also knew we were going to be a bad team, but I thought that meant I'd get a chance to really develop because I would get a lot of minutes. But about a week before veterans camp started, I was playing in the Hall of Fame game in Springfield, Massachusetts, and I broke my foot for the first time. I rested for eight weeks and then came back to play 25 games [averaging 8 points and shooting only 37 percent], but I could tell that my foot wasn't right. Then I re-broke my foot, had surgery and sat out the rest of the season. For the first time in my life, I had to fear that I was a failure. They were saying that Philadelphia had wasted the No. 1 pick in the draft on me. That really inspired me to prove those people wrong. During the summer, I worked my fanny off to come back."

In his second year, Doug averaged 18 points and shot 49 percent. The next season, it was 21 points and 51 percent from the field. He just kept getting better and would have been one of the league's great guards, but his feet wouldn't hold up. As it was, he played eight years and made the All-Star team four times, but by 1981 he was 30 years old and knew he was through as a player. Most guys with Doug's injuries would not have lasted half as long.

"I am not a quitter," Doug told me. "No matter what I've faced, what has been put in front of me, I never gave in. I'm one of those guys who runs into an obstacle and finds that it gives me extra incentive to show what I'm made of. I was raised never to fold, never to bow to adversity.

"The year before I came to Philadelphia, the Sixers were 9–73. We won 25 games in my first season and were 9–16 in the games I played. The next year, we jumped to 35 wins. After that, it just kept getting better and better and we were consistently winning 50 games. Of course, we also had a lot of great talent with people like Julius Erving.

"What I'm saying is that I consider myself a winner. I had operations on my feet and battled back. I tore up a knee and they told me that I'd never play again and that it would be at least a year before I could do much of anything on the leg. But six months after blowing out the knee, I was back starting for the Sixers and had 18 points in the home opener. I could tell that I wasn't running well. I ended up with more foot problems and had to sit out the rest of the (1980–81) season. In September of 1981, I was trying to come back again playing at Penn, and I ripped up my other knee. That's when I knew it was over. I was afraid that I would cripple myself. I had seven different operations in eight years. I remember there was a time when I was sort of down because of all the injuries and I talked to Will Robinson about it. Will told me to quit feeling sorry for myself, to be grateful for what I had as a player because most guys would give about anything to have one good season and I had eight as a pro.

"I knew that I wanted to stay in basketball and I wanted to coach. I went to work for the Sixers as their broadcaster and I also was a volunteer coach for Bob Weinhauer at Penn. The broadcasting went well and I was hired by CBS, but I missed the feel of the game. In the broadcasting booth, you're watching basketball, you're close to it, but you're not really a part of it. At the network level, one day you do the Bullets game, the next it's the Celtics and then it's the Lakers. You don't build up any attachments. You just walk into the arena, do the game and then you leave. You don't care who won or lost. Your heart doesn't pump when the game is on the line.

"I also was working as an assistant for Bob Weinhauer when he went to Arizona State (in 1982–84), but I wanted to coach my own team. When the Bulls job became available in 1986, I was 34 years old. I love pressure. I love stress. I love the feeling of being in the arena. I missed that and I missed the feeling you get in your gut, the feeling of, 'We gotta win this game.'

"I wanted the chance to coach in the NBA, but I wasn't going to take anyone's job. I consider myself a very principled person. Stan Albeck was still the coach of the Bulls when Jerry Krause talked to me. I like and respect Stan, and I told Jerry, 'You already have a coach. If you're interested in talking to me, you must first make a decision on the coach you have. If you decide that there's a vacancy, then I'd like to talk to you.'

"About a week later, they let Stan go and they flew out to my home and talked to me. Jerry Krause spent the day with me, and I asked him [for] two things:

"First, I must be allowed to be the spokesman for the team. My voice is the one that has to be heard in the newspapers and I want you to let me set the tone for the franchise.

"Second, I need you to give me an opportunity to set a tone of discipline, of sensitivity and of teaching for the team.

"I told Jerry that we'd become successful, but it wouldn't

happen overnight. He agreed to what I asked and I took the job. I wanted the job very much. I always wanted to play for the Bulls because Jerry Sloan was my hero. When the Bulls hired me (on May 22, 1986), I felt I was ready."

————●

Not everyone felt the same way about Doug.

I remember when Albeck was fired. I kept thinking, "Stan got fired? Wow." Stan had worked under very difficult conditions with Michael only playing 18 of the 82 games and it seemed like he did a decent job. The fans were shocked and unhappy. The general mood of the media and the public was that Albeck got the short end of the stick.

Also, people were asking—who the hell is Doug Collins and what makes him think he can coach the Bulls?

It was true that Doug was an assistant at Penn and Arizona State, but he had never been a head coach anywhere. He was only 34 and that made him the youngest coach in the NBA. Meanwhile, Albeck was established with a pretty good track record.

But something was bothering me. I kept thinking that there must be more to this story than we were being told. One thing that was apparent was that Stan's style of basketball—a lot of isolations and little ball movement—wasn't very popular. Jerry Krause didn't like it. The owners didn't like it. I didn't enjoy watching it. There are certain times in the game when you want to run a clear-out and a pick-and-roll play—the two-man game that coaches talk about—but why do it constantly? Who wants to watch two guys play while three other players are standing around on the other side of the floor just watching? You should have sold those guy tickets instead of paying them salaries if all you ask them to do is watch.

Sometimes people close to a basketball team forget that the purpose of the Bulls and every other NBA franchise is entertainment. Isolation basketball is not entertaining. If the public doesn't come out, we can all go home. I admit that I didn't hear the fans complaining much about the style of the Bulls and maybe that was the only strategy Stan could use because he was hampered by injuries. But there was something about the situation that did bother me, and it bothered Jerry Krause, too. And for the record, there were a lot of stories about Doug that weren't true. He never travelled with the team while Stan was still the coach. Some people said that Doug was watching games and evaluating the Bulls for Krause, but I don't remember seeing Doug Collins at a game anywhere that season unless Doug was broadcasting it. I know I would have noticed Doug because he's 6-foot-6 and we've known each other for quite a while. That's why I never believed any of those rumors about Doug undercutting Stan Albeck, and the more time I spend with Doug, the more I know that it wasn't true. Doug wasn't out of work. He wasn't desperate. He wasn't the kind of guy who'd say to Krause, "Hey, Jerry babe, give me a shot at your team and I'll take you to the top." Doug has tremendous confidence and he knows that he is talented. He never has had to go behind anyone's back.

Here's how Jerry Krause explained Collins' hiring to me.

"At the end of Albeck's first year, I looked at the situation and I tried to see what the future would be. I felt strongly that a coaching change was needed. I went to (Bulls owner) Jerry Reinsdorf and told him what I thought and he said, 'Well, if you think that's what has to be done, go ahead. I'll back you.'

"So I went looking for someone to replace Stan. Doug Collins had been on my mind for a long time. The previous year (1984–85), I tried to hire Doug as an assistant coach but he was making a lot of money with CBS and couldn't leave television for financial reasons. I always liked Doug very much and had a gut feeling that he'd be an outstanding pro coach.

"I first talked to Doug while Stan was the coach, and Doug showed me more morals than anyone I have ever been around in the coaching business. We talked about the NBA in general, but when the subject of the Bulls job came up he absolutely refused to discuss it because Stan was still the coach. Believe me, not many guys who had coaching aspirations would have acted as Doug did. In this cutthroat business, most people will go after another man's job if they think they have a shot at it. After the end of the season, I went to Doug and told him, 'Stan is gone. Now we can talk further,' and that's when it became serious.

"Firing Stan was a very controversial move as far as the media were concerned. But I told Albeck that I'd never publicly give the real reasons behind the move and I still won't. But I had good reasons for doing it and Jerry Reinsdorf knows those reasons.

"Anyway, I was criticized heavily for firing Stan and in some respects, I also was criticized for hiring Doug Collins because he had no coaching experience. I remember Jerry Reinsdorf saying to me, 'Doug Collins...wait a minute, isn't that the television guy?' And I said, 'No, that's a guy who is going to be an outstanding coach.' The fact that Doug was in the media at the time was a plus because handling the press is a big part of a coach's job.

"Look, the easiest thing to do would have been to keep Stan as the coach. No one would have said anything. Stan was liked by the press and he was well-known. From a personal standpoint, it would have also have been the easiest move for me because this was the end of only my first year as general manager, and that's pretty soon to make tough decisions. In other words, the conservative approach would have been to let things ride, but I felt strongly that we needed Doug Collins coaching the Bulls. I stuck my neck out an awfully long way to hire him, and some people in this business said I stuck it out too far. I'm sure that if Doug hadn't worked out, the fellows behind the typewriters would have chopped me off at the neck."

———●

Firing Albeck and hiring Doug was everything Jerry Krause said—bold, gutsy, controversial and seemingly a big gamble.

You can think that a guy will be a good coach, but you'll never know how a man will react until he is on the front line. The key was Krause saying he had a "gut feeling" about Collins. Jerry and Doug had known each other for a long time. Krause didn't just run into this guy, have one conversation and then come away dazzled. Jerry remembers scouting Doug Collins at Illinois State and he remembers watching Doug with Philadelphia. Jerry was a scout for the Bulls when they tried to work the draft-day trade for Doug.

The point is that Jerry Krause always had good feelings about Doug Collins. Before Doug was hired, he and Jerry talked for days. They discussed every aspect of coaching the Bulls—How do you handle the player's egos? What kind of style do you like? What is your overall philosophy? How do you view Michael Jordan? Both men made sure that they were on the same page with respect to the team.

Jerry Krause and Doug Collins had several things in common, although tailors and diets aren't two of them.

Doug is almost a foot taller than Krause and probably 75 pounds lighter. Doug is the kind of guy who looks good in anything he wears. I know how Jerry Krause feels because neither one of us is ever going to make the cover of *Gentleman's Quarterly* and I don't care if you take the world's greatest tailor and have him make the world's most expensive suit for either of us.

Also, Jerry and I are guys who have never missed a meal. Doug appears almost skeletal. He is so nervous and so detached from the world that he seems to forget about eating. Doug is so wired that I worry about him. It reminds me of a biology course I took at Illinois. We had to inject small doses of strychnine into frogs and the frogs would lie there as if they were sedated. Then the instructor would come up behind the frogs, bang his fist on the table...*pow!*...and the frogs would jump up, throw all their legs out and then...*bang!*...they'd just die.

I keep thinking that if Doug isn't careful, he could end up like that. He is so into everything, so hyper that it's almost scary.

But it's that intensity that binds Krause and Collins. I swear, neither of these guys sleep. All they did, all they talked about was basketball. They committed themselves to the Bulls.

Also, the Bulls are the first team to give Jerry Krause a chance to be general manager and Doug Collins a chance to coach. Both men knew and appreciated that fact. They had a feeling that they were in this thing together and they both wanted to pay back Jerry Reinsdorf for the opportunity.

I have asked myself why Collins was an immediate success as a coach and one of my theories is that he was born to coach.

We say that some people are natural players. Michael Jordan was obviously born to play basketball. If that's the case, why wouldn't some people be born with the ability to coach?

If you look at Doug's record you can see that he has been under the gun of all his life. He was a highly-recruited player at Benton High and he went to Illinois State, where great things were immediately expected from him. He went to the Olympics and if anyone is a hero from that 1972 team, it is Doug Collins. Then he was the No. 1 pick in the 1973 draft and again greatness was expected. He continually came back from injuries—the man had seven different operations! Then he became a top-shelf broadcaster at the NBA level. He also was an assistant college coach. He had all the basketball credentials except pro coaching, so it would seem that coaching would be the next logical step for him.

What Doug lacked was experience and the only way to get it is to go out there and make your mistakes. And Doug does make them, but there are fewer now than when he was a rookie coach, and that's how you should judge him. I do wish that he wasn't such a perfectionist. There were games when the Bulls would fall behind 6–2 and after two minutes he called a time out and he was enraged at the guys. There were times when he needed to lighten up, something he never did.

"If you want excellence, you have to demand it," Doug told me. He certainly did that—perhaps too much.

What makes me think that Doug will eventually become a great coach is that he keeps learning. I saw improvement in him from month to month, sometimes even game to game. He is such a positive person and he has a brilliant mind. His memory must be photographic because he can remember so many details of games from years ago—names, scores, places, you name it.

People have asked me if I miss coaching and I always say, "As much as I can." I never liked the idea of five guys running around the court with my paycheck in their pockets, and that's how a coach often feels.

Coaching is a brutal job, one that has become far more difficult than it was when I coached the Bulls from 1966–68. Just as playing is a young man's game, so is coaching. That is why I marveled at veteran NBA coach Jack Ramsay and how he continued to coach into his 60s. The guy is in amazing physical condition. He bicycles, he lifts weights, he runs. But Ramsay is the exception while guys such as Doug Collins and Phil Jackson are the wave of the future.

What I'm talking about is energy. It takes more energy to coach than it does to play. When I coached the Bulls, it was a six-month job. There was the season and the off-season and the off-season meant just that—a lot of time off. But the modern NBA coach has virtually no time off, especially if his team advances deep into the playoffs. They start training camp in late October and they are playing the NBA finals in the middle of June. The NBA draft is in late June. The NBA rookie camps are a couple of weeks in July. The NBA summer league in Los Angeles is a few weeks in August, and that's only part of it.

Twenty years ago the players spent their off-seasons working. Not working out, but working at other jobs to supplement their income because there just wasn't that much money to be made in basketball. When you're making twenty grand a year and then have a chance to pick up another five for driving a beer truck in the summer, you drive the beer truck and hope to practice a little ball on the weekends.

Now, the coaches put players on summer work-out programs designed to improve their skills. Remember, it was a summer in the gym that made Michael Jordan a good jump-shooter. Since these guys are all making six and even seven-figure salaries, they are expected to get better during the off-season. It's the coaches who set up the programs and monitor the progress.

And once training camp starts, the coach goes to more meetings than Lee Iacocca. He has breakfast meetings with his assistants, lunch with the general manager, after-practice film sessions—one with the team and one with the assistants. At night, he often makes public appearances at banquets or press functions and then watches more films at home on the VCR before he hits the sack.

Coaching in the NBA is a 25-hour day, 8-day week job.

No wonder Doug Collins looked like a ghost.

The game itself also has changed, and that's because of the coaches.

In this decade, the accent is on complex defenses, doubling-down and all kinds of tricky stuff like that. For the most part, the NBA was 1-on-1, my best shot against your best defense. But now a player such as Michael is constantly having to cope with double, even triple-teaming defenses designed by the opposing coach to stop him. Meanwhile, Doug and his assistants—John Bach, Phil Jackson and Tex Winter—drew up new plays to deal with the new defenses.

"You know, you can't even run a regular play anymore,"

Doug told me one day. "The way everyone scouts and has films of everyone else, the other team recognizes your hand signals and knows your numbered plays as soon as you call them out. Of course, you know the same thing about the other guys."

For example, one standard play is two-down. This means there are two men on one side of the court and the other three guys take a coffee break. Usually, it's the center and the guard—Magic and Jabbar with the Lakers, Isiah Thomas and Bill Laimbeer with Detroit or Michael and whoever is the center with the Bulls.

But the minute someone yells two-down, the defense is almost double-teaming the center before he even gets the ball because the defense knows the play and where the pass is headed.

I'd say I had about a dozen plays when I coached the Bulls. Doug probably had 40, maybe more. He had a guy who sat by the bench; Bob Sullivan, an outstanding former high school coach whose job is to chart every play run by the Bulls and by the opponents and to record if the team scored on the play or missed. That way, the Bulls will know that the Celtics have run three-down on six occasions and scored five times, so during a key part of the game the coaches will tell the players to look out for three-down. Or else Doug would know not to call a certain play because the Bulls hadn't scored on it all night. A guy such as Bob Sullivan and this information just didn't exist 15 years ago for a coach.

So preparation is one of the major ingredients in good coaching. The coaches have to know the Xs and Os and then they have to get their plans across to the players. That's what coaches mean when they talk about execution—taking those Xs and Os off the blackboard and making them work on the floor. This is the area where Doug was the strongest—communication, motivation, dealing with people. A coach has to be able to get into the heads of his 12 players, and we are talking about 12 very different personalities and 12 very big egos. It's a lot more than the pick-and-roll play. A coach finds out that one of his players isn't getting along with his wife, or that another player has a child who is very sick. A third player has money problems and a fourth is unhappy because he is sitting on the bench. It is so much different from when you played. As a player, you look out for yourself. The world is so much smaller. If one of your teammates is having marital troubles, you may think that's too bad but it's *his* problem. But if you're that player's coach, his problem is also *your* problem.

When Doug and I talked, here is how he characterized his approach to coaching:

"In life or in basketball, victory goes to the aggressor unless you happen to be born with a silver spoon in your mouth. Even then, you have to watch out because there is someone hungrier than you are who is trying to take it away from you. I live with one motto—it's better to have respect than popularity. It's easy to be popular, to do what other people want you to and to join the crowd. To be respected, you sometimes have to do things that will set you aside from everyone else.

"What makes me most proud is that in the short time I coached the Bulls, we've gotten respect. When teams play us, they know that it's going to be tough. When they drive down the lane against us, we're not going to step back and let them have a lay-up. We'll go for the block or even smoke them good. That's the aggressor mentality I'm talking about.

"When I was hired by the Bulls, the team was at an all-time low. Michael was coming off the broken foot and there was all kinds of controversy. The team was divided by a lot of different personalities who didn't want to fit in. I spent a lot of time talking to the players and some of them just weren't right for what I wanted to do. Several times, I told Jerry Krause that this guy or that guy wasn't going to be able to play for me and we usually were in agreement. Jerry has the final say on things, but he respects my opinion and takes my advice. We both want the same thing for the Bulls. Jerry made some great trades that dramatically improved the team.

"A big plus when I took the Bulls job was that there was a lot of heat on the front office for letting Stan go, and that meant they had to be patient with me and give me a real shot to do it my way. If they had wanted to win big immediately, it never would have worked out. I was a young coach and we were in the process of putting together a young team, and that meant all of us needed patience.

"In my first year with the Bulls, I wanted to establish two things. First, I wanted the players to get to know me as a coach and to learn how I approached the game. They needed to see how I prepared and how I wanted them to prepare. Secondly, I wanted us to start earning respectability and to play hard every night. I didn't want a team that quit, a team that would beat itself. I wanted us to be in every game. In our first year, we were 40–42, which was ten games better than the Bulls were before I came. We also were 5–16 in games decided by three or fewer points, so we were in position to win a lot of other games. The point I'm making is that we were competitive about every night.

"I'm a confident person and I believe that if you surround yourself with good people, by that I mean a good staff, and if you work hard and have a consistent attitude with the players, you can create a positive environment. That's crucial. The setting has to be positive and the players have to understand that they must work hard, but they can also have fun. A coach doesn't have to be a hard-ass all the time.

"Chicago is a very unique city and it takes a lot to be a coach here. It's more than the basketball—dealing with the players, owners and general manager. The media are so important in creating that positive environment I talked about. The one thing I'll never do is be negative in the newspapers. I won't rip guys in public. If I'm upset, I keep it in my own private world. If I have a problem with a player or something I'd like the front office to do differently, I talk about it behind closed doors. I don't believe in airing out a team's linen in public. When a coach starts saying negative things in the papers, it drags the whole team down. I'm talking about the feeling around the team, and not only must it come from the coach, but from the owner, the general manager and the front office people and I even mean the secretary who answers the phone. When a team is in turmoil, everyone can tell. You hear it in the tone of people's voices and I think that tone changed with the Bulls in the last few years."

———●

One of the reasons Doug Collins was effective with the players was that he wasn't far removed from when he used to play. On the rare occasions when I mention something about when I played, the guys on the Bulls now look at me as if the 1960s were the Stone Age. Say Oscar Robertson and they ask,

"Who's that, Alvin Robertson's father?"

Are you kidding me? Alvin Robertson is a good player, but there was only one real Robertson in basketball and his first name is Oscar.

But Doug was still playing in 1981 and he played against a number of the guys who are still in the league.

Another factor is Doug's background. When a rookie said to Doug, "Gee, Coach, this is really tough. I'm a No. 1 draft choice and there are all these great expectations about me. You don't understand, I was the fifth guy taken in the draft and I got this big contract and everyone thinks I should be able to..."

Doug cut the guy right off and said, "Wait a minute. I was a No. 1 draft choice...No. 1 in the whole draft. I played on the 1972 Olympic team that lost to the Russians. I had to cope with seven operations. I know about pressure and I know about expectations because I've been there. Believe me, I know what you're going through. I know it isn't easy. Here is how it is going to be and here is what you must do..."

What Doug did was speak from experience and speak from the heart. His point is not, "Hey, I had to put up with it, so can you." Rather, it's, "This is how to handle the situation..."

Whenever any of us faces adversity, we often feel like we are the only person ever to run into that kind of problem. It is a relief to talk to someone else who has been in the same spot and lived through it. Why do people with back troubles like to talk to other people with bad backs? Why do psychologists put together groups of divorced fathers or unwed mothers? Because people with the same backgrounds can help each other.

That's one of Doug's big assets.

Some coaches never played in the NBA. They had very little talent and never were expected to produce on the court. So when they see a guy with a lot of ability who is struggling, they become very impatient and they don't comprehend why the player doesn't perform as he should. Their entire view of the world comes from being a coach.

But Doug walked that line between both worlds. He was a coach, he looked at the big picture, but he also empathized with the problems of the individual player. And when Doug talked to a player about dealing with pressure or trying to get the most out of his talent, he was talking straight from experience. He didn't say, "I did this . . . I did that." He said, "Maybe you'd want to try this because it worked for me . . ."

This also is why Doug had such a solid relationship with Michael Jordan.

Believe me, both men have very big egos and both have tremendous pride. They are convinced that they will succeed and they know that they are winners. Guys I know who are successful in business have the same attitude. It's not that they brag, rather they give off this feeling of tremendous confidence. When that type of person speaks, you believe him because he is so self-assured. When Michael Jordan is on your team, you know that you have a great chance of winning the game. When Doug Collins is coaching your team, you know that you'll be prepared.

Michael and Doug also have a lot in common. They were high draft choices and Olympic heroes. Michael is a high-scoring guard and so was Doug. Of course, Michael is a greater player than Doug was, but an advantage Doug has is that he played with Julius Erving in Philadelphia.

"There are a lot of similarities between Julius and Michael," Doug told me. "At least in terms of what the fans expect from them. Every night, Julius prepared himself for the challenge. He never had a mental let down, a night when he just wasn't mentally there. That didn't mean he played well all the time, but he always knew what he was supposed to do. Michael is the same way. Also, Julius ran into incredible expectations from the fans. It wasn't good enough for his team to win and for him to score 25 points. Julius had to have X number of dunks and X number of plays that bring the fans out of their seats. Those same expectations now surround Michael. There was a playoff game where Michael had 28 points and I picked up the paper the next day and a guy wrote, 'While he had 28 points, it wasn't vintage Michael Jordan . . .' That's amazing! Don't people know how hard it is to score 28 points, especially in the playoffs when the defense is so intense? Ninty-five percent of the guys in the league would give their right arms to score 28 points in a playoff game. What I admire about Michael is what I saw in Julius—both guys handle everything with class. They don't complain when the press is unfair and they never are rude to the fans. They have a smile for the outside world, even in the bad times."

When Doug was hired, he was Michael's third pro coach in

three years. I think that Doug was the first coach to really yell at Michael. Not that he did it often, but I've seen him do it. The other coaches tended to speak in general terms. They'd say, "We're not rebounding," or "we're forcing shots," to all 12 guys and hope that the player they want to get the message is listening. Doug wasn't like that, and that's why he not only had the respect of Michael, but of the entire team. Doug knew that Michael needs his space and that Michael is different from the other 11 guys on the team. That was why Doug was more patient when Michael took a bad shot than he might have been with some of the other players.

But Doug also will get in any player's face, eyeball-to-eyeball, and tell the guy he messed up, and that included Michael. Doug did it in the dressing room and few people knew about it, but it happened. During a game, I saw Doug look at Michael during a time out and say, "Listen, your guy has already scored 13 points off you this half, you gotta tighten up," and Michael did. Other coaches would just say, "We have to play better defense," and pray that Michael knew the coach meant he had to play better defense. They don't want to offend the star, but Doug was secure enough with himself to correct Michael.

"I remember a game we had at Utah," Doug told me. "We were on a long trip and the guys were tired. The night before, Michael had only 16 points at Golden State, but we won anyway. On this night, I knew we'd need more from him. I told Michael, 'We have to get 48 from you tonight.' Then both of us started laughing. I do think Michael knew I didn't expect him to score 48 points, but that we did need a big night from him if we were going to win. Well, in the game the guys were really sluggish, but Michael was playing sensationally. He just carried us, scored 47 points and we won. In the dressing room, I went up to him and said, 'Michael, you disappointed me. You were a point short.' We both laughed again."

Michael listened because he knew that Doug was a good coach. Doug knew the value of a very demanding practice. Some pro coaches stand off to the side, drink coffee and read the morning paper while letting the players go through the motions during practice. Doug was out on the floor, his practices were quick— bam, bam, bam—and demanding. The message was clear, "We're here to work, all of us." Doug also knew when to pull back and let the team relax. Before some games, he'd say, "You give me a good 48 and I'll give you 48." That meant if the team played hard for the 48 minutes of the game, Doug would give them the next 48 hours off to rest.

"I mentioned earlier that my first meeting with Michael didn't go that well," Doug said last season. "He was under a lot of stress because of his broken foot, and that was something I could identify with. Later on, we got together in Phoenix for two days and spent a lot of time on the golf course. I could see that Michael was watching me on the course, how I handled myself and how I dealt with other people. I think we found out that we were on the same wavelength and that was really when our relationship began. Michael has never said it, but I believe he does like playing for me and he appreciates how I approach the practices and the games. I realize that Michael is a superstar and the NBA is a star league. No one pays to see a coach. Also, a coach should never try to detract from a superstar. I want my players to do well. I want them to make big money. When Michael signed a $25 million contract or whatever, that makes me happy. Because it says what we are doing in Chicago is working."

The only conflict between Doug and Michael was early in the 1987–88 season when Michael walked out of practice after he thought that Doug wasn't keeping score correctly in a pick-up game.

When it happened, people in Chicago acted as though the Hancock Building had fallen down. This was the first (and only) crack in the armor. Fans said, "Michael's mad, what the hell is going on?"

Actually, the whole thing was pretty stupid, and that's exactly what Michael and Doug would tell you. Michael is very competitive. As his father told me, Michael wants to win at anything no matter if it's golf, Ping-Pong or a 10 a.m. scrimmage. Michael thought that Doug was cheating his team out of points, and he blew up and left practice.

The next day, Michael was back at practice. All the reporters and the television people were there and they were asking Doug about his problem with Michael.

"What problem?" asked Doug. "Hey, Michael, come over here."

Michael went to Doug.

"Do we have a problem?" asked Doug.

"What problem?" asked Michael, then he gave Doug a kiss on the head. It was the perfect comic gesture that put the entire incident in perspective. Now if it had happened again, there indeed would have been a problem. And maybe if it were some-one else besides Michael, Doug would have handled it differently. But it was a rarity and Michael is a good person, so they let it slide and Michael literally kissed his coach to make up.

"The one thing I don't like is confrontations," Doug told me. "That's why I don't like to talk to a guy when the emotions are out of control. If you confront a guy when he's angry, the natural reaction of the player is to defend himself. He thinks, 'The coach is getting in my face, he's letting me have it in front of the 11 other guys. I can't let him do that.' "

Which explains why Doug decided to let Michael walk out of practice and go home. Twenty-four hours later, they talked it out and everything was fine.

"When I correct a guy, I prefer to do it as teaching," said Doug. "I'll say something like, 'Sam (Vincent), you've got to do a better job with your passes. I know you're trying to make the good pass, but we need better judgment. We work so hard to get the ball, let's not just give it back to them.' Or I'll say, 'Michael, I need you to pick up the level of your defense. So-and-so has 16 points at the half and he's only averaging ten a game. We need your defense to win.' I try to take a negative and make it into a positive. Look, players will make mistakes. It is the nature of most players to go out on the limb and try something to win the game. I'll tell the guy that he tried to do too much, but I won't jump all over him unless he makes a habit of it. You have to be very careful with criticism. You don't want to make your players timid, yet you want them to play under control. It's a delicate balance."

The biggest challenge facing Doug was with the other 11 players.

Again, the subject is egos.

Think about this for a second. All of these guys were stars in high school, stars in college, stars of the neighborhood and stars on the playground. Suppose you are Michael's teammate and Michael scores 54 points and you get six and the Bulls win.

In the dressing room, it's no problem. Winning is the most

important thing, it doesn't matter who gets the points. But when you go home and run into your buddies, they say, "Hey, man, I don't get it. Michael got 54 and you got six. What's six points? You used to get that much in six minutes. What happened to you?"

These guys don't want to hear about team concepts or offensive strategy. They judge a basketball player by the number of points next to his name in the boxscore.

"One of my main messages to the players is that the guys who play well get to stay on the floor," said Doug. "That may sound obvious, but some coaches will get good minutes from a guy off the bench, but then they'll put the starter back in the game and forget about the substitute who played so well. Basketball is based on rewards, and not all of the rewards are monetary. The most precious commodity in basketball is playing time. If a guy plays and his team wins, he'll make a lot of money and he'll stay in the league for a long time. So if a starter is having a rough time and a guy comes off the bench and does the job, I'll stick with the guy off the bench. But after the game, I'll go over to the starter and say, 'Listen, Paxson was giving us good minutes tonight so I had to stay with him. It's a long season, so let's encourage the guy, but I am going to need you tomorrow night so stay ready.'

"Our team is very young and it's my responsibility to give my experience to some of the players, that's my experiences on and off the court. I talk to the players about all aspects of the game. I warn them about drugs and I worry about drugs. I keep my eyes open for it. It's not like I'm a snoop or anything, but I look for behavior changes and things like that. People don't realize the insecurities that some of the players suddenly feel the first time they are hit with adversity. Often, it is the first time their confidence has been tested and then you watch how they react. Do they fight back? Do they sulk? Do they grab the first thing that makes them feel good?

"When times are hard, I don't want guys who will go south on me. By that, I mean I don't want them to start feeling sorry for themselves and then decide that no one loves them and suddenly they have a phantom injury that is impossible to detect. All you can do is take a player's word for it, and all a player can do is rest it and take a little whirlpool bath. I think if you reward players for doing the job, then you create good morale on the team and keep more guys involved. Because Jerry Krause and I have the same feelings on this subject, we were able to shape a roster that is not just talented, but has good people. We have a group of guys who get along."

So what about Charles Oakley?

Unlike some people, I don't think that the main reason Oakley was traded to New York for Bill Cartwright and Will Perdue is that Oak had a conflict with Doug Collins. It may have been a factor, but not the overriding one.

Charles didn't understand what Doug was doing for him. The fact that Charles signed a six-year, $6 million contract before he was traded should have told Charles that Doug was making some very good decisions.

Oakley is a 6-foot-9, 230-pound muscle forward. His official position is power forward, but what he does is muscle people. From 1986–88, no one in the NBA got more rebounds than Charles Oakley.

But Charles wanted more. He wanted to score and he wanted plays run for him to take the shot. All of that would have been fine if he kept those complaints in the dressing room, but Charles often mentioned them to reporters and they appeared in the newspapers.

Doug and Charles sometimes fell into that type of father-son relationship where they both wanted the last word. It could be something like this:

Collins: "Go to your room."

Oakley: "No."

Collins: "Don't slam the door."

Oakley slams the door.

Collins: "Don't talk back to me."

Oakley: "I won't talk to you at all."

Obviously, this is not the actual dialogue, but it sometimes reflected the tone of their relationship. I watched a practice at Loyola-Marymount where the Bulls were scrimmaging and Charles was complaining to Doug about the calls. Finally, Doug got tired of listening to Oakley. He stopped the practice, walked out on to the court and handed Charles the whistle.

"Here, you do it," he told Charles.

That shut up Oakley for the rest of the day.

Doug used to joke, "Charles and I have a love-hate relationship. I love him and he hates me."

Actually, Doug did love Charles as a player, but Charles didn't appreciate Doug as a coach. Charles is not a good offensive player because he still needs to develop some moves in the low post so he can get shots near the basket. His outside shot also is erratic. Doug would tell Charles, "You can get 15 points a night without me even running a play for you, all you have to do is hit the boards." But Charles had the big man's ball-and-chain complex. He thought he was being shackled. Like everyone else, he wanted to shoot.

Doug would tell Charles, "Why do we let certain guys shoot more than others? Because we want to win the game and they're the best shooters. Why else play the game if not to win?"

In his two years under Doug, Charles did make a lot of progress. I think that Charles would have felt that he fit better into Doug's system if Charles had stayed around. But the reason he was traded was very simple—the Bulls need a center and Cartwright and Perdue are centers. I'll talk more about that later on. Doug and Charles could have continued to live with each other. Charles would have always made Doug's life interesting, but Charles also always played hard and Doug respected that.

Doug Collins was good for this team. Even though he is from a small town, he likes the big city. He played in Philadelphia and he loves Chicago. He really could have been born in the city because he strikes me as a city guy. Doug also is interested in big business, marketing and the media. Stick a microphone in front of him then just sit back and listen because Doug knows when he's "on" and what he's supposed to do. He is a lot like Michael in that respect—he knows there is a lot more to basketball in Chicago than what happens on the court. You have to sell the sport and sell the team and that's what Michael Jordan and Doug Collins did for the Bulls.

5

The Man In The Middle

The Chicago Bulls' next great center will be their first. Every Bulls fan knows that. It also is why the fans should take it easy on Dave Corzine and Bill Cartwright, the men in the middle right now.

For years, that was how Corzine was introduced at Chicago Stadium:

"The Man in the Middle, Dave Corzine."

That also is putting a player on the spot. Everyone else is a forward or a guard, but Corzine or Cartwright is The Man in the Middle. He is the biggest of the big guys. There was a period in the middle 1980s when the Chicago fans booed Corzine. The team was losing and it had to be someone's fault. Corzine was The Man in the Middle. He should do something about it. When the losing got worse, so did the booing for Corzine.

Okay, that's a side issue. What I'm really talking about is the relationship between the fans and The Man in the Middle.

When was the last time someone ever said: "We lost because our guards stunk up the joint"?

Or: "We lost because the small forward shot so badly that he could've stood in the middle of the Golden Gate Bridge, dropped a beach ball off the side and missed the San Francisco Bay."

Or: "We've got no bench."

Those things may be mentioned, and of course the coach can count on being verbally lynched when the team is getting beat, but usually it's: "We got hurt in the middle."

Or: "We got hurt on the boards."

Or: "We've got to get more out of the guys in the paint."

Like every center, Corzine has heard all that. One day, he did something about it—he threw the ball to Michael Jordan and that's always a smart move. The better Michael became, the more the Bulls won and more fans started saying, "You know, that Corzine ain't too bad. He works pretty hard out there."

Corzine always worked hard out there, only he wasn't working next to Michael Jordan, and that's what should be remembered.

We like to think of our centers as the Lone Ranger, a guy who rides into town and single-handedly brings law and order. Once in a while, that happens when the center's name happens to be Russell, Chamberlain or Jabbar.

Remember something about the Lone Ranger—he always had Tonto.

So those Lone Rangers won championships, but they were helped by Tontos who also happened to have great jump shots and passing skills. Before Kareem Abdul-Jabbar won a championship in Milwaukee, he needed Oscar Robertson in the backcourt. In Los Angeles, Jabbar teamed with Magic Johnson. Before Wilt Chamberlain won a championship, he needed Jerry West in Los Angeles or Hal Greer in Philadelphia. As for Bill Russell, he came to a team with the Jones boys at guard—Sam and K.C. Later, he played with John Havlicek in Boston.

I'm not putting Corzine in this class since our premise is that the Bulls have never had a great center. But Corzine did look much better after Michael Jordan rode into town. Most centers are like Corzine. The game doesn't come easy. At times, they seem overmatched and awkward. They have one or two things they do well—in Corzine's case it's a 15-foot jumper and a willingness to put a body on the man he's covering—but they don't have the all-around game in the pivot.

In other words, they're human.

They also are about seven feet tall and that's the problem.

The average fan sees the average center and thinks, "This guy is a foot taller than I am. Look at the stiff out there. He can't even jump. If I were that tall, I'd be twice as good as that guy."

Fans have no idea of the sheer size of The Men in the Middle. When you watch a basketball game from 40 rows up in the stands or on television, the guys just don't seem that tall because everyone looks about the same size, unless you are talking about extreme cases such as 7-foot-5 Mark Eaton or 5-foot-3 Tyrone Bogues.

Charles Oakley...Dave Corzine...Moses Malone...Larry Bird...Robert Parish—they all look like people with normal builds when you watch them play basketball. But when you walk up to one of these men in the mall, you say, "My God, Martha, that guy is huge!"

I'm 6-foot-9, which made me a center in the 1950s and 1960s, but I'd be a power forward now and looking up at every starting center in the league, not to mention 6-foot-10 point guard Magic Johnson. When fans see me away from the court, they say, "I never thought you were that big."

I never thought of myself as small until I started watching the guys in the NBA now.

What centers need is their own advertising agency. They've been getting bad publicity for years and it's simply because of their size. To the fans, the center is Goliath. When David grabbed the slingshot and went after the Bible's Man in the Middle, nobody was cheering for Goliath to take little David and turn him into a potted plant.

It was, "Go David, kill the big guy," and that hasn't changed.

How many people are enamored of their team's Man in the Middle? Kareem Abdul-Jabbar has scored more points than anyone in the history of the NBA. He is more than just tall, he is talented and probably the most skilled center ever to step on the floor. Any basketball fan has to love his hook shot.

But they don't love Jabbar.

For most of his career, Jabbar was booed, and not just on the road. Now he is cheered primarily because he's still there, still floating in the skyhook at age 140 or whatever. But listen to the fans when they clap for Jabbar. It's polite applause, a grudging respect but no real emotion and certainly it's nothing like the love the fans reserve for Michael Jordan or Magic Johnson.

It's almost like Kareem is the guy who fixes your car. You say, "Hey, nice job." But that's it. You don't run out and embrace your mechanic.

The center has a ball-and-chain on his leg. It's as if the man who plays the pivot is a prisoner to his position and to the fans' expectations. Some of the most hated folks in NBA history are centers. Detroit's Bill Laimbeer is despised to the point that he has to register at hotels under a different name when the Pistons play in certain cities. Wilt Chamberlain spent his career on the defensive, explaining why he didn't win more titles, or score more points, and trying to answer the latest charge made against him.

So I guess it should come as no surprise that the Chicago fans were rough on Corzine. Dumping on the big guy is human nature.

But believe me, Corzine's not bad. Not at all. And neither is Bill Cartwright. You don't know what it's like to be *the big man*. I was always *the big man,* even when I was just a little kid. I was always the guy they told to stand in the middle of the back row for the team picture. In class, the big kids are sent to the back of the room because no one can see around them.

I've had old ladies come up to me and say, "My dear, how many times do you bump your head?"

"Usually just once," I say.

Then the lady looks at me a little confused.

"Hey, lady, I'm tall, not stupid."

"Oh," she says.

"After I hit my head once, I duck."

"Oh...well...that's wonderful," she says.

Or you hear that original line, "Hey, buddy, what's the weather like up there?"

Then the guy laughs until he cries as if he thinks he's the first guy in the world to ask that question.

Of course, there have been some people in the NBA who were asked, "Hey, buddy, what's the weather like up there?"

They spit on the guy and say, "It's raining."

That's not my style. Usually when someone asks if I was a basketball player, I say something like, "No, I was a jockey for dinosaurs."

What are you supposed to say?

The point is that big guys are always being asked stupid questions . . . usually by little guys. In basketball, big guys are always being told how they should play . . . usually by little coaches.

I remember when I was The Man in the Middle for the Syracuse Nationals and I played another Man in the Middle by the name of Wayne Embry, who was with the Cincinnati Royals. Embry weighed about 3,000 pounds (okay, 300 pounds) and when he leaned on my back, it felt like I had a Mack truck pushing me out of the key. I had a coach who'd see Embry shoving me out of the key and he'd shout, "Kerr, hold your ground!"

Hold my ground?

Embry had his forearm on me and I was trying to hold my ground. My body wanted to stay still, but my feet were moving. I could smell the rubber burning off the soles of my tennis-shoes. After a quarter against Embry, I could look at where I was standing and see skid marks.

Don't people realize that guys like Wayne Embry or Karl Malone or even a middle-of-the-pack center like Mark West are so strong that they do arm curls with pickup trucks?

The officials understand that the big men are different. Under the basket is the only place where the officials let you lean on each other. If a forward and a guard match up and start shoving, it takes about a half-second before you hear a whistle. Centers play under another set of rules. Centers bump and grab and push and the officials stand there and nod as if to say, "Those two guys are beating the hell out of each other . . . that's what the NBA is all about."

A funny thing happens when you start leaning against another guy and he leans back. Suddenly, you realize that you're both in trouble.

"What if one of us steps out of the way?"

That's a frightening thought because we'll both end up on our cans, the fans will laugh and the coaches will be all over us because we didn't hold our ground.

If the big guy does fall down . . . you'd have thought the world got knocked off its axis. If it happens on offense, the coach is yelling, "Get outta the lane. Crawl. Hey, Fred, pull the big guy outta there, will ya?"

Does the coach worry that you might get a footprint on the back of your head? No way. All the coach wants is for you to move out of the lane so your team won't be called for a three-seconds violation.

Once I remember hitting the deck, hearing the coach scream and trying to get out of the key on all fours, but the floor was wet because these big bodies were banging and sweating all over the place. People were walking on my hands and finally I slipped and fell flat on my face.

Centers wake up at three in the morning in a cold sweat after having a nightmare where they fell down in the key and got called for three seconds.

Coaches are wonderful. A lot of them are former 5-foot-9 guards telling you what it's like under the basket. The coach can say, "Hold your ground" with a straight face because he never got within 30 miles of the ground you're trying to hold. So the little coach tells the big guy to get tougher. He tells the big guy that he's soft. He is looking up to the player who could mash him into a sardine can with one hand and the coach is telling the big guy that he has no guts.

And the centers stand there and take it. That's the most amazing thing.

I've always wondered about Atlanta coach Mike Fratello, who is about 5-foot-9 in high heels. The Hawks are a team loaded with big guys, and Fratello's screaming, "Get on the boards, will ya already?"

I bet some of those players are wondering, "How can he talk about that? He's never been under there."

That's why it will be interesting to watch what happens to some of the teams that are now coached by former centers—Wes Unseld in Washington and Willis Reed in New Jersey. These guys were exceptional centers. When they talk to their big men, they are looking at them eye-to-eye and speaking from experience. They know what it's like to take an elbow to the gut or a forearm to the nose. They have walked a few miles in those size 16 Converses.

Of course, the guards will wonder what Reed and Unseld are talking about when they start complaining about a guard throwing the ball all over the gym against a full-court press. So maybe the key is for big head coaches to have little assistants and for small coaches to have tall assistants.

I do believe that the big men need special care.

If you're the center and you're playing under the basket against a 7-foot-5 monster like Mark Eaton and you're doing all you can to *hold your ground,* you deserve a little reward.

Hey, how about the ball? Just let me see it . . . touch it . . . just once . . . all I want is a shot.

During a timeout at the 1988 College All-Star Game in Orlando, a big center from Louisiana State University named Jose Vargas told Al Attles, his coach, "Let Jose have some ice cream."

Attles said, "What?"

"Ice cream," said Vargas.

Vargas is originally from the Dominican Republic, so Attles decided to humor him.

"What flavors, Jose?" asked Attles.

"It no matter," said Vargas. "Chocolate, vanilla. It's all the same. To the center, the basketball is like ice cream. Give me a taste."

Watch the big guys. You can see that message in their eyes. Nothing is more deflating to the center standing in the low post, his arm raised and holding his ground than to have the guard who is dribbling the ball look right at him and pass the ball to someone else.

After a while, the big guy starts to wonder, is it me? Do I have bad breath? Are we dating the same girl?

That's why when I work at a basketball clinic, I ask the kids, "Who are the centers?"

A bunch of kids will raise their hands and I'll take them down to one end of the court. I tell them: "If you're a center, the first thing you've got to do is catch the ball, no matter where it is thrown. What happens is if the guard throws you the ball and you don't catch it, the coach will probably blame the guard for a bad pass. But the guard will start to think, 'I threw the ball in there and the big fella didn't get it.' Soon, the guard is going to say, 'Forget the big fella, I'm going to someone else with my passes.' "

Then I tell the centers this: "No matter how awful the pass happens to be, tell the guard, 'Hey, man, my bad. I shouldda had it.' I don't care if you couldn't have reached the ball standing on top of the Hancock Building, always say, 'It's my bad.' Then tell the guard, 'Don't you worry, I'll catch the next one.' Then if you have to grab a chair and knock out the guy guarding you to get open, do it so you can get the next pass. When the guard throws you the ball, no matter how mundane the pass, tell him, 'Great pass. Way to thread the needle.' After the game, take the guard out for a chocolate sundae or fix him up with a date with your sister. Pretty soon the guard is thinking, 'The big fella is all right.' Soon, the ball starts going into the low post more often."

My message is that the big man has no choice. He has to be nice to the guards. One guard can stand out there dribbling the ball all day, or he can throw it to the other guard, who can stand out there dribbling the ball all day. Even the forwards can go out to the top of the key to get the ball.

But The Man in the Middle, the ball-and-chain man, is supposed to stay in the paint—hold his ground. Whatever he does, he is not supposed to dribble the ball because the little guys will run in and take it from him. Coaches consider a big man who dribbles worse than an ax murderer.

All the centers hear is what I call "Don'ts":

Don't dribble.

Don't go farther than a few feet from the basket.

Don't try to play defense in the open court because we want you under the basket so you can play defense and block shots.

Don't go to the foul line to catch a pass because we want you under the basket so you can rebound.

Don't take a jump shot from more than five feet away.

Don't try any difficult passes.

When I played, I sometimes felt like the polar bear at the zoo, who is behind a moat and all he can do is stand there and wave his paw, hoping someone will throw him a peanut.

Smart point guards understand this. Magic Johnson makes sure that Jabbar sees a lot of the ball. One of the greatest attributes of New York point guard Mark Jackson is how he uses his center, Pat Ewing. If you watch the Knicks, notice that Jackson is always talking to Ewing, patting the big fella on the butt and telling him what a great rebound Ewing just hauled in. Jackson knows that if the Knicks are going anywhere, it will be Ewing who takes them there. I've seen Jackson out ahead of the pack on the fast break and he'll stop and wait for Ewing, giving him a pass so Ewing can slam.

The problem is that there aren't enough guards who understand the game as Magic and Jackson do. That's why too many Big Men end up going through ten minute stretches where they just don't see the ball, and then they decide that, "If no one will pass it to me, I won't rebound."

Pouting?

Of course. But Big Men have feelings, too.

Perhaps the most humbling of all experiences for the Big Men is at the foul line. They usually are miserable free throw shooters, and I think part of the reason is a lack of practice. It's the ball-and-chain routine, never being allowed to get the ball at the foul line during a game situation. All that coaches stress to the Big Men is rebounding. There is a tradition of centers being lousy free throw shooters so I think coaches just assume that the big guys won't make their free throws.

Another factor is that the Big Man feels naked when he's at the foul line.

When a guy is fouled, the game stops. The Big Man goes to the line, the officials hand him the ball and then the other nine guys on the floor and the 20,000 people in the stands are all watching him. He can feel them staring and he knows that they're thinking, "This big stiff can't even hit a foul shot."

So the inevitable happens. He misses, they laugh and he's embarrassed. Then the official hands him the ball and tells him to try it again. Now, the Big Man is thinking, "If I miss two in a row, the coach will be all over my case. The guards won't throw me the ball. The fans will boo me. They'll forget about all the rebounds I got and the picks I set."

The whole thing is psychological.

That's why Wilt Chamberlain could never make free throws. He tried everything—underhanded, one-handed, two-handed, from the side, from five feet behind the line. In college, he even attempted to run from half-court and take off at the foul line. He wanted to dunk it, but they changed the rules to end that strategy.

The reason I insist it's all in the Big Man's head is that some centers are superb free throw shooters—Bill Laimbeer, Jack Sikma and Corzine are all shooting nearly 90 percent.

I played a game at the old Madison Square Garden where

I stood at the line and I could swear I saw the rim moving. At first, I thought I was choking. I was afraid to say anything because if anyone heard me, they'd grab a big net and haul me off. But I looked above the basket and I saw a guy lying on the cable running from the second balcony, and he was pulling it back and forth.

So the basket was really moving.

But I never said anything. I figured no one would believe me. That's how it is for a Big Man—even when he knows he's right he still figures that he's wrong.

———————●

I was the Bulls' first coach in 1966. I would have loved to have been the Bulls' first center, but my knees were pretty much shot.

How did I know I was finished?

One day I drove the lane and got called for three seconds before I could get to the basket and take my shot. That's when you know your wheels are about to fall off. Besides, I always wanted to tell other big guys what coaches told me. At home I'd practice screaming, "Hey, hold your ground out there."

Boy that sounded good.

Then reality hit. I remember when I was hired to coach the Bulls, I could look down at my starting center.

That, friends, is a bad sign.

The sportswriters used to joke that I was the best center on the team, not poor Erwin Mueller, even though I was the coach. He was the Bulls first starting center, my center, to be exact. He was 6-foot-7.

Talk about bad signs.

In pro basketball, a 6-foot-7 center is like a 120-pound bodyguard. All you can do is pray the guy knows karate. I don't mean to knock Erwin Mueller. He wasn't bad. He couldn't shoot from the field very well. . . his foul shooting wasn't the best. . . he didn't even lead our team in rebounding—6-foot-6 guard Jerry Sloan did. But Mueller did jump fairly well and he could get out and run on our fast break. Hey, what could I really expect? When we drafted Mueller, he was a 6-foot-7 *forward* at San Francisco University.

Talk about bad signs.

You're supposed to take college centers and make them into NBA forwards, not the other way around. We had the whole thing backwards. So that's how the bloodline of Chicago centers began. When we were putting together the Bulls in the expansion draft, we wanted a big guy, and we took a fellow from Boston named John Thompson, who was Bill Russell's back-up. Thompson never showed up for training camp. I always wondered whatever happened to him after he retired. Of course, Thompson ended up coaching Georgetown, where he could tell his own big guys to hold their ground. Another center we had was Nate Bowman, at 6-foot-10, whom we drafted from the Cincinnati Royals. Jerry Colangelo (then the business manager of the Bulls, now the owner of the Phoenix Suns) and I used to play 2-on-2 with Bowman and Dave Schellhase (our No. 1 draft choice from Purdue) and we consistently beat them. Colangelo was a good college guard, but never played in the NBA.

Talk about bad signs.

So we settled on Mueller, who did well enough to make the NBA All-Rookie team. Like Corzine, he wasn't bad. And like Corzine, he had to live with people saying, "The trouble with the Bulls is that they got nobody in the middle."

No matter what a coach tells you, when he doesn't have a good center, he feels as if someone just tied both of his hands behind his back and sent him into the ring with Mike Tyson. Before a game, I'd look down, yes *down,* at Mueller and I'd start to say something like, "Hey, try to get the opening tip." But then I'd stop. Why say that? He's 6-foot-7, Chamberlain is at least 7-foot—why waste your breath?

When we were playing Philadelphia, I didn't want to upset Mueller. He was going to face the greatest offensive force in the game, a guy who was averaging 50 points, playing all 48 minutes a night and getting 25 rebounds. I sure as hell didn't want to talk about the night Chamberlain scored 100 points. I looked around the dressing room and I saw poor Mueller sitting there and I decided I wasn't going to say a word about Chamberlain. When I told the guys about the matchups, I said, "Sloan, you take Jones. Guy Rodgers, you take Greer. Bob Boozer, you've got Luke Jackson. Jimmy Washington, you guard Walker and Mueller, you've got the big guy."

I just sort of tossed it off—"Mueller, you've got the big guy."

Well, at the half, the big guy had 42 points. As we were leaving the court for halftime, I couldn't wait until we got into the dressing room. I grabbed Mueller and said, "I told you to watch the big guy."

"I did, coach, and he's great," said Mueller.

So how do you handle a situation like that?

Before another game, I tried psychology. I said, "Washington, pretend you're the greatest defensive rebounder in the NBA. Rodgers, pretend you're the best point guard ever to dribble a ball. Sloan, pretend you're the toughest defensive player in the history of the game. Boozer, pretend you're the best 15-foot shooter in the history of the game. And Mueller, pretend you're the premier center in the league."

I forget to tell these guys that they were playing Bill Russell and the Boston Celtics. And to no one's surprise, we lost the game. I was walking off the court with my hands stuffed in my back pockets and my head down. Mueller came up to me and said, "Coach, coach!"

"What?" I asked.

"Pretend we won," said Mueller.

So here's today's lesson:

If you're going to win—and I mean win big—you need a great center.

Just good isn't good enough. Championship teams have All-Stars in the middle. That's what history tells us. The old cigarette advertisement about "It's what's up front that counts" is right. If you were to list the championship teams since the late 1950s— the advent of Russell and Chamberlain—you'd discover that great teams have great centers.

There is only one exception, the 1974–75 Golden State Warriors, who won it all with Clifford Ray in the middle. Irony of ironies is that Clifford Ray was a former Bulls center who was traded by Chicago to the Warriors for a No. 1 draft choice and Nate Thurmond. I considered Thurmond a championship caliber center even though he never played on a team that won a world title. Jabbar has often said that Thurmond was the most difficult defender he has ever faced.

I left the Bulls for the Phoenix Suns and Dick Motta took over as coach. He thought that they couldn't win an NBA title with Ray at center. Thurmond was 33 at the time and Motta was convinced that Thurmond's experience and defensive presence—the man knew how to block a shot—would help the Bulls in the playoffs. As it turned out, Thurmond had a quadruple-double in his very first game with Chicago—double-figures in points, assists, rebounds and blocked shots. It was a truly great performance. But for Thurmond, it was all downhill, and I mean way downhill, after that. Thurmond was supposed to split the center spot with Tom Boerwinkle, and these two old warhorses were supposed to become one very excellent center. On paper, it seemed good. In the bars where scouts get together and pour out the gossip while the pour down the beer, they'd tell you that Motta's thinking was sound.

Except true to the history of Bulls centers, it didn't work.

Thurmond never fit into Motta's offense. He was a low-post center ordered to play the high post. That's like trying to shove a square peg into a round hole.

As for Ray, he was decent with the Warriors and decent in Chicago, but nothing special at any point in his career. His one attribute was that he was a real load—6-foot-9 and about 250 pounds. When Clifford Ray set a pick on you, you suddenly started thinking about dentures for the first time in your life. Hitting Ray was like dropping down into a sprinter's stance and running head-first into the Berlin Wall.

What Ray also knew how to do was give the ball to the forwards, a couple of guys named Rick Barry and Jamal Wilkes. While they shot, Ray pounded the boards to the tune of 11 rebounds a night. He averaged only 9.4 points on 6.6 shots per game.

I put an asterisk next to that 1974–75 Warriors team. It won a championship—once and only once. In fact, the Warriors never again made it to the NBA finals.

Okay, so we've given Clifford Ray his due and mentioned that for one season the theory of great centers and championships did not hold up.

But here is how it breaks down.

In the 1980s, only three centers have played on the championship teams—the Laker's Jabbar, Boston's Robert Parish and Philadelphia's Moses Malone. All of them are All-Stars.

In the 1970s, the championship centers were Seattle's Jack

Sikma, Portland's Bill Walton, Washington's Wes Unseld, Boston's Dave Cowens, New York's Willis Reed, Chamberlain with the Lakers in 1972 and Jabbar with Milwaukee in 1971. Again, all of these players were All-Stars.

As for the 1960s, it was all Russell and Chamberlain.

What I'm saying is that when it comes to putting together a championship team, there can be no gimmicks. You need the horse in the middle. You must have that player who can score, who can block shots and get rebounds. Even if Sikma and Parish don't end up in the Hall of Fame, they are tremendous centers.

But there really are four centers who have shaped the NBA.

George Mikan: The First Big Man

Even by today's standards, George Mikan was a big man at 6-foot-10 and 250 pounds. But when he played at DePaul and in the NBA from the middle 1940s to the middle 1950s, the guy was a giant. Most centers were a half-foot shorter and the key was only six feet wide compared to the 16 feet it is today.

So all old George had to do was go near the basket, stand there and put his hand up. No one was strong enough to move him out of the lane. When Mikan got the ball, he was so close to the basket and so much taller than anyone else and so damn strong, about all he had to do was turn and shoot, and his shots were more like lay-ups than hooks.

What Mikan did was show what that size meant to a basketball team. The fact that he was more than big, that he had some coordination and a few moves, enabled him to become the first dominant center in NBA history. When Mikan retired at the start of the 1954–55 season, his Minneapolis Lakers had won three consecutive titles and five of the last six. I think it's somewhat ironic that 1954–55 also was the season when I came into the league with Syracuse, and we won the title that year. Mikan had quit to coach the Lakers, and the Lakers found out they were a better team with a guy named Mikan in the middle rather than on the bench.

The following season Mikan came out of retirement to play for the Lakers. I had heard about him for years. He was Mr. Basketball, the man who invented how the center position was played. So I was psyched up the first time I played him. Early in the game, he did the same thing to me that he did to everyone else. He took me under the basket, caught the ball, sort of swatted me out of the way and scored. He got about 12 points off me in the first half and I didn't know what was going on.

In the dressing room, Coach Al Cervi jumped on me. "Johnny, you've got to run the guy. You're quick, he's an old man. Make him chase you up and down the court. You can't stand under the basket and play his game, he's too strong for you."

I did just that and I scored something like 17 points against Mikan in the third period. Actually, I scored because he couldn't catch me. I was beating him down the court, getting position near the basket before he could get to me. So after the game, I was feeling pretty good. We'd won, I'd scored all these points against George Mikan, who was at the time the greatest center in basketball history.

Now I can look back and realize that Mikan was 32 at the time, in bad shape because he had come out of retirement. This was the first year of the 24-second clock, and by the fourth quarter, poor George needed an oxygen tank. The George Mikan I faced was not the same guy who had averaged 23 points and 14 rebounds for nine years.

The other irony is that if Mikan were to play today, he would be one of the smallest centers in the league. Even Dave Corzine at 6–11, 260 pounds is taller and heavier. I'd like to think that Mikan could have adjusted to modern basketball, that his little turn-around hook and his strength would have kept him in the league, but I just don't know.

I'd say if Mikan were to show up at a training camp today, he'd never have a chance. Of course, he'd also be something like 65 years old. But if a young George Mikan tried out for the NBA, the best he probably could hope for would be to be a back-up center or power forward.

Nonetheless, when Mikan retired, there was a void in the middle. That's when my Syracuse team sneaked in and won a title. We thought we could win a few more, but we didn't know about Bill Russell.

Bill Russell: Candle Snuffer

George Mikan brought the hook shot into basketball and Bill

Russell swatted it away.

No man has ever blocked shots as well as Russell, and play-ing against him was amazing because his style was very different than the one used by most centers. We've already talked about life in the middle—the body banging, the elbows and the bloody noses. If you tried to go somewhere under the basket, you had to *fight* to get there because someone was always leaning on you.

Not Russell.

He'd let you go anywhere you wanted. He never tried to take away your position. Want to stand six feet from the basket on the right of the key? Fine. Eight feet on the left . . . that's okay with Russell.

If Russell were like the other 99 percent of us who made our living on the boards, you'd think the guy was crazy to play like this. But there was also a very scary part—you never knew exactly where Russell was standing.

The guy was always sneaking up on me. I'd think I had good position in the low post, I'd put up my hand and ask for a pass. I didn't feel Russ on my back, I didn't see him so I'd think he was off somewhere not worrying about me. Then the pass would come my way and Russ would bolt out of nowhere to steal it.

And true to the big man's code, all I could do was look at the guy who threw me the pass, shrug my shoulders and say, "Hey, don't worry. My fault."

No matter what happens, it's always the center's fault when he doesn't catch a pass.

Against most mortal centers, body contact told you a lot. If the center was leaning on your left side, you could sort of posi-tion your body so you could catch a pass to your right. You'd shield the defender from stealing the pass with your body. The same thing after you got the ball. If you felt the guy pushing you from the left side, you'd spin right and take your shot.

But you never felt Russ anywhere. You just knew he was there.

So you might turn right for your shot, and there he'd be, making you eat the ball. All you could do was guess about Russ, and most of us guessed wrong. Sometimes, it seemed like he was playing you on all sides because he was so quick. I played a lot of high-post center. That means I'd go out to the foul line and catch a pass so I could either take my shot or pass to a teammate cutting to the basket. When I'd catch the ball at the high post, Russ would drop off me a bit. I'd think that I had room to take a shot, but I was worried. I'd see Russ in the key, bent over in that defensive crouch of his. He'd be staring at you with those piercing eyes. He had that scraggly beard, and he usually had a couple of his crooked fingers taped together, and a lot of the time he was coughing or wheezing or something. He acted like an old man who was going to die.

Then I'd try a move.

And it was a medical miracle. The man was cured. He would spring at me like some huge cat and he'd block my shot. Russ really frustrated me. I never was certain where he was or exactly where I should go to get my shot off against him. I will say this— Russ made me and a lot of other centers better passers. The coaches saw him blocking all of our shots and they started using us as decoys. We'd get the ball at the high post and they'd send cutters to the basket for us to pass to, trying to take Russ away from the hoop.

It was, "Kerr, you keep Russ busy so the other guys can score."

While Mikan demonstrated the value of size, Russ showed what size and athletic talent could do on the floor. He was the next evolutionary step up from Mikan. Russ also was only 6-foot-9, and I always was convinced he was taller. It was hard to imagine a 6-foot-9 guy blocking shots as he did.

We don't know how many shots Russell blocked in his career. The NBA didn't start keeping track of blocks until the 1973–74 season, when it picked up the idea from the old American Basketball Association.

Furthermore, Russ was an intelligent player with ability, which made him all the more devastating.

One example was how he blocked shots. More to the point, how Russ understood the value of the blocked shot. Actually, I prefer the term "spoiled shot," because that's the most important aspect of shot blocking.

When Bill Russell blocked a shot, it was like snuffing a candle. He didn't knock the ball into the stands or past half-court. I call that slam-blocking. The shot goes up, the guy slams it to who knows where in the second balcony. That serves absolutely no purpose. Suppose Michael Jordan drives down the lane and

Manute Bol whacks Jordan's shot halfway to Evansville.

What happens?

The Bulls get the ball again. They pass it in to Michael, who gets to drive again. In the boxscore, that goes down as a blocked shot. In my mind, it was pretty much a waste of effort because the ball didn't change hands. Chicago had it before the block and Chicago had it after. The crowd got to go "Oooooo..." but that was it.

Another useless block is the In Your Face. That's when Michael Jordan drives to the basket and Manute Bol takes the ball and shoves it right back into Jordan's face. Most of the time, an In Your Face block becomes a foul because you are swinging down at the man whose shot you're trying to block and that creates contact. Again, the fans see it and get excited. They stand and yell "Face...face...face." Maybe a foul isn't called, but usually the guy taking the shot ends up with the ball because it was shoved right back at him.

Russ snuffed candles. When the ball went up, he just flicked it enough to spoil it. Either he caught the ball himself or one of his teammates ran it down. Russ was so good that he could block a shot in the direction of another Celtic so that player could take possession and start fast breaks.

What confuses me is why more players today don't follow Russ' lead. They still insist on slam-blocking. They jump both vertically and horizontally—in other words, they don't just jump straight up to block the shot, they jump at the man taking the shot so they can get an In Your Face. Most of the time even when they block the shot, they end up whacking the shooter and being called for a foul.

I suppose much of this is a product of the playground. Kids grow up dreaming of In Your Face dunks and In Your Face blocks. It's a sign of power. It's macho. It's also dumb basketball.

As I mentioned, Nate Thurmond was a great player but he was into power blocking. So was Wilt Chamberlain.

But Russell just Snuffed the Candle. He controlled the game. He might only block five shots a night, but you never knew which five or when he'd do it. And he was rarely in foul trouble because he jumped straight up instead of at the man whose shot he wanted to snuff.

Would Bill Russell be able to play today?

You bet, even if he is about 55. Russ is a center for all the ages. The Celtics won 11 titles in the 13 years Russell played. The common thread between the first and last championship was Russell—all the other players on the team had changed. That also was true of Mikan. He was the only player from the first championship won in 1949 to be around when they won their last one in 1954. That's what Russell and Mikan meant to their teams.

Wilt Chamberlain: Docile Giant

I was stretching a point with Russell. He wouldn't be a factor today, not in his middle 50s, though the Bill Russell who made the Boston Celtics would make any of this era's teams a champion. But one retired center who could step on the court tomorrow and give a team 15 good minutes a night is Wilt Chamberlain, and I don't care if he's in his early 50s.

I remember a game where Wilt dunked a ball that almost broke my toe.

That's right, not my arm, my toe. He hammered the ball through the rim with such force that it slammed against my foot before it hit the floor. I ran down to the other end of the floor and there were tears coming from my eyes. I was convinced the toe was broken, but it turned out to be a severe bruise.

Wilt was over 7-foot-2 and 275 pounds, all of it muscle. I know that Wilt was measured at 7-foot-1 ⅛th, but some guys measured the ceiling in the shower room in Philadelphia and it was 7-foot-2, and Wilt had to duck when he went in there. So the guy was at least 7-foot-2—in his bare feet.

When I got the ball at the low post, I could see his shadow looming over my shoulder. He was just so damn big.

All I can say was, "Thank God he was docile." If not, he could have destroyed continents. Those of us who played against him would have had to spend a lot of time making sure our wills were up-to-date.

What helped against Wilt was him being so passive. He was the center with that ball-and-chain on his foot. If you went out to the foul line to catch a pass, Wilt would stay under the basket. If you wanted to take a 15-footer, he'd let you. He waited for people to come to him before he'd block their shots, while Russell would chase you everywhere. I've taken 20-footers that were blocked by Russell.

Facing Chamberlain, you knew he'd get his points. Hey, the guy *averaged* 50 one season and once scored 100 in a game. His career average was 30. Wilt had that famous finger-roll lay-up, and he also had a short fade-away jumper. Wilt's fade-away jumper must have driven his coaches crazy. Wilt was the biggest guy on the floor, why did he have to take a shot where he fell away from the basket?

There is no answer to that one.

Just like why didn't Wilt learn a hook shot, which would have been perfect for a guy his size?

Again, there are no answers other than Wilt was Wilt and Wilt did what he wanted on the court.

Early in his career, Wilt wanted to score. That was when he was good for 50 points a night. Then people said Wilt couldn't pass, so he went for the assist title and won it with an 8.6 average in 1966–67. And that's still a record for centers.

In so many ways, Chamberlain's career is measured by numbers. He's another guy who had Lord knows how many blocks because they weren't counted. And no one counted his toe-breaking dunks. That's where Wilt got his revenge. Defensively, he seldom leaned on you (Thank God!) and he pretty much let you roam outside. That meant you could score on Wilt if you had a decent shot from 15 feet. But then you had to guard him.

No one could guard Chamberlain.

No, not even Russell. Russ' teams usually beat Chamberlain's, but Wilt averaged 28 points against Russell. The NBA record for rebounds is 55 and Wilt did that against Bill Russell.

It was fun to watch those battles. Russ was the master psychologist. He didn't like the press and seldom spoke publicly about Wilt. Chamberlain reveled in the attention and was always shooting off his mouth. The day before he'd play the Celtics, Wilt always would tell reporters, "Russell doesn't own me."

I always pictured Russell at his kitchen table in the morning, sipping his first cup of coffee and smiling as he read about Wilt popping off in the newspaper. It would seem like Wilt would go out and have a big game against Russell, but Russ would make some play down the stretch that would change the momentum and help the Celtics win. When it was over, the reporters would dwell on the fact that Russell beat Chamberlain. . . again. And that would set Wilt off. . . again.

It was like these two men had been severed from the rest of their teams. They were both literally and figuratively bigger than the guys they played with because they were always the focal point.

For example, Russell never averaged 20 points per game in a season while Chamberlain averaged at least 33 in each of his first seven seasons. Both guys averaged 20 rebounds per game for their careers.

Yet there is a side of basketball that can't be measured in numbers. Often, it is not how many rebounds a player gets, but when does he get them? Does it happen in the middle of the second quarter when no one else is under the basket or does it happen late in the game when everyone is jumping over your back and trying to tear your head off to get the ball? The same with blocks. Do you swat the shot when it doesn't matter or during the last minute of play when a basket can decide the game?

Russell appealed to those with an artist's sense of the game. His baskets, his rebounds, his blocks all seemed to come when it really meant something. His main job was defense. Chamberlain's strength happened to be whatever he wanted it to be that particular season, and he often changed his on-court personality from season to season.

What we are talking about is *how* these guys played. No one ever doubted that Russ played hard. He sweated, he leaped, he left his soul on the floor.

Tom Meschery, a former pro basketball player who wrote poetry, compared Russell to a condor that sat on top of a mountain and waited for the prey to come into his territory. When it did, the condor would swoop down, striking quickly and lethally. Russell was always there, waiting, staring. He was a real contrast to Mikan, who was like some grumpy bear roaming around, wanting to cuff you, maybe even maul you if he was mad enough.

Wilt was a happy guy, but he also was very passive. The game came so easily to him. He was not a mean, physical player like Wes Unseld or Willis Reed. He just did his thing, and the facts show that for most of his career, he'd play the entire 48 minutes and seldom missed a game. So he played hurt and played all the time. It was almost as if Wilt was a friendly elephant.

It would have been nice to see Wilt play with Russell's old Celtic teams while Russ played with some of Wilt's so-so teams in Philadelphia and San Francisco. When Wilt went to Los Angeles, he finally was surrounded by the likes of Jerry West and Elgin Baylor. Wilt was still great, but not as awesome as he once was, so I guess we'll never know how big a difference his teammates would have made to Wilt's game.

Kareem Abdul-Jabbar: The Dinosaur

If only we had called tails.

That's what I think about whenever I see Kareem Abdul-Jabbar play.

And if I had called tails, I might still be coaching and Jabbar might be my center. I came very close to being a great coach, much closer than my 93–190 lifetime record shows.

That's because I was a coin toss away from being Jabbar's first coach. Instead, I got to be Neal Walk's first coach. Believe me, there's a difference—sort of like being on "Let's Make a Deal" and having a chance to win a deep sea fishing trip and ending up with a can of Starkist Tuna instead.

I don't mean to knock Neal Walk, a workman-like 6-foot-10 pivot man from Florida who turned out to be a respectable center. But Jabbar never had to stay up nights worrying that Neal Walk was going to break his records.

I was coaching the Phoenix Suns in 1969 when Jabbar (then called Lew Alcindor) was coming out of UCLA. The Suns and the Milwaukee Bucks were the two teams with the worst records in the NBA. The team that would receive the first pick in the draft was to be decided by a coin flip. In Phoenix, we ran a contest asking the fans to pick what we should call—heads or tails.

They picked heads.

I always said never let the fans coach, and this just proved it. They can't even get a coin flip right.

Anyway, we were sitting in the office of the Suns' general manager Jerry Colangelo. The press also was there and we were all staring at this little brown box on the table.

From the box came Commissioner Walter Kennedy's voice, "Are you ready Phoenix?"

Colangelo said, "We're here."

Kennedy said, "Richard, are you there?"

"I'm here," said Richard Bloch, the owner of the Suns who was on the conference call in Los Angeles.

Kennedy asked, "Milwaukee, are you there?"

"We're here," said Bucks' Coach Larry Costello.

Kennedy said, "I'm going to take this Kennedy half-dollar and toss it in the air, catch it in my right hand and turn it over."

We're all holding our breath. Actually, we were going to call heads anyway because we had checked with someone in Las Vegas who told us that coin flips come out heads 52 percent of the time or something like that. Of course, that's if you flip the coin 1,000 times.

Kennedy said, "Phoenix, what do you call."

Colangelo said, "Heads."

Kennedy said, "Phoenix calls heads...It's tails."

We heard this roar coming out of the little brown box. It was the Milwaukee people going crazy. It was complete pandemonium breaking loose while we're all standing there, lumps in our throats and feeling like we're going to cry.

Finally I said to Colangelo, "Maybe they'll take Neal Walk."

No laughs. No smiles. No center.

Later, we started to rationalize. Jabbar liked playing on the West Coast and maybe he'd refuse to go to Milwaukee. He said that he liked UCLA because of the warm weather, perhaps we could work a deal. On and on, but of course that never materialized.

I ended up with Neal Walk and by the middle of that season, I ended up out of work.

Jabbar went to Milwaukee, where he played for Larry Costello. I played with Larry and I always considered him a super coach for a big man. He designed more plays to get the ball into the post than any other coach. I think he had more than 40 plays to get the ball to Jabbar. Costello was a genius when it came to the Xs and Os. Of course, it helped that Costello had Jabbar to work with. Kareem came out of UCLA as a finished product. He had the whole package—he could run, shoot, jump, block shots. He was listed at 7-foot-2, but I always thought Kareem was taller than that.

When Jabbar first came into the league, he was kind of a

skinny kid and the other guys tried to lean on him. But he was too quick and had an inner toughness. He wasn't going to be intimidated.

Jabbar had superb coaching by John Wooden at UCLA. That was something that put him way ahead of Chamberlain, who played at Kansas and with the Globetrotters before he came to the NBA. I really don't know what kind of coaching Wilt received, but his certainly wasn't as strong as Jabbar's or what Bill Russell had at the University of San Francisco. I'd say that 90 percent of the big guys coming into the NBA were ball-and-chain types. They couldn't shoot, they weren't allowed to go more than a few feet from the basket, and they sometimes acted like the basketball was a hand grenade when they touched it because they were so excited to finally get the ball. None of that applied to Kareem. He entered the NBA knowing what it meant to win, knowing about pressure and having played at the top level of college basketball. He played three years at UCLA and they won three national titles. They were expected to win a national title each year, so you knew that Kareem had to have some ice water pumping through his veins. He also had been surrounded by all kinds of zone defenses in college. The rules committee even tried to stop him by putting in the No Dunking Rule for college games.

One of the factors that made Jabbar a great player was that he was a fine passer. If he is double-teamed, he'll drop off a pass to a guy cutting to the basket. He understands team basketball and he did from the moment he stepped off the UCLA campus.

Passing is a lost art with most centers. It is that ball-and-chain mentality. You don't want to trust the big kid to think about giving the ball to someone else. Hell, you don't even want to trust him with the ball, period.

When I played, I liked to pass the ball and that's why I've been partial to centers who could do the same. That's also why if I were going to start a franchise and had the choice of any center, I'd pick a healthy Bill Walton. Like Kareem, Walton played for John Wooden at UCLA. He was even a better passer than Kareem, and that's saying a lot. Both guys could hurt you in so many ways. Leave them open, they hit the shot. Double-team them, they hit the open man with a pass. Defensively, they roamed the key and blocked shots, Jabbar not as well as Russell, but close enough. It's just a shame that Walton had foot injuries so many times in his career because he would have ended up on this list of centers who changed the face of the game.

So passing, especially from the high post, is something I miss in basketball. So is the hook shot.

The irony is that Kareem didn't need the dunk because he has the greatest hook shot the game has ever seen.

I love Kareem's hook. Maybe it's because that shot is from my generation, but I say that hook is for all generations and the young guys today just don't know it. They see Kareem throwing in the skyhook at 40 years old and they say, "Look at that guy," as if they just caught a glimpse of a dinosaur. Or they watch the Laker games on television and act as though Kareem were caught in a time warp.

"Jabbar's shot is nice, but we don't do that anymore."

Why not?

The hook is what is keeping Kareem in the league. It is what has made him the all-time highest scorer in NBA history. They couldn't block it then and they can't block it now. Don't tell me that the shot isn't hip, which is what the young centers are really saying when they don't practice the hook. Dunks are in. Turnaround jumpers are in. But all a hook shot does is go in.

George Mikan was the first guy to bring the hook shot into basketball's mainstream. When he played at DePaul, his coach was Ray Meyer and Ray made Mikan practice for hours, hooking with each hand. But because Mikan was so much bigger than everyone else and because the lane was only six feet, it wasn't the sweeping skyhook that Kareem has. But if you were a big kid who wanted to play ball, you saw what Mikan was doing and then you worked on the hook.

What I can't figure out is why kids today don't do the same.

All right, Russell took the hook out of basketball. Russ was so quick and his timing so perfect that he was one of the few men who could block the hook without fouling. Back then, there were only eight teams in the league so you got to face Russell a lot, and that meant you had to change your game and forget about the hook, at least when you played the Celtics. But Kareem brought the hook back into the NBA. People think Kareem invented the shot. Now that Russell is gone, no one can block it, but no one shoots it.

Look around the league. Who consistently takes a hook shot?

Moses Malone has scored eight million points or whatever and he doesn't have one. Neither do Robert Parish, Bill Laimbeer, Akeem Olajuwon or about anyone else. Once in a while, these guys heave a "half-hook" at the basket, but that is not a real hook. The guy just puts the ball above his head in one hand and flips it at the basket. That's a tougher shot because the man really isn't shooting it, he is throwing it and hoping for the best.

I know a lot of people say that zone defenses are the reason that no one takes hook shots. They say that when a kid gets the ball near the basket, he has to turn and shoot it fast before he gets double-teamed, which is why so many big guys have turnaround jumpers.

Yet when Kareem faced collapsing zones in college, he got off the hook.

The problem is the high school and college coaches. They just don't teach the shot. They tell their kids, "Now, son, don't you worry about hook shots or anything, you just keep the ball-and-chain on your leg, get rebounds and tip-ins. Once in a while, we'll give you the ball, but only when you're close enough to get a lay-up. Don't think out there, just jump and hit the boards. We have the little guys to shoot 3-pointers and they'll take care of the offense."

That's not coaching a kid, it's restricting him.

I've been to a lot of basketball camps and they give all the kids shooting drills. Go to this spot on the floor and take a jumper. Go to that spot and take a jumper. Take two dribbles to your right and take a shot, two dribbles to your left . . .

Or they say, "You're a center, go under the basket and jump up and touch the rim a hundred times. Work on your legs."

Why don't they have drills so big men can practice hook shots?

There also is the Magic Johnson factor.

Kids see Magic, who is about 6-foot-10, playing guard, dribbling the ball through his legs and passing it behind his back. So the big kids go to the playground and they all want to be 6-foot-10 point guards.

But if you've noticed, Magic recently came up with a new shot—a hook. He learned it from the master. Magic went to Kareem and asked Kareem to teach him a shot that he could get off in traffic under the basket.

If the hook is good enough for Kareem and Magic, two of the greatest players in NBA history, why does everyone else ignore it? This just drives me absolutely crazy. During a Bulls game I'll be sitting at the press table next to Jimmy Durham, and I'll say, "Jimmy, if only this guy had a hook shot!" Jimmy has heard me say that (almost in despair) about a million times.

That's why I'll miss Kareem.

Okay, as a person, Kareem seemed to feel that people were trying to take advantage of him or that they just didn't like him. He didn't have the playful personality of Wilt Chamberlain, or even that cackle of a laugh that Bill Russell made famous. Kareem seemed to stare right through you with those suspicious eyes. Of course, he did leave college in the late 1960s when the country was in a state of semi-rebellion with all the riots over Vietnam on campus. That also was in the middle of the civil rights movement. Kareem is a bright guy and all these things had an effect on him. Kareem is a hard person to get to know off the court. But on the court, he and I understand each other perfectly every time he catches the ball and takes that skyhook.

So what would be my advice to anyone who ever had to guard Kareem?

Breathe on his goggles and pray they steam up.

The Search For Size

If you're a Bulls fan, you noticed that Mikan, Russell, Chamberlain and Jabbar never showed up in a Chicago uniform. As mentioned before, I had Erwin Mueller in my first year with the Bulls. As has been the case with about every Bulls team since then, I was looking for someone taller, someone bigger, someone better.

Here is how coaches think:

In my second season with the Bulls (1967–68), I really wanted a 7-footer and I heard that Reggie Harding was available. Harding met my first criteria—he was 7-foot, which was much taller than Mueller. He also was one of those first hardship cases, who skipped college and went straight to the pros with the Detroit Pistons.

Everyone in the NBA knew that Reggie Harding was trouble.

He came from the worst ghetto in Detroit. I'm thinking, "Well, we'll take Reggie away from Detroit and all of his friends in the inner city. Maybe that will straighten him out."

So where do I bring Reggie Harding?

To Chicago, which has more crooks and street hustlers than Detroit.

No matter, I was going to save Reggie Harding. I was going to be the one coach who could do what no one else ever did—communicate with the kid.

For a while, it worked. Reggie had a couple of good games. Then one night we were playing in San Francisco and I got a call from Harding's high school coach telling me that Reggie's mother had died. It was about four in the morning and I called Reggie's hotel room. He wasn't in so his roommate, Flynn Robinson, answered. Flynn had a stuttering problem and the guys on the team called him Freddie Flintstone.

Kerr: "Flint, I need to talk to Reggie."

Robinson: "He's...he's...he's...not here."

Kerr: "Where is he?"

Robinson: "He's...he's...you know...he's eating...you know...breakfast."

Kerr: "He's eating breakfast at four in the morning?"

Robinson: "You know...he's...well, he's..."

Kerr: "I know. Just have him call me."

The phone rang about nine in the morning and I told Reggie to come to my room. When he got there, I told him about his mother and said he should go home to help his family.

For two weeks, I never heard a word from Reggie. Once in a while, someone from the front office would call but had no luck. Finally, I got in touch with Reggie and he said that he was the executor of his mother's will and he had to take care of the estate.

The estate?

This guy was from the projects in Detroit. The family couldn't have had $1,000 in the bank.

From there, it was just one dumb thing after another. Reggie later was arrested when he tried to rob a store. He knew the store owner. He was 7-foot and he walked in wearing a Lone Ranger mask. The owner recognized him right away and said, "Reggie, you don't want to do this."

But Reggie wanted to do it. He did it and the next day the

cops went to his house and picked him up.

That's the mindset. Coaches will try anyone from anywhere if he's 7-foot. It used to be that we just scoured the country for talent, now it's the globe.

Take a guy like Manute Bol. If he was a regular 7-footer, he couldn't play in the league. But he's 7-foot-6 and pretty much lacking any semblance of athletic talent. He's from the Sudan where he used to herd sheep and kill lions. His passport says he's 5-foot-2. He says they took his picture sitting down. His age? Who knows. Cleveland State Coach Kevin Mackey brought Bol to the U.S. and he says that Bol's birth is "a moveable feast. Your guess is as good as mine." The whole thing is crazy. I look at Bol and I think that this is a guy who must be standing on stilts. No one can be that tall without breaking in half. And he really can't play basketball. Chuck Nevitt is 7-foot-5 and he never gets off the bench. I think he has more ability than Manute. Mike Smrek is 7-foot-1 and I know he has more ability than Manute, but Smrek never plays. Manute plays more than those guys because he is so tall.

Imagine what Manute's resume would look like—back-up NBA center, shepherd, lion killer.

If Bol had turned out to be a player, some agent would have signed up the entire Dinka tribe and auctioned all those guys off for a million bucks a pop. San Antonio had this guy from Iceland, Petur Gnudmundsson. Is he a center or the Abominable Snowman? He grew up in Reykjavik and when he was 13 his goal was to be a team handball player. He already was 6-foot-5. Now he's almost 7-foot-3. He's just one of the guys keeping the key warm in San Antonio until David Robinson gets out of the Navy.

Mark Eaton is 7-foot-5 and about 3 million pounds. He is a monster in the middle for Utah. He is so big and so wide that Jabbar couldn't even deal with him in the 1988 playoffs. He's another guy who wouldn't be in the league if he were 7-foot. When Eaton was at UCLA, he never got off the bench. As it is, Eaton has been a starting center for the Jazz since 1983 and never scored 20 points in a game. He leads the league in blocked shots. He doesn't just stand in the key, it seems like he's grazing in there.

There is one exception to the Goliath Rule about centers.

That's the Freak Factor, the tall guy at the end of the bench who never gets in.

In Chicago during the 1987–88 season, it was Granville Waiters. The fans liked him because he was about 7-foot and bald and his nickname was Granny. So when the Bulls were blowing someone out, the fans chanted for Granny.

Whatever team has Chuck Nevitt finds that it also has a guy the fans love. Suddenly, the big guy has become the underdog because he is so tall it appears he might break in half. Or because the game just seems so hard for him and he's so uncoordinated that he is very, very human. That's why fans go nuts when Manute Bol scores a basket. If you watch Manute do anything but take his flat-footed dunks you start to think that it would take this poor guy an hour to make ten shots from the foul line in an empty gym. He doesn't shoot the ball, he throws it at the basket like a guy would flip a dart at a board.

In my era, the guy the fans loved was Swede Halbrook, who was a legitimate 7-foot-3. In 1960, 7-foot-3 was what 7-foot-7 is today. We used to take a picture with him standing flat-footed and holding the ball above his head and against the rim. Swede was my backup. I'd play about 40 minutes and take a pounding under the boards. The fans would give me nice, polite applause when I left the game. Swede would come in and someone would try to throw him a long pass and he would sort of catch it and then fall flat on his face and the crowd would give him a standing ovation.

One good thing about being the 12th man—the fans always love you and it's unshakeable love. No matter what you do it is great because you aren't supposed to be good enough to do anything.

Swede did have one specialty. He gave Wilt Chamberlain a hard time. I asked him, "Swede, you can't play anybody in the league but Wilt. I don't get it."

"Oh, you can stop Wilt," he said.

"Really?"

"It's easy," said Swede. "The first thing you do is stand behind him and then when he gets up in the post, you put your elbows down on his shoulders so he can't get the ball."

"Elbows on his shoulders?" I said. "Jeez, you have to be taller than Wilt to do that."

Swede would just smile.

I guess everyone can do something and coaches continue to look at centers from anywhere.

The best of the next generation of centers may be Houston's Akeem Olajuwon, who is a former soccer goalie from Nigeria. I was a former high school soccer goalie from Chicago. Wonder why I couldn't jump like Akeem? The other center prospect is New York's Pat Ewing, who was born in Jamaica, although he mostly grew up in Cambridge, Massachusetts.

There are reasons why centers today won't have the statistics, especially on the boards, that the pivot men did during Chamberlain's era. Players make far more shots today than they did 20 years ago. The more shots made, the fewer misses. The fewer misses, the fewer rebounds. Shooting percentages have increased from about 40 percent to 50 percent. Suppose there are 200 field goal attempts in an average game. Twenty years ago, there would be 80 shots made and 120 misses. Today there would be 100 shots made and 100 misses. That means there are at least 20 fewer possible rebounds per game.

Nonetheless, the need for size is all the more acute. Instead of eight teams, there will be 27 by the 1989–90 season, meaning the demand for big men has tripled in the last 25 years.

That's why I say that all coaches and general managers are like that guy with a lantern in the middle of the night. But they're not looking for an honest man, just a tall one.

6

The Search for a Good Big and Little Man

Name the best center in the history of the Chicago Bulls. How about the best point guard?

The answers are Tom Boerwinkle and Norm Van Lier. Boerwinkle was a bull, a massive 7-footer who was rather clumsy on the court except when it came to passing. Then he delivered the ball like a guard. Boerwinkle's personality was passive, almost gentle like the touch he had on his passes. Boerwinkle reminded me of a kind, obedient elephant. Van Lier was a wiry 6-footer with the personality of a wolverine—nervous, suspicious, expecting a fight.

Boerwinkle and Van Lier played together on the Bulls teams of the early and middle 1970s and they had plenty of help from Bob Love, Chet Walker and Jerry Sloan. But it is no coincidence that the strongest teams the Bulls have ever had were when they were the strongest in the middle and at point guard.

And what does that mean?

Not only do you need a good big man to win, you need a good little man, too.

That's why one of the first moves I made with the Bulls made was to trade for Guy Rodgers from the Warriors. He is one of the finest passers ever in the NBA and he was the main reason we were able to run a fast break offense in 1966–67, even though the Bulls were an expansion team and even though they had 6-foot-7 Erwin Mueller at center. Rodgers set a league record with 908 assists in 81 games that season. He was a 6-footer with an outgoing personality, always patting guys on the butt, telling them they were doing a great job and to keep hustling. A coach loves it when a point guard does that.

There are two elements to the fast break—getting the rebound and getting the ball to a man in a position to make a lay-up. It is the big man who has to get the ball off the boards. It is the point guard who has to pass the ball to the right man at the right time on the break. It all sounds elementary and it is, assuming you have the players who can do it.

But another subconscious part of the fast break is what people think. A coach wants his big men to get the ball off the backboard and run up the court, filling a lane to perhaps get a pass back for a lay-up at the other end of the court. If the big men believe that the guards will give them the ball, then they will run after they get the rebound and throw an outlet pass to the guard. But if they run down the court a few times and see the guard just take the shot himself, then the big fellas get their feelings hurt. When they rebound, they pass the ball out and say, "The hell with it, I'm gonna walk up the court." They may even become so annoyed that they'll also say the hell with pounding the boards, and then the team is in real trouble.

That's why a team needs a point guard who the big men trust, a point guard such as Guy Rodgers, Magic Johnson or any of the other greats who played the position. They understand that there is a responsibility to everyone on the court when the coach puts the ball in your hands.

But for the most part, the Bulls haven't had those guys at the point and they haven't had the really big men in the middle.

I mentioned that Boerwinkle was probably the best center in the history of the Chicago franchise. I also have to admit, I didn't like Boerwinkle when he played at Tennessee. General Manager Dick Klein and I were trying to decide between Otto Moore and Boerwinkle because we thought they both would be there when it was our turn to draft. This was taking place in the middle of all the turmoil I had with Klein and I also was sure that I was going to take the job with the Phoenix Suns.

Anyway, I went to watch the Olympic trials in Albuquerque in 1968 and Boerwinkle was there looking terrible. I swear, he was about 300 pounds, seemed totally out of shape and could barely make it up and down the floor. I felt so sorry for the guy, I wanted to call him a cab so he could have a ride from place to place. I kept looking at Boerwinkle, trying to find something positive, but he was so overweight and so slow that all I could think was, "Gee, this is a bummer."

Meanwhile, Moore was a 6-foot-11 sprinter from Pan American. The guy could flat-out run and there was nothing flat about his jumping ability. I saw him as a shot-blocker in the pros. As it turned out, I went to Phoenix and Klein drafted Boerwinkle, who was perfect for those Bulls teams of the early 1970s. As for Moore, he was a journeyman center for several NBA teams.

With no disrespect intended to Boerwinkle or any of Chicago's other men in the middle, one of the problems with the Bulls was that while they have often been a bad team, sometimes they haven't been bad enough.

Say that again?

Think about the great centers and where they were placed in the draft—Kareem Abdul-Jabbar, Wilt Chamberlain, Akeem Olajuwon, Brad Daugherty, Pat Ewing, Bill Walton and even Ralph Sampson were the first players selected. Bill Russell went third. Until the lottery system was installed in 1985, the first draft pick was decided by a coin flip between the teams with the worst records in their respective divisions, meaning the Bulls never had a chance to draft an elite college center.

That's why the Bulls made one of their biggest, most controversial trades on draft day of 1988, sending Charles Oakley and their first round pick to New York for Bill Cartwright and the Knicks draft pick, which became Will Perdue. Everyone said that the Bulls would never compete for a championship until they got a player who was a force in the middle. Even Michael Jordan begged the front office to find someone to help out David Corzine at center.

Corzine is 6-foot-11, 260 pounds but his strength isn't blocking shots, nor is it scoring near the basket. He is a shooter, a guy who is best from 15–20 feet. In many ways, he is a lot like Jack Sikma and Laimbeer. All three of these guys come from white, upper-middle class families. When you watch these guys play, you know that they spend a lot of time practicing their shooting. They have good basketball skills for men their size and are almost 90 percent foul shooters. But they also remind me of backyard shooters—they practiced a lot by themselves. I don't think they often shot at a rim that didn't have a net. If any of them had gone to camp, it probably included a swimming pool, horseback riding and shuffleboard.

These guys are studied, methodical players. They are smart, play almost mistake-free and they work hard and keep in shape. But they don't have the physical skills to shut down the middle, to block shots, to score down low under the basket.

The Bulls won 50 games with Dave Corzine as their man in the middle in 1987–88, and clearly they thought that was the best they could do, which was why they traded Oakley.

It almost sounds like a move out of desperation—trading the league's premier rebounder, Oakley, for a 31-year-old center with a history of broken bones in his foot and for a rookie out of Vanderbilt who was not considered a franchise talent.

I did find it interesting that on draft day of 1988, the two top rebounders in the league—Michael Cage and Oakley—were traded. Both are power forwards, both are fanatical about rebounding and both have questionable offensive skills. The conventional thinking in the league is that you can find another power forward, but it is easier to discover the Dead Sea Scrolls than a new center.

The fact is that this team is still searching for a center and wants to see if Cartwright or Perdue can be the guy. What's more, I can't blame the Bulls for looking, especially when I think about the guys they've tried in the middle.

Mueller was the Bulls first center and he was really a forward. Then we traded for Reggie Harding, and that poor kid just was too immature and too much of a head case for him to play well for anyone. Then came Boerwinkle, who still has the team record with 37 rebounds in a game. There was Clifford Ray, but he had some knee problems and played at the same time as Boerwinkle.

There also was Jawann Oldham, another promising player from the neck down. He could block shots but he never had a feel for the game or understood the goaltending rule. He wanted to block everything, even when the ball was on the rim, which is why he has been traded several times. Oldham is known as a guy who is never content with his contract, a guy who thinks he's much better than he is and is never happy with his coach. The Bulls' coaching staff considered him a pain in the ass and I don't blame them. My favorite Oldham story was when he was with New York and the Knicks had just fired most of their front office. Oldham told several writers, "I wish the Knicks would hurry up and hire a general manager so I'd know who to tell that I want to be traded."

Wallace Bryant wandered through here for a short time in 1982 and what I remember about him was that he and Rod Higgins got tangled under the basket in a game against the Knicks at Madison Square Garden. Higgins drove the lane and someone kicked his legs out from under him, causing Higgins to come down flat on his back, his head banging against the floor. In the process, Higgins cut the legs out from under Bryant, and he came down right onto Higgins' skull. It was eerie, because for the longest time Higgins didn't move. Seriously, I was scared that he had died out there.

But it turned out that Higgins and Wallace Bryant were all right, but the Bulls just died when Bryant tried to play center.

Mike Smrek was another Bulls center. Smrek liked to block shots and unfortunately for him, there were times when he just couldn't do that. Instead of blocking, he ended up fouling. And Smrek wasn't the most graceful guy ever to wear sneakers. Well, let me put it to you this way—it got so bad that Michael Jordan didn't want to play in scrimmages when Smrek was on the other team because Smrek was continually, although unintentionally, taking Michael's head off. As a coach, I wouldn't be thrilled with my back-up center trying to send my star to an early funeral, so there was almost a sense of relief when Smrek moved on to the Lakers, and then to San Antonio. There was an exhibition game with Los Angeles when Smrek had to play because Jabbar was hurt. Michael took one look at Smrek and raised his hand, which is a signal to Doug Collins to take him out of the game for a rest. Of course, the game hadn't started and this was all done facetiously, but the message was clear—Michael did not want to take an early retirement because of Mike Smrek.

The most interesting center the Bulls have had is Artis

Gilmore, who played in Chicago from 1976–82 and again briefly in 1987. Gilmore is 7-foot-2, 270 pounds and a case can be made that he was the strongest player in the NBA after Chamberlain retired. Gilmore was a star in the American Basketball Association for Kentucky, and he came to the Bulls when the ABA folded and a dispersal draft was held to distribute that league's players. Artis was a low post center, where his size and sheer physical power was most effective. If you have a guy as big as Artis and as strong as Artis, then you should play him near the basket.

There was one problem—the Bulls didn't do that.

Gilmore joined a Chicago team that was still dominated by the forwards. The strategy was the same the Bulls used in the early 1970s—Boerwinkle at the high post throwing the pass while the forwards (Chet Walker and Bob Love) worked down low. It was absolutely the worst offense for Artis because he was asked to pass from the high post, which was new to him. He also was too far from the basket, which frustrated him. Under this system, he even set a league record for turnovers in 1977–78 that still stands.

Artis is a beautiful man, wonderful to be around. Like Wilt Chamberlain, we all can be grateful that Artis was docile on the court or there would have been corpses everywhere. When you tried to push Artis out of the key, it felt like you were on the corner of State and Madison putting your shoulder against a brick building. The guy was an unmoveable force. But as I said, he was a great guy, a guy who preferred to get along and go along. That's why he played out of position for so long. Artis was too nice to tell the coach that the offense didn't fit him. Instead, Artis tried to make it work.

While Artis has astounding power in his legs and lower body, his hands are very small. If you saw his hands, you'd figure he was maybe 6-foot, not 7-foot-2. Those hands gave him problems because he had trouble catching the ball and hanging on to it in traffic. Artis took to using Stick-um on his fingers so he could snatch the ball and keep it. It's funny, most of my teammates in Baltimore and I used that stuff in 1965 because it really did give you a better grip on the ball. We were playing against Chamberlain one night and he kept complaining to the officials, "Hey, the reason Kerr handles the ball like that is because he's got stuff on his hands. Get that firm-grip junk off him." We used to hide the stuff on our shoes so all you had to do was reach down and get a dab. They passed a rule saying it was a $25 fine if you were caught with the stuff. Then we put it other places such as behind the backboard. We'd reach up there during free throws to get some.

The officials started shaking hands with players before the game, giving you the old "Hi, how are you? How's the family?" routine. Of course, they really wanted to see if you had Stickum on your hands. When you saw a player greet an official with his hands doubled up in fists, then you knew the guy was guilty. I never knew where Artis hid the stuff, I just knew that he did. And I suppose it helped him some, but no one will ever say that Artis had good hands.

What people remember most about Artis is his face. The deadly, almost blank glare, the goatee, the long sideburns. From a distance, you'd see him and figure there is one mean, unhappy man. But he was just the opposite. He was friendly when you got to know him and I never recall him being in a fight on the court. If anything, he played absolutely void of emotion. When he blocked shots, he did it with little flair. He seldom dunked, preferring just to softly drop the ball through the rim. Sometimes, you wondered if Artis was breathing because his expression and body language seldom changed.

In six years with the Bulls, Artis averaged 20 points, 10 rebounds and shot 59 percent. He was surrounded by mediocre players and the team never won more than 45 games with him in the middle. In terms of raw talent, Artis was in a class by himself when it comes to Bulls' centers. But for a variety of reasons, that talent was never used correctly by the coaches or by Artis and he never became an impact player who could carry the team to contention.

Of course, Artis also played with those Bulls teams that were really hurting at point guard.

We all know that the point guard is important; he is the coach on the floor—the guy who sets up the offense and gives up the ball—the player in charge of keeping the other four guys happy and standing in the right place. But now a guard has to do even more—he has to be able to make the outside shot, especially if he is the guard playing next to Michael Jordan.

Because Michael is such an overwhelming presence on the floor and because he receives so much defensive attention, the guard playing next to him has his own set of problems.

For example, the Bulls' guard must make sure that the ball is distributed enough so that the Bulls don't fall into the habit of standing there and watching Michael go 1-on-1. But with a guy like Michael, I can see why that happens. So the other guard must have enough confidence and be outgoing enough to talk to the other guys on the floor and *tell* them to move. He must know that there are certain times in the game when the ball should go to someone else besides Michael, and that must happen for two reasons:

1. Michael gets tired and shouldn't be asked to score every time down the floor.

2. To keep their attention and to keep them moving, the other players need to touch the ball and shoot it occasionally. The easiest team to defense is a team that plays in cement sneakers.

Yet, there are times when Michael must have the ball. The game is close, the clock is running down and who else but Michael would you want to take the shot? You figure that when Michael goes to the basket, three things usually happen and they all are good.

1. He scores.

2. He is fouled but he is an 85 percent foul shooter, so being fouled is the same as scoring.

3. He scores and is fouled and that's a 3-point play.

The simplest way to get Michael the ball is to throw it to him in the back court and let him dribble it up the court and create his own shot. That also makes it very easy for the defense to guard him—remember the rule about the offensive team that stands around being the easiest to beat.

That means the point guard playing next to Michael must do more. He must be able to penetrate and he must be good enough to finish off the play if the defense doesn't guard him.

Here's how it works: Sam Vincent is playing next to Michael in the back court. Sam is quick and he sees an opening because the man guarding him is really paying more attention to Michael. So Sam has to take the ball to the basket and either force his man or someone else to stop him. If no one does, then Sam has to take the shot and make it. That's called finishing the play. If someone does switch off to guard Sam, then Sam must get the ball to Michael or whoever is left open. By going to the basket, Sam demands that the defense respect him and that means it is less likely that two guards will double-team Michael.

Another example: Michael has the ball and he is looking for an opening, but there is none. He is double-teamed by his own man and the man who is guarding Vincent. Michael won't force the shot, he'll pass it back to Sam, who is open from 18 feet. To make Michael and the Bulls effective, Sam has to catch the ball and take the shot without hesitation. He also has to make it regularly, or Michael will be battling a double-team all night and Sam and the rest of the Bulls will be frustrated by the 18-footers that are missed. If you don't make the outside shot, the other team will exploit you. Indiana's Bobby Knight did it in the 1987 Final Four when he left Nevada-Las Vegas' point guard Mark Wade wide open for the whole game, and Wade couldn't hit a 15-footer to save his life. A few years ago, the strategy against the Boston Celtics was to let their guards shoot, especially Danny Ainge. But Ainge spent his summers in the gym and made himself a reliable outside shooter and one of the best 3-point men in the league. Ainge didn't want anyone to consider him a weak link, and that's what a non-shooting point guard becomes in the playoffs. The days of the point guard who only had to worry about passing are over. He needs some offense.

The best point guard the Bulls have had until Michael was Van Lier, who was a ferocious defensive player. Van Lier spent a short part of his career with Cincinnati. At one point he got into a fight with Jerry Sloan and the brawl spilled into the hallway. Bulls' coach Dick Motta loved what he saw, said that Sloan and Van Lier were made for each other and a year later, they were playing together and pounding the hell out of the other team instead of each other. Van Lier also was a brilliant penetrator. When he went into the middle with the ball, he knew just where to find Love or Walker with a pass when the defense collapsed on him. Van Lier was not much of an outside shooter. What we are really talking about is chemistry. Van Lier was perfect for the old Bulls, a half-court, take-your-time-before-you-shoot style offense. The Bulls with Michael like to run and have been searching for a point guard who has a mix of speed and outside shooting ability. Toward the end of the season, Michael moved to the position. The results, as I'll show later, were dramatic and inspirational.

They used to say on draft day that there were a thousand guards, five hundred forwards and two centers. Well, there's still only two decent centers—if you're lucky—in most drafts. And there are about a thousand guards, but there are only two of them who really can play the point in the NBA. What that means is regardless of Michael's greatness, the Bulls won't be ready to play for a championship until they find guys to handle those two positions, which is the challenge facing Doug Collins and Jerry Krause.

7

At Last, A Real General Manager

The Chicago Bulls had been in existence for 19 years when Jerry Krause was hired as general manager in the spring of 1985.

That's a fact.

Jerry Krause also is the first legitimate general manager in the history of this franchise.

That may sound like an opinion, but it's also a fact.

And part of the reason the Bulls have pulled themselves together in the last half of the 1980s is that they have Krause in the front office. It was Krause who hired Doug Collins. It was Krause who drafted Charles Oakley, Scottie Pippen and Horace Grant and it was Krause who acquired Sam Vincent, Craig Hodges, Bill Cartwright, and John Paxson.

Not all of Krause's moves have worked out, but most have. Best of all, he has complete authority to hire and fire coaches, to draft the players he wants and to make the trades he believes will benefit the Bulls. That sounds like the job description of any general manager, but it has not been like that for Bulls general managers.

When I was the Bulls' coach in 1966, Dick Klein was the team's general manager and president. He knew just enough about basketball to be dangerous and that's what he became, a guy who could have submarined the franchise. Pat Williams followed Klein and he was more of a marketing and business guy than a man who knew a good player from a bad one. Eventually, Williams lost a power struggle with Dick Motta, the coach. Motta then did both jobs. . . kind of. He wanted the authority to make trades, but he couldn't scout the college players because he was coaching the Bulls. I was brought in as business manager from 1973–75 and I worked with Motta, scheduling exhibition games, negotiating some of the contracts and doing much of what Jerry Krause does for the Bulls today.

The Bulls' next general manager was Rod Thorn, and he was the first real basketball man to hold the job. He was an All-American guard at West Virginia, the second pick in the 1963 NBA draft by Baltimore and he played in the league for four years before an injury forced him to retire. Then he was a head or assistant coach with several NBA teams and the St. Louis Spirits of the American Basketball Association.

When the Bulls hired Rod in 1978, I was happy. I thought that here was a guy who had been around and knew what to do. He was energetic, a guy on the move. He loved the action, the arena and being a part of basketball. He talked to a lot of people and knew all the rumors and basketball gossip. There weren't enough hours in the day for him.

Rod Thorn could have been a good general manager, but he wasn't and I don't blame him for it.

When Rod was in charge of the Bulls, he really wasn't in charge of the Bulls. The team was ruled by a committee of owners. Rod would have a trade he wanted to make, and he couldn't just do it. He had to get it approved and he would be told, "Let's see. Rod, I think that Jonathan Kovler is in Palm Springs. . . Art Wirtz is somewhere in Canada (because he also owned the Chicago Black Hawks and was at an NHL meeting). . . Phil Klutznick is the ambassador to Israel.

The fastest way to mess up anything is to assign a committee to handle it, and that was so true of the Bulls. By the time Rod contacted all the owners, the proposed deal may have fallen through or it had changed. He'd call one of the owners and interrupt the guy's dinner. The guy is sitting there with his wife and friends and he's had a few pops and Rod is trying to find out if it's okay if he trades Dwight Jones, and Rod is telling it to a guy who doesn't know Dwight Jones from K.C. Jones or even Casey Jones. I know for a fact that Rod had a deal all set to bring Maurice Lucas and Lionel Hollins to Chicago without giving up much, but by the time Rod checked with all the owners, it had collapsed.

"Let's just say the situation was difficult," said Thorn. "We had a lot of very successful and busy men as owners and they just weren't available all the time. Many things you try to do in basketball must be done right now, and we couldn't get an answer immediately because our owners were spread out. We did have a deal worked out with Portland before the 1979 draft. Portland wanted Artis Gilmore and we were going to get Maurice Lucas, Lionel Hollins and Tom Owens. Then we planned to draft Bill Cartwright instead of David Greenwood, but all the owners couldn't be found and I also had a feeling that Jonathan Kovler just didn't like the trade and maybe he was stalling because he liked Gilmore. Jerry Sloan was the coach and Jerry and I liked the deal, but we had only a week to get it done. We finally got the okay, but it was too late and Portland changed its mind. But that is one deal I wish we could have made because it might have changed the direction of the franchise.

"In all fairness, I knew the situation after six months and I believed I could work under it. No one forced me to stay there for seven years. I signed two contracts to remain with the Bulls when I had other opportunities in basketball, so I don't want to throw all the blame for what happened on them."

So it is hard to assess what kind of general manager Rod was in Chicago. About all I can say is that Rod was lucky he didn't end up with permanent whiplash from having to spend so many years looking over his shoulder. Rod is now Director of Operations for the NBA and I would like to see him get a shot at running his own team, his own way.

Rod also had some very bad luck, and believe me, I know exactly how it felt. We are talking about the coin toss of 1979 between the Lakers and Bulls to see which team would get the first pick.

In this case, this first pick wasn't someone like LaRue Martin, it was Magic Johnson, and everyone had a very good idea that Magic was unlike any player we had seen before—a legitimate

6-foot-10 point guard.

"Obviously, we wanted Magic," Rod said.

Obviously, he didn't get Magic.

"After we lost the toss, our choices with the second pick were David Greenwood or Bill Cartwright," Rod said. "We thought about this for a long time. Cartwright was a center, Greenwood a power forward. I guess it came down to the fact that we already had Artis Gilmore at center, so we went with Greenwood. It's always hard to turn down a center and maybe we should have taken Cartwright in retrospect, because it would have forced us to trade Artis earlier than the Bulls did and maybe Chicago would have gotten more for him than Chicago did get when he was traded. I don't know . . . the thing was that the best player after Magic in that draft was Sidney Moncrief (who went fifth to Milwaukee). Sidney had some knee problems in college and we and some other teams were concerned about that. As it turned out. Sidney played a long time on those knees."

This shows you how drafting can drive a guy out on the ledge of the Hancock Tower. In 1979, doctors put a red flag on Moncrief's knees. Teams pass on him, he turns out to be a Hall of Fame-caliber player. In 1980, that same red flag is there on Ronnie Lester, Thorn gambles and goes for Lester figuring Lester can beat the odds as Moncrief did, but Lester never fully recovers. In 1984, it was Portland taking a chance on Sam Bowie instead of taking the sure thing with Michael. Bowie and Michael are both hurt in their second pro seasons, but Michael comes back and Bowie doesn't.

———●———

Two things turned the Bulls around.

The first was the drafting of Michael Jordan by Rod Thorn.

The second was that Jerry Reinsdorf bought the Bulls in March of 1985, followed by Reinsdorf's decision to hire Jerry Krause. This set up a very clear chain of command—Reinsdorf to Krause to the coach. Reinsdorf was not afraid to delegate authority and he essentially put the Bulls in the hands of Krause. Working with Krause was Irwin Mandel, the team's vice-president and financial officer, a wizard when it comes to figuring out how to deal with the NBA's mind-boggling salary cap.

As the Bulls began their first season under Krause (1985–86), they were coming off a 38–44 record. They had losing records in seven of their last eight seasons and had nothing in common with those great Bulls teams coached by Motta in the early 1970s. The starting lineup was Ennis Whatley and Michael as the guards, Caldwell Jones at center and Orlando Woolridge and David Greenwood as the forwards.

Jerry told me that he didn't like the makeup of the team, so he made changes—a lot of changes.

"We don't have the right kind of guys," he said. "Red, a lot of these guys just don't play hard. They don't have the proper attitude. These are not our kind of guys and I'm going to do something about that."

I had known Jerry Krause for years. He was a scout for Baltimore when I played for the Bullets in 1965–66. I know that Jerry was the guy who suggested that Baltimore draft Jerry Sloan. Baltimore did, but Sloan still had another year of eligibility and he stayed in school. Jerry pushed Baltimore to draft Sloan for the second year in a row, and they did. That's how Sloan ended up as my roommate in Baltimore and it's how I got to know Sloan well enough to draft him for the Bulls when I became the coach in Chicago.

Jerry's other claim to fame with Baltimore was as the man who discovered Earl Monroe. Since then, a lot of people have tried to take credit for finding Monroe at little Winston-Salem State, but I'm convinced that Jerry was the first scout to have a serious interest in a guy who became one of the game's great guards. I was with the Bulls when Earl Monroe came to Chicago to play in a black-college tournament at the Amphitheater. Jerry was also there and every time Monroe would make a good move, he would look up at the stands at Krause. It would only be for a second, but you could see Monroe making eye contact with Krause several times during the game, and Earl didn't look at any of the other scouts. He knew that Krause was the guy who had been on his trail the longest and who liked him the most. They had a special relationship, and it was because of Krause that Baltimore drafted Monroe.

What I like about Jerry is that he is an old-fashioned scout. He would be the kind of gardener who'd grab every tree and shrub and shake it to see what falls out. It seems as if he knows every college player of any significance playing anywhere in the country. A lot of people in Jerry's business wouldn't put in the hours he does and travel to the ends of the earth as he has to to watch a kid who probably has no shot at the NBA. But Jerry will take the chance, spend that extra time and take that one more trip. He was one of the first guys to get on the trail of Scottie Pippen, and Scottie Pipen didn't go to Alabama or even Arkansas. He went to Central Arkansas and he's from Hamburg, Arkansas. The only way to go visit Scottie Pippen is by two planes, a bus and a burro.

After years of hearing about some sleeper in Drowsy, Louisiana, and then going there only to find out that he's not 6-foot-9, he's 6-foot-6 and that he has been arrested for assaulting the rim with his foul shots and that he's so dead on the court they ought to call the coroner for an autopsy, most veteran scouts have decided to skip those trips to Drowsy, Louisiana. That's because 90 percent of the sleepers you hear about are just that— asleep—and they should stay that way.

On the road, Krause tends to stay by himself. He's almost a man from out of the legend of the great detectives. Raymond Chandler invented Phillip Marlowe, and Chandler said that the first characteristic of a private eye is that he is a lone wolf. That's Jerry Krause. On the road, scouts get together for dinner, a trip to the race track and then they go to the bar for a few pops. Seldom will you find Krause out on the town. If he's in town, he's not looking for the company of Jack Daniels unless Jack Daniels is 6-foot-11 and can make a hook shot with either hand.

While Raymond Chandler might conjure up a guy with Krause's determination, it's doubtful that Chandler's hero would look like Jerry Krause. This is not the guy they send you from central casting. Jerry is a small man in a big man's game. He's 5-foot-8 and he's somewhat overweight. It seems that about everyone in general manager positions is a former player and/or coach and these guys are all at least 6-foot. Some of them still look like they can play. Some of them jog, play tennis, even surf. But that's not Jerry Krause.

He would be great on "What's My Line?" because days would go by before anyone would guess that Jerry Krause was involved with pro basketball. You put him next to 6-foot-6 Doug Collins and you truly have an odd couple. One guy was a No. 1 draft choice, a basketball hero, a highly personable guy who became the youngest coach in the NBA. Jerry Krause was none of that. He waited for everything, success and opportunity came to him late and the one reason it came to him at all was because he persevered.

Doug Collins comes on like a comet while Krause is a plugger.

That's also part of what I like about Krause. He doesn't look like he belongs, he just performs like it. He is the underdog, the guy who never was given anything and maybe even was held back because his looks didn't match the part. Jerry Krause became a general manager because he worked harder than 90 percent of the people in his profession. He waited for his chance, he didn't get discouraged when he had a few career setbacks. The remarkable thing about Krause is that he has been a successful scout in two sports—baseball and basketball. He was a special assignment scout for the Philadelphia Phillies, the Chicago White Sox and several other big league teams. The guy has worked for three Chicago teams—the White Sox, the Cubs and the Bulls. Jerry Krause lives to scout, and that's exactly what the Bulls needed when he took the job.

The public reaction was not totally positive when Krause was hired by the Bulls. He had spent the previous five years working for the White Sox, and some people were asking why the Bulls would hire a baseball guy as an NBA general manager. But the Bulls had just been purchased by Jerry Reinsdorf, who also owned the White Sox. Reinsdorf had complete faith in Krause. It worked like this—Reinsdorf owned the team, Krause was his man and that was that.

Krause also had been with the Bulls twice before. He was hired as their scout in 1968, but he had a personality conflict with Coach Dick Motta. That meant Krause was a member of a very big group because there were more people in the "I Don't Get Along With Motta" Club than there are in Cook County. Motta replaced Krause with Phil Johnson in 1971. Jerry came back to the Bulls in 1975 and then left again a year later, this time in the middle of controversy about offering the Bulls' coaching job to DePaul's Ray Meyer. That was back when the Bulls were owned and run by a committee.

"The last time I was with the Bulls, I left with my tail between my legs," Krause told me. "I was accused of doing things that I didn't do. That was probably the lowest point of my life. So I had a lot to prove when I was hired by Jerry Reinsdorf. The image I had was of a short, squatty, roly-poly guy who didn't look good no matter what I wore. My experience was as a scout, and that meant I wasn't supposed to be able to run a front office. I know some guys on the street were saying, 'What the hell is Reinsdorf doing, putting Krause in charge?'

"Despite all that, I knew my capabilities. When I was with the White Sox, I worked under Bill Veeck and Roland Hemond and those men had a tremendous influence on me. They helped me mature. During the five years I was away from the Bulls and in baseball, I still stayed close to my friends in basketball and I kept tabs on the NBA. But a lot of people didn't know me. The media didn't know me. I wasn't in any clique so I didn't have a bunch of guys who would step forward and say that Jerry Krause was great. I had to prove myself."

It may sound a bit strange, but in some respects it might have been an asset that Krause wasn't directly involved with the Bulls before he became the general manager. He watched the team closely, but he had some distance and that distance led to real objectivity. He wasn't making judgments based on personalities. Being the Bulls general manager is the job he wanted, the job he has spent his life preparing himself to do. The Chicago Bulls were always his team even when he worked somewhere else. I have always felt the same way. When he took over, Jerry had a very accurate view of the situation.

Jerry Krause told me:

"I was on the West Coast scouting for the White Sox when Jerry Reinsdorf called me to talk about the Bulls. He said that no matter what I decided, he was going to hire a new general manager. That's how we started two days in which we discussed the team, the job of general manager and everything about the Bulls. I told Jerry (Reinsdorf) that I had seen the Bulls play 25–30 times a year and it was a bad ball club because it had bad chemistry. Michael Jordan was a rookie and I loved him, but I didn't like the players around Michael. There were a lot of negatives. Even the training facility was in poor shape and it was a bad atmosphere for the players. The fans had lost faith in the team. the organization hadn't been stable. A lot of changes had to be made.

"I knew that with Jerry Reinsdorf and the new ownership, the mood around the franchise would get better. I did tell Jerry that the Bulls were run by committee and that would never work. You can't go to five guys for approval every time you want to make a trade or sign someone, and 99 percent of those guys on that committee didn't know a damn thing about basketball. Arthur Wirtz was a very tough man to work for. I know because I worked for him for five and a half months and it was an impossible situation, no matter what you did. Rod Thorn learned the same thing when he took over for me. Rod was frustrated by the setup and I don't see how anyone could have succeeded under Arthur Wirtz and that ownership.

"I think back to the great Bulls teams of the early 1970s— Jerry Sloan, Norm Van Lier, Chet Walker, Tom Boerwinkle and Bob Love. Those guys all grew old at once. Walker had a personality problem with Dick Motta and then he had contract trouble with the ownership and he became discouraged and just quit when he probably could have played two more years. At the same time, there was some bad drafting going on and there was little talent to replace the guys who were getting old. One year, Tate Armstrong was the first-round pick. Another year, it was Scott May. In 1979, the Bulls and the Lakers had a coin flip to decide who would get the first draft pick. The Lakers won and took Magic Johnson. The Bulls got David Greenwood. Can you imagine where the Bulls would have been with Magic? So you take a team with age, some poor drafts, a history of contract hold-outs and some bad luck and that was the Bulls in the late 1970s until we came in. There were too many cooks in the kitchen and no one was really making anything.

"When we took over, we built a new training facility and we modernized the dressing rooms at Chicago Stadium. We also were at the salary cap, which meant that we didn't have any extra money to spend for free agents. After six months on the job, I told Jerry Reinsdorf, 'This is even worse than I thought it was. We really have to build from the bottom up with Michael as our base.' "

The first major move Jerry Krause made was to replace Kevin Loughery as coach with Stan Albeck. The most natural thing for a new general manager to do is to bring in his own coach. But Krause also made the right decision to fire Loughery, because the team wasn't organized. The Bulls were in a shambles. No one knew their roles.

"Jerry Reinsdorf gave me total control to hire and fire coaches," Jerry Krause told me. "I looked at the team and tried to analyze how Kevin Loughery fit in with the Bulls. I was hired right at the tail end of the 1984–85 season and I traveled with the team so I could get a better feel for things. It became apparent to me that a coaching change was necessary. I had been director of scouting with the Lakers when Stan Albeck was an assistant coach with that team, so I had known Stan for some time. We talked several times before I hired him to coach the Bulls."

Albeck got the job one day before the 1985 draft, a draft when Krause was to make his first real impact on the team. He pulled a trade with Cleveland, giving the Cavaliers the Bulls' first-round pick (No. 10) and guard Ennis Whatley for the Cavs' first-round pick (No. 9) and their second-round pick (No. 30).

"The idea of the trade was to make sure we got Charles Oakley," Krause told me. "I took the Bulls job on March 26th and three days later, I saw Oakley play for the first time. Charles was playing for a Division II school, Virginia Union, and I just liked him. I didn't care that he was from a small college. Earl Monroe was from a small college and he did pretty well for himself. People kid me about the fact that I've drafted a lot of players from small schools. Well, it takes the same skills to play in the NBA. Just because you are at Notre Dame doesn't mean you automatically have those talents and just because you are at Winston-Salem State doesn't mean you don't have a chance. I drafted Oakley because he had the ability and I didn't care where he was playing.

"I wanted to make sure that no one took Oakley before we had a chance to get him, so we set up a deal with Cleveland. The Cavs wanted Keith Lee and we wanted Oakley, and the trade hinged on those players being available and that's what happened."

To be exact, what happened is that Krause wound up with a guy who would become one of the league's premier rebounders. The second-round pick, Calvin Duncan, didn't make the Bulls. As for the Cavs, they got the 6-foot-10 Lee, who was a star at Memphis State but has had several serious injuries as a pro and has sat out more games than he has played. Whatley was cut by the Cavs.

I have a distinct memory of that draft day. I was sitting in the room with Jimmy Durham and the Bulls announced that they had drafted Keith Lee. I never was a Lee fan, so I booed along with the fans.

Then the Bulls said they had a trade in the works. I got excited and said, "That makes sense. I couldn't believe that Krause would take Lee. I don't think Lee can play a lick."

Then the Bulls said they had traded Lee for Charles Oakley.

Well, the fans and I booed again—shows you what we know.

Who was Charles Oakley? What could be so great about a guy from Virginia Union? None of us really knew Oakley.

This was a very gutsy move by Krause, using his first draft as a general manager to draft a nobody from a school whose biggest rival is Norfolk State. The newspapers were rather critical, the fans didn't like it and Krause immediately found himself on the hot seat.

———•———

That first season (1985–86) was a nightmare for Krause. He thought he had a good start on his long range plan to rebuild the Bulls. It was almost like one of those connect-the-dots picture. His first dot was getting his coach (Albeck). No. 2 was drafting Oakley. Then the whole picture went fuzzy, like a tube blew out on a television set.

It all happened so fast.

First, Michael broke his foot. Then it became apparent that Oakley was not ready to start immediately. He needed experience, or at least Albeck thought he did.

Finally, there was Quintin Dailey.

I want to say that Quintin Dailey could have been a helluva player. He was just that at San Francisco, a 6-foot-3 guard with an accurate jump shot. He had a pro body, pro moves, pro everything. He came from Baltimore, where he was a very good student at Cardinal Gibbons High. As a college junior, he averaged 25 points and shot 55 percent. But he also was arrested for assaulting a nursing student, which became a real source of controversy.

It's easy for a guy to second-guess, especially in light of what has happened since the Bulls drafted Dailey in 1982. But from the start, I just didn't think it was a good idea, regardless of his talent. The Bulls had the seventh pick in the 1982 draft and they took Dailey, whose legal problems were still pending. This was not an especially strong draft. The best players taken behind Dailey were Clark Kellogg (No. 8), Fat Lever (No. 11), Sleepy Floyd (No. 13) and Paul Pressey (No. 20).

The Bulls were 34–48 in 1981–82 and despite the losing record, there seemed to be some hope for the future. Reggie Theus, David Greenwood and Orlando Woolridge were develop-ing...I don't know, I just wouldn't have taken a chance on Dailey. Ability aside, with this hanging over a player's head and the team being in one of the major media markets in the world, drafting Quintin Dailey was not a good idea.

Making matters worse, the Bulls had a press conference after the draft and Dailey just wasn't prepared for the questions it seemed obvious that he would be asked. Bob Woolf was Dailey's agent, and he didn't come to the press conference. I remember being there and the first two questions were about basketball. Then a writer named John Shulian asked Quintin about the incident with the nurse. You would have thought that Dailey and the Bulls would know this was coming and they should have worked out something that Dailey could say. Instead, Dailey almost shrugged it off, almost saying what happened to the nurse didn't matter and he wanted to just talk about basketball. You'd think the guy would want to apologize or something, but he didn't show any remorse at that first press conference. I don't think Dailey meant it like that, but it came off badly. That obviously didn't do much for public relations and it didn't help the Bulls or Dailey. So he started off on the wrong foot and then stumbled several times later.

In his first exhibition game with the Bulls, in Peoria, Illinois, Dailey was picketed by the National Organization of Women. It was a real foreboding of what was to come. I have to admit that I like Quintin Dailey. I know what he did was terribly wrong, but I didn't see him as a loner, a kid who sulked or a guy who would cause problems.

But then he got caught up with drugs right after Krause took over the team. It was during the exhibition season in 1985 and we had a game at the Genesis Center in Gary, Indiana. Right before the game, Krause took Jimmy Durham, the Chicago writers and myself into a room and said, "We've got a problem here...Quintin Dailey has a drug problem."

Jerry Krause remembered the incident:

"When I got the job in March of 1985, one of the first things I did was sit down with Quintin and talk to him. We went over what had happened to him in the past and what he could do in the future. That summer, he received a community service award from the NBA because he was taking part in a lot of social service programs, being a real asset. I thought he was getting over his problems and he was acting as though that were the case. But then at our first exhibition game in Gary, I got a call from the state police and a patrolman told me,'Quintin Dailey is trying to get in touch with you.' Right before that, I had been in our dressing room and noticed that Quintin wasn't there. The players said, 'Quintin missed the team bus, but I think he's driving himself to the game.'

"At last, Quintin was on the telephone and he was in tears. I could hear this man crying and I knew something was awfully wrong. He said that he had a severe problem and the problem was drugs and he wanted help. It shook me to the Nth degree. I don't know if I was naive or what, but I thought that I had examined the situation, I'd talked to Quintin and thought he was going to be all right.

"Quintin asked me to get him admitted to one of the NBA's drug rehabilitation facilities, and I called the league office for direction. There were a lot of calls back and forth between myself, the league and Quintin. It was decided that someone from the drug program would fly to Chicago that night to meet with Quintin. The next morning, Quintin's wife and I took him to the airport where he met with the counselor, who went with Quintin to California.

"This was one of the most emotional things I've ever been through. Quintin was crying, his wife was crying and I was in tears, too. Later, I went out to California and I spent a day with Quintin at the center. I believe I was the first general manager to spend a day with a player at a drug rehabilitation center. Eventually, the doctors told us that he was ready to come back, and Quintin did come back to play and it didn't work out for a second time. Quintin had two more setbacks and after a while, the emotion isn't there anymore because you become hardened to it. I still like Quintin as a person, but I found out a lot about the drug scene that year and I learned just how hard it is to stay clean."

Jerry Krause never imagined his first season would see Dailey in a drug rehab center and Jordan on crutches, but that's what he faced. He also was in the middle of the crisis with Michael wanting to play and the doctors saying he should rest.

"There were so many problems, more problems than any of us could have imagined," Krause told me. "Part of the trouble with Michael's injury was due to the media, which really didn't understand the situation and the whole thing kind of blew up and got out of hand. Between Michael's injury and Quintin's drug troubles, there was a lot to handle. Some people in the media tried to make it seem as though Michael and I were having problems, but it was nothing personal. He was in a frustrating situation and that just made it tough on everyone. It wasn't Michael's fault and it wasn't my fault."

———————●

So Krause made it through his first year as general manager. It was impossible to judge the man—so much had gone wrong and his hands were tied. The situation with Michael could have been damaging to the franchise for a long time. The unfortunate thing is that I believe Krause ended up as the heavy. He took the heat from Michael. That's because it was Krause telling him that the doctors said he couldn't play. Krause was doing what any general manager would—taking care of the guy who is the future. The simplest thing for Krause to do would have been to say, "Go ahead, Michael." Then Michael would have been happy. The fans and writers would have been happy. Everyone would have been happy because everyone wants to see Michael play. But if Michael had come back too soon and broken the foot again, then fingers would have been pointed everywhere.

Okay, perhaps Krause was being overly cautious, but I can't blame him. It was apparent that the Bulls weren't going anywhere with or without Michael in 1984–85. It's just too bad that Michael's first contact with his new general manager came under these circumstances. Krause was trying to protect Michael from himself, the same way a father has to tell his son, "Just wait a few more months before you get your driver's license."

And once the season was over, Krause made another move—firing Albeck and hiring Doug Collins. Canning an experienced and well-liked coach such as Albeck in favor of Collins was asking for criticism—and Krause got it.

"I've never been a popular guy and I never will be," Krause told me. "All that matters is what happens to the Bulls. I was convinced that we had to make a lot of moves to straighten this thing out. I loved the old Bulls, the Bulls of Jerry Sloan, Norm Van Lier and Chet Walker. A number of the players on those teams were my kids, players I had scouted for the Bulls and recommended that they draft. When I came back to the Bulls, we didn't have those kind of people. The franchise lacked that old Bulls attitude, and one of the major reasons I hired Doug Collins was that he's a tough guy, just like the old Bulls were. Doug also is extremely bright, and tough people who are smart go a long way.

"I wish I could get 12 players just like Jerry Sloan, but that's impossible. But what Doug and I do want is 12 guys who will bust their ass every night. It took me a couple of years to get those players together, but the reason we were able to come so far so fast was that we have a great work ethic on the Bulls. Our one advantage was Michael. We knew that we could draw well for a while because people want to see him play, but there also was a fear that the novelty would wear off. We had to start winning and we had to give the fans more than just Michael. Drafting Oakley was a start in that direction, because Charles is a hard-nosed guy, a real ass-kicker. He also brought toughness to the team."

If you were to break down the decisions made by Krause, almost every one was against standard public opinion—drafting Oakley, firing Albeck, hiring Collins—and that trend continued.

In the 1986 draft, the Bulls had the No. 9 pick and everyone wanted them to pick Johnny Dawkins. On draft day, Jimmy Durham and I were standing in front of 2,500 season ticket holders, and the fans were all shouting, "We want Johnny, we want Johnny."

I turned to Durham and said, "I don't think they're calling for me."

We both laughed, but no one was laughing when Krause

picked Ohio State's Brad Sellers instead. Instead, they were booing just as they did for Charles Oakley a year before.

Dawkins was a 6-foot-2 guard from Duke whose team was in the Final Four. Everyone saw him on television and the conventional thinking was that he would be the ideal guard to play next to Michael. Sellers was a 7-footer from Ohio State, a team that didn't even make the NCAA tournament during Sellers' senior season.

Sellers has never been quite what the Bulls expected and he has been under a lot of pressure ever since he was drafted.

Most people still don't realize that Orlando Woolridge forced Krause to draft Sellers instead of Dawkins. Woolridge was the Bulls' small forward from 1981 to 1986. He was an explosive player capable of scoring 25 points any night. But entering the 1986–87 season, Woolridge's contract was up and he wanted outrageous money. I liked Woolridge, but it always bothered me that he was a guy who could jump over the moon, yet he never rebounded well. I know that also drove the Bulls crazy. Maybe Woolridge didn't have the toughness Krause talks about or maybe he just didn't know how to use that leaping ability, but he wasn't a factor on the boards. So he wanted a superstar's contract, and Krause wasn't sure if Woolridge was the kind of guy he wanted with the Bulls. It became obvious that Woolridge was going to sign somewhere else, so Krause knew he had better get someone in the draft to play small forward. That's what happened a few months later when Woolridge got a $4 million, five-year deal from New Jersey. The Bulls received a first-round pick in 1989 and a couple of second-rounders in exchange.

In Sellers, the Bulls saw a guy who led the Big Ten in rebounding. He was a 7-footer who could shoot like a guard. It turned out that Sellers was booed by the fans from Day One for no other reason than he wasn't Johnny Dawkins. Sellers hasn't developed as fast as the Bulls thought he would. He can hit the outside shot, but has trouble going to the basket. He also hasn't rebounded as well as they thought he would. And Brad's jump shot is strange—it isn't the textbook jumper—it almost squirts out of his hands.

It's funny, we see Michael Jordan in a 6-foot-6 body and he plays like a 7-footer. Then we see Sellers in a 7-foot body and he plays like he's 6-foot-6. By nature, Sellers isn't an aggressive person. He doesn't like to slam dunk, throw elbows or do the things we are used to seeing from a 7-footer. It's his personality—Brad Sellers is a nice, bright, academic kid—but he doesn't have that killer instinct. This is Krause's one borderline move with the Bulls.

"I think the unpopularity of the draft has hurt Sellers," Krause told me. "I'm not saying it affected him a great deal, but it can't be much of an asset to a guy when he is booed every time he steps on the home court. We drafted him for very logical reasons—we knew that Woolridge was a free agent and we were going to lose him. We had to get a big guy, and I had some reservations about Johnny Dawkins as a point guard. In fact, I still do, but I think Dawkins does have a lot of ability. Anyway, we had to get a small forward and we liked Sellers. Some people in the NBA say it's better to make a mistake on a big guy than a small guy. I just felt we had to take a chance on Brad."

In the 1987 draft, Krause returned to his scouting roots—the small colleges. He took Scottie Pippen, a 6-foot-7 small forward from Central Arkansas. Pippen was a guy Krause followed, and some people asked, "What about his competition and what about his coaching?" It was just like Oakley or even Earl Monroe. Krause got on Pippen's trail early and stayed there. By draft day, a lot of other teams knew about Pippen because he had played so well in the post season All-Star games and Krause had to work a deal with Seattle to make sure that he got Pippen in the same way he set up a trade with Cleveland in 1985 so he would be certain to get Oakley. Krause had two first-round picks in 1987 and he used them on Pippen and Horace Grant, a 6-foot-9 forward from Clemson. It will be viewed as one of the best drafts in Bulls history. Grant has matured so quickly that he enabled the Bulls to trade Oakley to New York for Bill Cartwright and Will Perdue.

When I think of Jerry Krause, I see a guy who finally is permitted to do the things a general manager must to make the Bulls into a winner. I see a man who is very single-minded and not vulnerable to public pressures. He has made coaching changes and draft picks that were extremely unpopular, and they have turned out well. He has made several small deals that have become very big such as signing John Paxson as a free agent, trading Sedale Threatt for Sam Vincent and Craig Hodges for

Ed Nealy.

But most of all, Jerry Krause is a scout, a guy who finds players everywhere. A lot of general managers take the express. They hear about a player and they jump on the bandwagon. They let someone else make all the stops. Krause takes the local. He goes to every gym and sees everyone play, and he usually sees them first.

8 ⏺——————————————————

Coaching The Bulls

The image anyone has the first time they walk into Boston Garden is the banners. The legendary players and legendary teams are honored with their jerseys and the championship flags hanging from the rafters.

Walk into Chicago Stadium and you only see one jersey up there—No. 4—which belonged to Jerry Sloan. I keep thinking that with all the coaches who have passed through this building since 1966 and failed miserably, they ought to hang about ten of us up there—in effigy.

For better or worse, I was there when the Bulls started.

The year was 1966 and I was literally on my last legs as a center with the Baltimore Bullets. I really wasn't sure what I would do after I retired, but toward the end of my career a sportswriter named Lenny Lewin wrote, "Kerr is a smart-thinking redhead who would be fine coaching material."

I read that and said to myself, "That's not a bad idea at all."

Then it seemed that other people were mentioning a coaching career in connection with me.

At this point I was thinking, "Hey, why not?" I figured that

Me at six years old, at Sister's Lake, Mich. Would you believe that this body would go on to play 844 consecutive NBA games?

My son, little Jay, gets a ride on my shoulders. I played center in basketball, but my position as father was even more exciting to me.

1966-67 The Kerr Family—The Bulls were in their infancy, and so was my family: The children (l-r) Matt, baby Jim, Ed, Bill and sister Essie. My wife Betsy and I are in back.

Here's the more current version. Front row (l-r): Therese Kerr (daughter-in-law, Matthew's wife), Essie Harrington (daughter), Neil Harrington IV (grandson), Neil Harrington III (son-in-law, Essie's husband), Tammie Kerr (daughter-in-law, Bill's wife), John G. Kerr II (grandson); second row (l-r): Matthew Kerr (son), John G. Kerr, Ed Kerr (son), Bill Kerr (son).

Tilden Tech Coach Bill Postl with George Macuga (r) and a center he found on the soccer field named Kerr. We became Chicago Public League Champs.

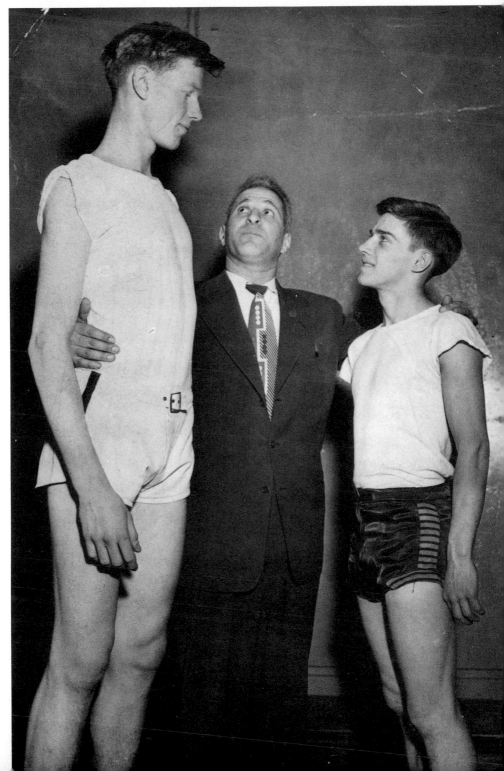

A young John Kerr with the Syracuse Nationals. It's hard to tell from this picture how excited I was to be playing pro ball.

Opposite page, top. Illinois vs. Butler at Huff Gym in Champaign, Ill., 1953-54. Can you spot anything unusual? Count the officials. The NBA thought three officials would be an innovation for 1988-89, but we had three officials three decades ago.

Below. That's some "In Your Face" defense. Plays like this were common when I played. Here Jungle Jim Loscutoff of Boston applies his idea of pressure defense to me. *Below, right.* Me and my "drill sergeant" Al Bianchi (r), ten-year teammate and my first assistant coach with the Bulls, 1966-67.

A technical problem in the Kerr family: I got a technical while coaching the Bulls and father-in-law Ed Nemecek got the thumb from officials and was escorted from the stadium by ushers.

Coach Dick Motta discusses strategy with (l-r) Bob Weiss, Tom Boerwinkle, Chet Walker and Jim Fox in a 1970-71 season game.

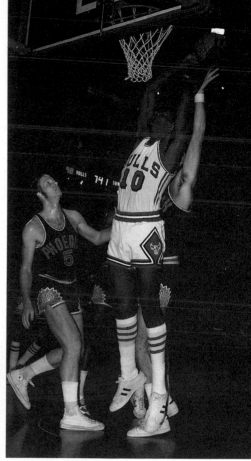

Above. Bob Love puts one
up despite tough
opposition from the
Phoenix Suns. (Dick Van
Arsdale - #5)

Jerry Sloan—the only
Chicago Bull to have his
jersey retired.

Stormin' Norman Van Lier drives to the hoop during a game in the 1971-72 season. *Below, left.* Tom Boerwinkle and Jerry Sloan trail the Milwaukee Bucks' Kareem Abdul-Jabbar to the basket. *Below, right.* Doug Collins at Illinois State: not only were his moves flashy, but check out these shorts.

(Courtesy Chicago Bulls)

Until the arrival of Michael Jordan at guard, Van Lier was in a class by himself.

A young Doug Collins with his coaching mentor Will Robinson.

(Courtesy Chicago Bulls)

(Courtesy Chicago Bulls)

Opposite page.

Top. Jim Durham and yours truly: two guys with the best jobs in the world—watching Michael Jordan and the Bulls.

Center. Billy Crystal, one of the Bulls' biggest fans, telling me that I look "maahvalous."

Bottom. The best choice the Bulls ever made—drafting Michael Jordan. General manager Rod Thorn and Coach Kevin Loughery hold up Michael's jersey.

Left. Doug Collins—striving for perfection, intent on coaching his players to their maximum performance.

Below. The Bulls brain trust ponders the game with Scottie Pippen.
(l-r): Phil Jackson, Doug Collins, John Bach.

(Courtesy Chicago Bulls)

(Courtesy Jerry Luterman)

(Courtesy Chicago Bulls)

(Courtesy Chicago Bulls)

Above. It's hard to say who's supporting who— we're both excited at the win over the Cleveland Cavaliers!

Right. Leadership flows from the bench to the floor as Coach Doug Collins talks to Michael Jordan.

Right. Jerry Krause, the most effective general manager in Bulls history.

(Courtesy Chicago Bulls)

(Courtesy Nathaniel Butler/NBA)

The Man in the Middle, Dave
Corzine, was a solid player
for the Bulls.

It's a bird. . .a plane. . .it's Michael
Jordan levitating.

Oh-oh-oh! That's all I can say on some of Michael's moves.

Michael on the move.

Horace Grant (l) and Scottie Pippen—two No. 1
draft choices who have delivered for the Bulls.
How do you like us now? In '89, just fine!

My restaurant, Red Kerr's, at Adams and Clinton. Attendance doesn't yet rival the Bulls', but we had a great crowd on opening night in June of 1989.

An interior shot of Red Kerr's, featuring my partners and me (l-r): Nick Kladis, me, me again!, and Fred Brzozowski.

(Courtesy Mitchell Canoff)

(Courtesy Mitchell Canoff)

guys dumber than I was had coached in the NBA.

What made it very interesting was that a Chicago business-man named Dick Klein put together a group of high rollers and bought the rights to an expansion team for $1.6 million. In 1966 that sounded like a fortune, but expansion teams in 1988 and 1989 are going for $32 million, while an established franchise in Portland was sold for $70 million in the spring of 1988.

But at the time, none of us knew what the future held for pro basketball in Chicago. It had already failed in 1963 when the Chicago Zephyrs left town and moved to Baltimore to become the Bullets. The Zephyrs had been in the NBA only two seasons and it broke my heart to see pro basketball leave my hometown.

That's why I desperately wanted to be a part of the Bulls. I knew I could help sell the team to the public, which just might be the most important job facing the coach of a new franchise. I also knew that my playing days were over. My legs were shot. I was 34 and had had 12 years and 905 games. Enough was enough.

Dick Klein was a massive guy—6-foot-3 and about 250 pounds. He was a fast talker, a salesman down to the last drop of his blood. He made his living by dealing in sales promotion premiums for various companies. His business manager with the Bulls was Jerry Colangelo, a young, aggressive guy who had been a fine shooting guard at the University of Illinois, averaging 15 points a game.

I interviewed with Colangelo and Klein and I thought it went pretty well. They asked me what kind of team I wanted to coach, and I said I wanted a club that ran the fast break and played good defense.

I figured that sounded pretty good—besides, what coach wouldn't want a team that ran the fast break and played good defense?

What are you supposed to say?

Hey, I like a slow team that can't even shut the door on a mailbox?

Actually, I wasn't the first choice to coach the Bulls. DePaul's Ray Meyer was and from what I understand, Meyer tentatively accepted the job, but was talked out of it by some of the priests at DePaul.

When I was thinking of trying for the Bulls job, I talked to

Alex Hannum, who was my coach in Philadelphia and also happened to be one of the smartest men ever to run a basketball team.

Alex said, "Red, Chicago is an expansion situation and you should let someone else coach it for the first couple of years and take the lumps. Then after that guy screws up, you should go for the job."

It was very good advice...and as you can see I certainly listened. I guess I was like the kid who is told by his father, "Don't touch the stove, it's hot." The kid nods, then touches the stove and fries his hand.

All I wanted to do was be a part of pro basketball in Chicago and I was willing to do it under almost any circumstances.

My boyhood buddy Stinky Fryer and his brother Reggie went around and collected a petition with 1,600 signatures from my old neighborhood asking the Bulls to hire me as their first coach. All these people promised to buy season tickets if I got the job. Actually, Stinky had faked a lot of the signatures, but who was going to check? Remember, this was Chicago and Richard Daley was the mayor, so we had a certain way of conducting business and Stinky Fryer was just following in our city's great political tradition.

Klein agreed to hire me, but then it got sticky.

We started our contract talks like this:

Klein: "How much does it cost you to live each month?"

Kerr: "I don't know...I really haven't thought about it...maybe $1,000."

Klein: "All right, I'll give you $15,000 to coach the team."

Kerr: "Dick, I don't know anyone who has a company worth $1.6 million that pays a guy only 15 grand to run it. It doesn't make much sense."

Klein: "What were you making in Baltimore?"

Kerr: "30,000."

Klein: "Okay, suppose I pay you $1,000 a win."

Kerr: "Dick, this is an expansion team. It's not going to win that many games. If I didn't have a family to support, I'd take it. But I can't take my family and leave them out on a limb like that."

Klein: "Suppose we say that you have a base of $15,000. If you win 25 games, you'll make $20,000. If you win 30 games, it will be worth $25,000."

(At this point, Klein had worn me down. I thought about St. Louis Hawks' coach Richie Guerin saying that the first Chicago team would be lucky to win 12 games. That meant I'd take a 50 percent pay cut from the $30,000 I earned in Baltimore, but I wanted the job so badly and I was afraid that Klein would hire someone else.)

Kerr: "Okay, I'll take it. But I want to hire Al Bianchi as my assistant coach."

Klein: "You've got a deal."

———●———

The next thing we had to do was find some players, and the NBA set up the expansion draft. It worked like this:

There were nine NBA teams with 12 men on each roster. The teams were allowed to protect seven of those players, and we could take two players from each of the nine established teams—that would become the Chicago Bulls.

Since I was still the property of the Baltimore Bullets, Chicago had to draft me from Baltimore in order for me to become the Bulls' coach. I was the first pick in the draft.

Klein and I tried to prepare for the draft. We said things such as, "If I were the Lakers, who would be the seven guys I'd protect?" Then we'd make a list of the seven players we thought Los Angeles would keep so we could figure out which of the remaining players interested us. We had no player-personnel guy following the league and scouting for us—as the current expansion teams had for a year before they entered the league in 1988. Klein did consult with the Boston Celtics' general manager Red Auerbach to get some ideas about the league, but basically it was just Klein and me, which sounds absolutely ridiculous today. But back then we didn't ask if we were qualified or if we had seen enough of the players, we just went ahead and picked. Someone had to start the team.

And Auerbach really wasn't a help.

Sending Dick Klein to deal with a basketball genius like Auerbach is like watching a blind bridge player try to play poker against a bunch of sharpies in a high stakes game in Las Vegas.

In exchange for Auerbach's advice, Klein agreed to pick John

Thompson and Ron Bonham from the Boston roster.

"What about K.C. Jones," I asked Klein. "There's a player who can help us and they didn't protect him."

"I told Auerbach that we'd lay off K.C.," said Klein.

I just shook my head. Jones went on to become a very successful coach of the Celtics, but few people remember that he also was one of the best defensive guards in NBA history.

Meanwhile, Thompson retired before training camp and Bonham was cut.

So much for Auerbach's advice.

———●

One of our first picks was Bianchi, who was with Philadelphia. Al had been my roommate in 10 of my 12 pro seasons and I knew him as a fiery guard from Bowling Green University. We were a Mutt-and-Jeff pair. I was the redheaded Scot, easygoing and not really worrying about much. Al was a hot-blooded Italian who had more intensity in one finger than I did in my entire body. He rarely started, but had several great games filling in for an injured player. He'd score 20 points purely on guile and emotion.

I loved Al because he refused to take anything from anyone.

There was a game where Hot Rod Hundley was showing us up, dribbling behind his back and putting on his clown act. Al was watching from the bench and getting very red and very mad. When Al went into the game, he floored Hundley. It was his way of serving notice.

In another game, Al went up for a lay-up and was undercut by Walt Hazzard, who had pulled this stunt before on other players. Al got off the floor and he was all over Hazzard. He got Hazzard in a headlock and used his skull for a punching bag.

Al also had a great feel for the game and players respected him because he played so hard. His specialty was defense. I knew that I could take care of the offense with the Bulls, but I wanted Al to handle our defense. Al would be my drill sergeant, the guy in the trenches. He could communicate well with players and when we held practices it was not uncommon for Al to have one group of players at one end of the court to set up the defense while I had the rest of the guys at the other end to work on offense. Then we'd switch groups.

So we drafted Al Bianchi to be my assistant coach.

The first player I wanted us to take was Jerry Sloan, who had been with me in Baltimore. Sloan was just a rookie who was stuck on the bench playing behind Donny Ohl, whom we called "Wax" because he used so much of it on his hair.

The veterans were tough on Sloan.

There was a game where we were getting clobbered and Sloan was sent into the game for Ohl with two minutes left. As he stepped on the floor, he said, "Hey, Wax, who are you guarding?"

"Rook, what have you been doing all night? If you watched the game, you'd know," said Ohl.

Sloan had to go through a lot of things like that.

I roomed with Sloan and really got to know him. One night I got in about two in the morning after having beer and pizza with some of the guys on the Bullets. The room was dark except for this small orange glow in the middle of the room. It was Sloan sitting on the bed, smoking a cigarette.

After I closed the door, he said, "Red, you know that play in the middle of the third quarter...."

He starting reviewing the whole game, almost play-by-play, and he hadn't left the bench all night.

Finally, I said, "Hey, Rook, give it a rest. The game is over."

That intensity impressed me.

Another image that stuck in my mind was when the Bullets brought a hot-shot draft pick to camp named Gary Bradds from Ohio State. This guy had scored a ton of points in college, and they sent Sloan to play him 1-on-1.

There is only one way to describe what happened—it was a blood-letting. The kid couldn't dribble the ball without Sloan taking it from him. He couldn't get off a shot without Sloan knocking it back in his face. It was like Bradds was caught in a human hurricane and I know he had never faced anything like Sloan in college. Sloan was all over the guy like Bradds had a second layer of skin.

This didn't help Sloan's stature with the Bullets, but it did tell the coaching staff that the NBA wasn't going to be easy for Bradds.

Sloan was from Gobbler's Knob, which is in the southern Illinois oil fields. His town was small but rough, like those small

Texas oil towns where guys think a great night out begins with a few beers and ends with a few broken bones. Sloan's father died when he was four, so he had to grow up fast.

The first time I saw Jerry without a shirt, I suddenly knew what people meant when they described someone as rawboned. His 6-foot-6, lean body was nothing but sharp angles, all knees and elbows. He looked like a guy who had come off the farm, taking off his suspenders and overalls, His eyes were deep set and his face was almost gaunt. It was a haunting look, the look of a man who had seen too much, too soon. He first attended the University of Illinois, but thought that Champaign was too big for him. He quit and returned home to work on an oil rig. Then he tried Southern Illinois University, but didn't like that either. Finally, Sloan ended up at Evansville College, where he became a pro prospect.

I knew we had to get Sloan in the expansion draft and I was ecstatic when we did. I talked to Jerry in the summer before that first season in Chicago and I told him, "All I want you to practice is your shooting. I can't tell you to rebound any harder. I can't tell you to play better defense or to hit the boards. I can't tell you to hustle more. You can do everything but shoot, so work on the 15 to 18-foot shots."

That's exactly what he did.

When Jerry came to camp with the Bulls, no matter what four guys I put him with, that team won the scrimmage. He still was far from a great shooter, but he made enough from the outside to keep the defense honest. But he was my best rebounder as a 6-foot-6 guard. I called him "Road Hog," because when the opposing guard brought the ball up the court Sloan would meet him at the half-court line and body the guy. Just dribbling the ball against Sloan became an ordeal and his tenacity set up our defense.

————●

As for the rest of the expansion draft, we did get some decent players, but no center.

From the Detroit roster, Dick Klein wanted to draft Bill Buntin from the University of Michigan, who was only 6-foot-7, but weighed 250 pounds, most of it right around his gut.

"Buntin will be good for us," said Klein. "He's from the Big Ten and he'll draw some fans."

"But Dick, he can't play center," I said.

"Red, you can teach Buntin to play center," Klein told me.

"Yeah, but I can't teach him to grow," I said.

We went around and around on that for a while, but I finally convinced him to pick Don Kojis, a 6-foot-5 small forward who was a very good athlete.

As for Buntin, he died a few years later of a heart attack, due in part to his weight problem.

The man who was supposed to be our center was 6-foot-10 Nate Bowman of the Cincinnati Royals. Bowman had the size to play center, but all he ever did for us was get in foul trouble, and that's why we ended up with 6-foot-7 Erwin Mueller in the middle.

Klein's first pick in the college draft was Dave Schellhase, a 6-foot-3 forward who had led the nation in scoring with a 32.5 average at Purdue in 1965. The writers called him Super Shell.

This was another guy Klein thought would be a local favorite and help at the gate. He was so sold on Schellhase that he paid him $35,000, which was not only more than the coach was earning, it was among the highest salaries on the team. The average player drafted by the Bulls in the expansion draft made $20,000.

I didn't care about the money that much. What really bothered me was Schellhase's size—6-foot-3 is just too small, even for a small forward. Making matters worse, he showed up in training camp about 20 pounds overweight. We had to move him to guard because of his size, and there he was chewed up by the likes of Jerry Sloan and some of our other veterans. In his two years with the Bulls, Schellhase averaged only three points per game.

In addition to Schellhase, Klein had another brainstorm.

"Red, let's hold an open tryout," he said.

"Why do that?" I asked. "We've got 18 guys coming to camp with NBA experience from the expansion draft. We have ten more guys we took in the college draft. Why do we need to look at guys off the street? We can only keep 12 players."

"Because it will be good public relations," he said.

Klein put an advertisement in the newspapers saying the

Bulls were having an open tryout camp for a week. About 180 guys showed up. We had fat guys, little guys, guys with tattoos that said "Mom," guys with headbands that said "Mom," guys who sort of looked like Mom. It was a mess and they were all over the gym.

I just said forget this and sat down behind a desk to work a crossword puzzle, leaving Al Bianchi to handle it—hey, what are assistant coaches for?

Al was going crazy because he was trying to bring organization to this chaos. After a while, he screamed at everyone to sit down and he came over to my desk.

"Red, what should we do with all these guys?" Bianchi asked. "They're out there pushing, shoving, scratching each other's eyes out."

"Al, I got an idea," I said. "Line them up against the wall and have them count off by twos."

"Then what?" asked Bianchi.

"Send the twos home," I said.

That's exactly what we did and we eventually told everyone to go home. There was no point to this tryout.

———●———

As the real training camp opened, the Bulls made a deal that was a pretty good one, but that could have been great. Klein traded Jeff Mullins and Jimmy King to San Francisco (now the Golden State Warriors) for Guy Rodgers.

After our first few practices, it was obvious that we needed a point guard who could push the ball up the floor and Rodgers could do that. He was starting to hit the downside of a super career, but I wanted him.

But I didn't want to trade Mullins, who was a shooting guard with a lot of potential. Al Bianchi and I told Klein to give the Warriors Gerry Ward and King. But Klein said that he had given the Warriors his word and he was not about to go back on it, so the trade was made.

Finally, I had set up a deal with St. Louis General Manager Marty Blake to trade a second-round draft pick for Paul Silas, who would become one of the greatest rebounding forwards in NBA history. But Klein insisted that we sell the draft pick to the Los Angeles Lakers instead.

I couldn't believe it.

We had been awarded that second-round pick by New York in exchange for not taking Michigan's Cazzie Russell in the college draft. The league gave us that pick to make us more competitive.

"You can't just sell it," I told Klein. "You help a team with players, not with money. They didn't give us the draft choice to make money."

"We're getting $25,000 and that will help us," said Klein.

So St. Louis kept Silas, who later played key roles on championship teams in Seattle and Boston. With that second-round pick, Los Angeles took Henry Finkel. Okay, the 7-foot Finkel wasn't another Wilt Chamberlain, but he became a reliable back-up center in the league for a long time. He could get up and down the floor without falling over, which made him better than most centers we've had in Chicago.

The reason I mention the drafting of Schellhase, the Rodgers deal, the Auerbach fleecing and the Silas fiasco is that they show that Klein and I were already having problems before the season began.

Then there was the hypnotist.

We were still in training camp and Klein brought this guy into the gym with him.

"I want you to meet this hypnotist," he tells me.

I stared at Klein.

"This guy is great," said Klein. "He says he cured cancer."

Al Bianchi was with me and he was rolling his eyes.

"Listen," said the hypnotist. " You give me any five players to work with and let me have them for three sessions and I guarantee you that my five players will beat any five you can put on the floor."

So I gave the guy Barry Clemens, a forward who had a stuttering problem. I gave him Nate Bowman, who was foul-prone to the extent that he had fouled out in the second quarter of an exhibition game. I gave him Larry Humes, who had a hitch in his shot. The other players were Keith Erickson and McCoy McLemore, who were respectable.

Three days later, the hypnotist returned and said he had taken care of Clemens' stuttering.

"Go ahead, Barry, say it," said the hypnotist.

Clemens said, "Peter Piper picked a peck of pickled peppers."

Clemens said it clearly, the best I had ever heard him speak. I said, "Barry, that's great!"

But Clemens ruined it by saying, "I. . .I. . .I always could say that one."

We then were set for the scrimmage.

"Hey, guys," I told my team. "If you let the witch doctor and his players beat you, you're going to run a thousand laps."

That may have been the best motivational speech of my coaching career.

My guys slaughtered them.

Larry Humes did get rid of his hitch, but he couldn't make a shot.

Barry Clemens went right back to stuttering.

Nate Bowman was fouling guys left and right until he fell down and sprained his ankle. Bowman was in pain on the floor and the hypnotist ran out there and said, "Nate, your ankle doesn't hurt. Just repeat after me."

"Man," said Bowman. "This hurts like a son-of-a-bitch."

Klein got rid of the hypnotist, and after that we always referred to the guy as the "Mojo Man," and he became a running joke with us.

The other comic relief in training camp was Izzy Schmissing.

One day I got a call from the coach of St. Cloud College in Minnesota.

"Would you like to look at the leading rebounder in our conference?" the coach asked me.

"How tall is he?" I asked.

"He's 6-foot-9, 260 pounds," said the coach.

"What's his name?" I asked.

"Izzy Schmissing," said the coach.

I laughed so hard that I almost fell out of my chair. I had never heard of the guy, but what a name! Izzy Schmissing—the writers would have some fun with that. And if the guy really was 6-foot-9. . .hey. . .you never know.

"Crate Izzy up and ship him down here," I said.

Izzy really was 6-foot-9. But Izzy really couldn't play at all and we had to cut him. We did get one story out of it as the *Chicago Tribune*'s Bob Logan wrote, "When the Bulls got ready for the exhibition opener, Izzy was among the missing."

Too bad. It would have been fun.

———●

My biggest job that first season was selling the Bulls. I went to every banquet and talked to every organization that would listen. Our public relations man was Ben Bentley, a Chicago legend who was a ring announcer for some heavyweight championship fights. He also did a lot of public relations work for boxing.

Ben would take me around to the newspaper and beg them to write stories about the Bulls. It was a completely different situation from today, when the Bulls own the front page of the sports sections during the season. Basketball writers do a million stories and a lot of the guys complain because their bosses won't let them do more.

At the time, there were four newspapers in Chicago and Bentley had contacts on each of them. When our straight pleas for coverage were ignored, Bentley went into action. He'd tell a reporter, "Hey, you owe me one. Remember when I gave you that story about Rocky Marciano...."

The reporter would nod.

"Listen," said Bentley. "If nothing else, you can do a story about Kerr. He's a local boy coaching Chicago's new pro basketball team. You know, you can do the Chicago kid comes home, blah, blah, blah...you got the idea."

And the reporter would interview me and we'd finally get something in the paper, even though you had to page to the back right near the obituaries to find it.

One time, Klein tried to organize a parade for the Bulls. People thought it was going to be 150 floats like a St. Patrick's Day parade or something. But all it turned out to be was one flatbed truck holding Klein, Bentley, me and a damn live bull. We didn't exactly draw a crowd.

On the court, things went much better.

Al Bianchi was invaluable to me. Together we got the team hustling, and Guy Rodgers was the ideal point guard for us. He used to throw the alley-oop pass to Don Kojis, who'd catch the lob near the rim and slam it. Kojis called it "the Kangaroo

Kram." I'm convinced that we were the first NBA team to consistently use the alley-oop play. And I also happen to know that 6-foot-5 Don Kojis could jump about five miles higher than 6-foot-7 Bill Buntin.

We opened the season in St. Louis, whose coach, Rich Guerin, had predicted we'd win only 12 games. After the night of October 15, 1966, we needed to win only 11 more because we beat the Hawks 104-97. Guy Rodgers was brilliant, scoring 37 points and pushing the ball up the floor. We won our home opener 119-116 against the Warriors before 4,200 fans at the Chicago Amphitheater and the next night we upset Los Angeles at home.

I was sitting there with a 3-0 record and I liked coaching a whole lot. It also seemed pretty easy. I watched Guy Rodgers handle the ball, I watched Jerry Sloan play defense and I watched our guys hit the boards. The pressure defense designed by Bianchi and me caught some teams by surprise.

One of my favorite moves was the defense—and I use the word as loosely as possible—Al and I designed against Philadelphia's Wilt Chamberlain. This was the season that Philadelphia would win the NBA title with a 68-13 record and it was the season when Chamberlain would average 24 points, 24 rebounds, and 7.8 assists and shoot 68 percent from the field.

Al and I and a very successful amateur coach of the Jamico Saints, Jack Mathis, were talking about how we could possibly be competitive with Philadelphia for even one night. We had the stat sheet and noticed that Chamberlain was shooting only 44 percent from the foul line.

Forty-four percent.

We talked about that for a while. That meant Wilt wasn't even making one of every two foul shots.

"You'd be better off fouling Wilt every time down the floor," said Al. "Just foul him before he can get a shot off."

"We'll do it," I said

Al just looked at me. At best, he was half serious.

"What have we got to lose?" I asked.

"You think we can?" asked Al.

"Why not?" I said. "There's no rule against it. Okay, we'll be in the penalty so that means whenever Wilt is fouled, even if he doesn't have the ball, he goes to the line for two shots. So what? Do you think he'll make both shots?"

Al smiled. That was all he said about it until that night. Before the game, all I told the players was, "If we get in a close game and Al and I decide to do something crazy, don't think about it, just do it."

The guys nodded but they had no idea what we were talking about.

We played Philadelphia very close and we were down six points with about four minutes left. I called time out and said to Al, "We've got to try it."

He smiled again.

Then I told the players. "We want you to foul Wilt every time he comes over half-court on offense."

"But that means he'll always be taking two shots," one of the players told me.

"So what?" I said. "We want him at the foul line."

That's what we did, and Wilt kept missing the free throws and we'd get the ball and go down to the other end and score.

After three possessions, Wilt sensed what was going on. He also was getting mad about being fouled, particularly when he didn't have the ball, and even madder when he missed the foul shots.

When his team got the ball, he started running around in the back court, away from our players who were trying to catch him and foul him. I mean, Wilt was maybe 50 feet from the ball and half of our team was chasing after him. Wilt was screaming, "I'll break your nose if you foul me."

Our players would still catch him and put him at the foul line. With a little over a minute left in the game, Philadelphia Coach Alex Hannum took Wilt out and replaced him with a better foul shooter. By then we were in deep foul trouble. They kept the ball in Hal Greer's hands and nipped us at the wire.

But we did find a way to drive Wilt out of the game.

When it was over, Hannum found himself in a delicate position when the reporters asked him about taking Wilt out of a close game. Instead of saying Wilt was killing Philadelphia with his poor foul shooting, Hannum said that the Sixers were on a long road trip and that Wilt had played a lot of minutes and needed some rest. No one believed that for a second, but Hannum did not want to make Wilt feel any worse by mentioning his foul shooting.

After the game, Al and I were buoyant. Everything had gone almost to perfection because we had to be in a close game before we could start fouling Wilt late in the fourth quarter, and it was very hard to stay with Philadelphia for three quarters. We felt like a couple of tax lawyers who had just found a new loophole that saved our client a million dollars.

But the next day, we got a call from the NBA office and they got all over us. The league said we had made a travesty of the game and we should never pull a stunt like that again.

To make sure, the league passed a new rule—any foul away from the ball was a technical. That meant if we fouled Wilt without the ball, they could use their best shooter for the technical and Philadelphia also would get the ball. So that would kill our strategy.

We ended with a 33–48 record which didn't keep Red Auerbach and the Celtics up nights worrying, but it was good enough for us to make the playoffs. Those 1966–67 Chicago Bulls remain the only expansion team in any sport ever to make the playoffs in their first year. I was voted the NBA Coach of the Year, and I was very sincere when I said that I wanted to saw the trophy in half and give part of it to Al Bianchi. After all, Al was a guard and I was a center and it's a big man's job to keep the guard happy or he'll never see the ball.

Actually, I didn't have to go out of my way to praise Al Bianchi, because he deserved it. There were so many times when I had to be away from the team to make public relations appearances and sell the Bulls to the fans, and that meant someone had to run practice. That someone was Al. The players said it was hard to tell exactly who was the head coach because Al and I worked so well togther. One of us would start a sentence and the other would finish. Our players fed off Al's intensity and a lot of these guys were determined to show the teams that had let them go in the expansion draft that those teams had made a mistake.

I took a lot of pride in Jerry Sloan being named to the All-Star team. He also was the first of two guards to ever lead the Bulls in rebounding—the other was Michael Jordan.

Despite our success, Klein wasn't happy.

At one point during the season, he sent a note to us saying we should play two five-man platoons—one group in the first and third quarters, another group of five in the second and fourth quarters.

That didn't sit well with Al or me.

Klein also insisted that Schellhase was a viable player and he wanted the guy on the floor. But I sure wasn't going to bench Jerry Sloan or Guy Rodgers to play Schellhase.

What really upset me was late in the season when we were in the middle of the playoff race, Klein ordered Al Bianchi to leave the team for a night to scout the DePaul-Notre Dame game. I couldn't believe it and Al was ready to strangle Klein. Al and I decided that Al would stay with us—I needed him more on the bench than looking at some college players.

We lost the game and afterwards Klein came up to Bianchi and said, "I ought to fire you right now for disobeying my orders, but I'll let you stay until the end of the season because I know you need the money."

That was the end for Al and the Bulls.

"I can't stand this guy (Klein)," Al told me. "As soon as the season is over, I'm outta here. I love working with you, Red, but..."

Al didn't finish the sentence and he didn't have to. I understood exactly. The problem was Klein and I was getting the feeling that the problem always would be Dick Klein.

At the end of the season, Al was hired by Seattle to be the first head coach of that expansion team. Now, we really were in trouble, and losing Al Bianchi was only part of it. Klein always had a lot of George Steinbrenner in him, and this was before we knew who George Steinbrenner was. Klein took credit for every victory and was constantly working to be in the public eye.

As Bulls' public relations man Ben Bentley said, "Dick Klein would jump out of a window to get his name in the newspaper."

Klein did have some talents. He was an outstanding salesman. When Jerry Colangelo told me that he was quitting as the Bulls' business manager to become the general manager in Phoenix, I asked him if he was going to personally tell Klein.

"No, I'll leave him a letter of resignation," said Colangelo. "If I know Dick Klein, he'll talk me out of it."

And Klein does deserve credit for putting together a group to buy the Bulls and then convincing the NBA to expand into Chicago only three years after the Zephyrs had failed and moved to Baltimore. These achievements show that Dick Klein could use the power of words.

But Klein really wanted my job, and that became even more apparent in the Bulls' second season.

I went in to negotiate my new contract and I figured I'd get a raise.

"Same deal," said Klein.

"Same deal?" I was shocked. "Dick, I was Coach of the Year. We made the playoffs. That should be worth something."

I guess I should have known that this was coming. I had heard that Klein was asked about me at a banquet and he told a room full of people, "Yeah, Kerr will be all right as a coach as soon as he learns how to use his time outs."

That's a helluva thing to say about your coach, a guy who was the Coach of the Year.

Anyway, I came back to the Bulls for about the same deal. I had no choice. I didn't want to leave Chicago and Klein knew it. Then Klein swung into action on the player personnel front, making several moves that would immediately hurt us.

Guy Rodgers was traded for a shooting guard named Flynn Robinson, and the absence of Rodgers meant we had no point guard. We had a disagreement on who to protect for the expansion draft, and Klein decided that we could afford to lose Don Kojis and we did, as he was taken by Seattle.

Suddenly, two of our most exciting players, the guys who invented the "Kangaroo Kram," were gone. We made several other questionable moves, and I knew I was in trouble. I didn't have Bianchi, who meant so much to the team on the bench and in practice. I didn't have Rodgers, whose leadership meant so much on the floor.

That added up to losing 15 of our first 16 games.

Klein was taking it very hard. In the middle of the game, he'd send me a note saying, "Nine turnovers so far."

No kidding?

Where did he think I was, in Siberia? I knew we had made nine turnovers! We had a young team with no point guard...what did he expect?

Klein started calling meetings with me. They were supposed to be lunch, but they were endless affairs—I'm talking about four hours. For the first three and a half hours, he'd ramble on and on, never getting to the point and smoking about three packs of cigarettes. Then he'd finally get to what he wanted to say—which usually was that I was a lousy coach.

After those sessions, I'd go home with my stomach tied in knots. I started making model airplanes, something to keep my mind occupied. It would take a lot of time to build them, using balsa wood, glue, paper, the whole bit. Then I'd turn the propeller, light the plane on fire with a cigarette lighter and sail it right into a wall.

Betsy would see me doing this and worry. I don't blame her. This wasn't normal behavior unless you were a guy who happened to be working for Dick Klein.

Klein was undercutting me to the press. On February 2, 1968, he told Bob Logan of the *Chicago Tribune*, "By NBA standards, John should have been fired in December. I can't believe that we won't make the playoffs. If not, I'll have to take a whole new look at the team, and that includes the coach."

Statements like that made me want to blow up Dick Klein's car, just as he turned the key in the ignition.

Our final record for 1967–68 was 29–53 and we crept into the playoffs, only to be immediately eliminated by the L. A. Lakers.

———●

Dick Klein would say that he fired me as the Bulls coach. I say that I left for a better job in Phoenix. Some of the reporters said I went before I was fired.

None of it really matters.

The point was that I couldn't and wouldn't work for Klein any longer, and the point was the Jerry Colangelo really wanted me to coach his new team in Phoenix.

That made me feel wanted. I had an offer from Colangelo while I was still the coach of the Bulls. The offer was for $30,000—none of this $15,000 base and $5,000 for 30 wins and so on. I also knew that Colangelo would be a good man to work for since he had been the Bulls' business manager during the first year of the franchise. We had a lot in common and Jerry helped me keep some semblance of sanity in my second year with the Bulls.

I kept thinking that I didn't want an ulcer and I was too young to watch all my red hair turn gray. The bickering with Klein had transformed me into this strange guy who sat around the house building model airplanes then setting them on fire and crashing them into a wall. I never got a pat on the back from the guy. Instead all I heard was that he was ripping me behind my back.

Who needed that?

As for Phoenix, I had never been there and didn't even know where it was but for $30,000 I knew I'd find it.

So I went to see Klein at the end of the second season and said, "If you want me to go somewhere else, then tell me."

Klein sort of talked around the subject for a while.

Then I said, "If you want me to stay, I want an unlimited expense account."

Klein wasn't paying me a decent salary, and I also was only getting the same meal money as the players on the road. This was embarrassing because there are times during a season when a coach wants to take the sportswriters and broadcasters to dinner—it's good public relations—but I had to pay out of my own pocket or else we went Dutch treat.

Well, Klein said forget the expense account, and I told him I was going to Phoenix.

End of story.

Klein did demand a second-round draft pick from the Suns as compensation for me, and that became Simmie Hill from West Texas State. I was the first coach who wasn't a player to be "traded," since the Suns had to give up that draft pick to get my contractual rights from the Bulls. That doesn't sound like being fired to me.

At my last press conference I was asked if I had any advice for the next Bulls coach:

"Yeah," I said. "Change the plays because I know them all."

After the press conference, John Hillyer of the *Chicago Herald* came up to me and said, "It will be a lot easier to knock the Bulls now that you're gone," and Klein found himself under a lot of heat from that moment until he was fired four years later in 1972.

Jerry Colangelo was in charge of everything in Phoenix. He was building the franchise from scratch—he rented the building, he hired the basketball and business staffs, he bought the equipment. It was a tremendous challenge with a lot of pressure and I think Jerry wanted a familiar face around, which may be part of the reason he hired me. I was named coach of the team before it even had a nickname, a schedule or any players. All Jerry and I had to sell was the fact that we would be in the NBA the next season. I'd go to banquets and tell people, "Look, I'm not sure who will play for us or even when we'll play, but it's going to be exciting, so buy your tickets anyway."

Colangelo ran a contest to name the team and got about 28,000 entries for everything from the Suns to the Gila Monsters. Three hundred people picked the Suns, and we held a drawing for the winner. I believe that all the winner received were Andy Williams albums because Williams was a minority owner of the team.

I brought my family to Phoenix in the summer and it was about 117 degrees and I could see that my wife and kids were looking at me as if to say, "Why is he bringing us here?" We did buy a house with palm trees, grapefruit trees and the mountains in the background. For survival, we had a swimming pool that we named the Expansion Pool. The new Phoenix franchise did not enjoy the same advantages that the Bulls had in 1966. In two years, the NBA had added four more expansion teams. The owners and the league also learned some more effective ways to make life miserable for its newest teams.

Instead of letting the established teams protect seven players as was the case when the Bulls began, the league made it eight players on the protected lists. Also, the Suns came into the NBA the same year as Milwaukee, which meant that the talent in the expansion pool was cut in half. Therefore, the situation in Phoenix was this—there were fewer experienced players, and those players weren't as talented as those the Bulls had in 1966.

Our first three picks in the draft were Tom Van Arsdale, Gail Goodrich and Dick Snyder. Goodrich was an established player, and Van Arsdale and Snyder became very good players for the Suns. But there was a problem—all three guys were guards and we had no big men.

I was the first coach in NBA history to coach two expansion franchises, and I learned the same lessons every expansion coach has endured ever since:

1. The moment you walk on the floor and you see your "talent," you know it's going to be a very, very long year. All it takes is one look and you know. What's more, as the practices go by, you discover that some of the guys you thought "weren't all that bad," are indeed that bad, which is why the established teams gave up on them in the first place. You'll have a few moments when you might dare to think that "we're going to be okay, not as bad as everyone thinks." This is called delusions of grandeur and don't worry, because the feeling will pass the next time you take the floor and get your brains beat in.

2. You'll have no center. You'll have no one who might even act like a center. You'll have some guys who claim they are centers but the moment you see them play you'll know they lied. None of them will bump his head on 7-foot doorways.

3. You'll say that you want your team to run. Every coach does. Then you'll see your team try to run in practice. Within a week, you'll have them walking the ball up the court. At least it will take more time off the clock before you make a turnover in a slow-down game.

4. Learn this phrase, "We'll play them one game at a time." You'll find yourself saying it 82 times a year. You'll also discover that you lose them one game at a time.

5. You'll spend an inordinate amount of time staring at the waiver list. You'll think that perhaps one of the established teams cut a player who might help you. Well, you're right. One of those teams will eventually cut a player who is better than some of the guys you have. But when you get him, it won't matter because you'll still get your brains beat in.

6. Remember: No matter what, you'll get your brains beat in. But remember that your wife still loves you and try not to kick the dog too hard.

7. Aim to lead the league in jokes. It's your only chance to lead the league in anything.

8. You'll soon realize that some of your players weren't bad supporting actors, but you have no leading men.

All of this is a long way of saying the 1968–69 Suns were not a good team. We won our first game and surprised everyone, especially me. But reality quickly set in. How does a 16–66 record sound? It sounds to me like a coach won't be around for a long time. Thank God I did lead the league in jokes and thank God there was no Dick Klein in the Suns' front office. That meant all the model airplanes around my house were safe.

Jerry Colangelo was great to me. We came off one trip where we'd lost something like seven in a row. I was nervous and worried when I walked from the plane to my car. As I backed out of the parking spot, I plowed right into Colangelo, who was pulling in. Jerry just said, "Don't worry about it. These things happen."

Our big moment in that first year with the Suns came on Christmas Day. We were playing the Lakers in a nationally televised game and they were asleep. In the middle of the second quarter, we had a 25-point lead on a team that was in first place in the Western Conference.

Well, I was feeling good. We're up by 25 and all my friends back in Chicago are watching it. I started to think about the guys on the end of the bench. They weren't very good, but they were nice guys and they tried hard and maybe they'd like to get on the floor so their parents could see them on television.

Thinking like that is why I've had a nice long career as an announcer.

This was the dumbest coaching decision I ever made—and that takes in some real territory.

Anyway, we blew the lead and played Santa Claus for the Lakers as we lost the game. That was not something I wanted seen by the nation as it ate its Christmas dinner.

It was a brutal year. We'd come close to winning a number of games, but there would always be a crucial turnover or a missed shot in the clutch. The team walked on to the floor thinking, "Okay, when does it start? When will we begin to blow this one?"

I'd go back to my room and would be up half the night thinking, "If only this guy had made a free throw...if only we had run the pick-and-roll...if only...."

Like every coach, I tried to have us prepared for everything the opposition threw at us. And it was the same for every coach in an expansion situation; it didn't matter because we just weren't good enough. We became accustomed to losing. I talked about the guys putting forth "a great effort." I talked about patience. I said I saw progress...blah...blah...blah.

What I really saw was Lew Alcindor (now Kareem Abdul-Jabbar) playing center for UCLA and knowing that the Suns or Milwaukee would have him next season.

The coin flip came between the Suns and Milwaukee for the rights to Jabbar.

We called heads.

The coin came up tails.

They got perhaps the greatest center in the history of the game.

We got Neal Walk.

In effect, you could have turned the hourglass over on my coaching career because it was just a matter of time before it was over.

Colangelo did try to upgrade the Suns by signing Connie Hawkins, a playground legend from New York who was a star in the American Basketball Association. Hawkins had been denied the right to play in the NBA because he allegedly associated with gamblers when he was at the University of Iowa, but Hawkins took his case to court and part of the settlement was that he'd be allowed to play in the NBA.

After Phoenix signed Hawkins to $2.5 million, one of the team's owners, Richard Bloch, said to me, "John, if this guy can't play, lie to me."

Hawkins could play...sort of...when the moon was in the right phase or when the mood struck him. He played well just often enough to drive me up a tree and demand that someone give me a banana. Hawkins would score 15 points in the first quarter and five for the rest of the game. Connie did not have a big build. In fact, I was shocked at how skinny the 6-foot-8 forward was. He was listed at 200 pounds, but it looked more like 180. I said he reminded me of a polio poster child. At the time, Hawkins was sick and had lost some weight because of a virus, but he was not the physical presence you'd expect from a guy who was supposed to be The Franchise.

Hawkins was very immature. I think it came from the fact that he never finished college and that he played for everyone from the Globetrotters to the Pittsburgh Condors. He had a playground, "me-first," mentality.

Phoenix sportswriter Joe Gilmartin put it best when he wrote: "The Hawk is a work of art. Some nights, it's poetry in motion. Other nights it's still life."

I'd look at Hawkins in the dressing room and know that he had no idea what team we were playing that night unless he'd read it on the tickets he was leaving for a friend. As for who he was supposed to guard, he had about as much chance of knowing that as he did the square root of 113.

One night we were playing the Chicago Bulls. It was an important game because we were losing and we needed a big night from Hawkins.

Right before the game I got a call from our trainer (Joe Proski).

"Connie won't be able to play tonight," said Proski.

"Why not?"

"He had a toothache and went to see the dentist and the dentist gave him some gas to relieve the pain. He's out of it."

I couldn't believe it. Connie didn't tell anyone that he had a dental problem and he didn't tell the dentist that he had a game that night. He just took himself out of commission.

And my job was riding on this guy.

Well, it didn't ride on Hawkins for long because Colangelo fired me when we had a 15–23 record and took over the team himself. In retrospect, he did me a favor because that got me started in broadcasting with Hot Rod Hundley, as we did the Suns' games together.

But I look back at coaching two expansion teams and I see my 93–190 record in the NBA and I still think I was a good coach, especially when it came to the Xs and Os. On the blackboard, my Xs and Os looked great but when I got on the floor I always discovered that their Xs were a lot bigger and faster than my Os. And that reminds me of several conversations I had with Alex Hannum right before I took the Bulls job.

"Johnny, you don't want to be the first guy who coaches an

expansion team," he said. "You want to be the second coach so you'll have another coach to blame for screwing up the team in the first place."

Boy was he ever right.

Officials

I want to start this discussion of officials with a quick story. The Bulls were playing a game in 1987 that was being officiated by Earl Strom, who is one of the greatest refs in the history of the NBA.

I was sitting at the press table doing the game on the radio with Jim Durham. During a time out, Earl came over to us and said, "I don't know what he ate before the game, but if (Dave) Corzine farts out there one more time, he's history."

I laughed. I have to admit that's one of the few times that I've ever laughed with an official. I've laughed at them enough, when they fall down or otherwise embarrass themselves. But it isn't often that you can laugh along with these guys.

That's because there is something about being an official that makes people do strange things, things they'd never even imagine doing to anyone else.

I'm talking about the night my father-in-law, Ed Nemecek, tried to strangle an official.

The official's name was Don Murphy and this was during my second season coaching the Bulls (1967–68). The game was in Chicago and we were getting our butts kicked, as usual. I also thought Murphy was making matters worse by missing calls. I kept telling him things like, "As lousy as we're playing, you're worse tonight, Don."

Finally, Murphy had had enough and called a technical on me. We went into the dressing room losing and I was worried.

At this point in the season, I was fighting with general manager Dick Klein and I also was fighting to keep my job. We had lost 15 of our first 16 games, Klein was openly second-guessing me and our crowds were small. I didn't have to be Sherlock Holmes to figure out that my future with the Bulls was very shaky. Being coach of the Bulls wasn't just another job, it was the job I always wanted because it was in Chicago, and never again did I want to leave this town.

If you get the sack as a director of one advertising agency in Chicago, you probably can get work at another one. The same is true in virtually all professions. But either you're the coach of the Bulls or you're not. If you wanted to be an NBA coach in Chicago, then there was only one place to work. My family knew this, especially my father-in-law. He was so happy to have Betsy and our kids close by, that he was feeling even more pressure than I was when things with the Bulls started to go sour. He knew that Klein wanted me to win at least 30–35 games or else I was out. Watching us lose night after night, Ed had the feeling that his family would soon move to who knows where, assuming I could find another NBA coaching job. To most fans, pro basketball is a game. To the coach and his family, it is a life.

So we were in Chicago and we were getting beat and Murphy was out there acting as though he needed a throat operation because he had swallowed his whistle—he never used it when my guys were driving to the basket and getting clobbered.

"Hey, Murph, no fracture, no foul?" I yelled.

Anyway, it was one grim day at the office.

My family was in the stands—my father and mother-in-law, Betsy, and her sister—being subjected to this fiasco. Ed was standing up and screaming at the officials. He was taking everything very hard and very personally.

The half ended and I walked off the floor and into the dressing room.

Ed was trying to climb out of the box seats to get on the floor.

"Lemme at 'em," he kept telling Betsy and his wife.

Betsy was pregnant and she was holding him back. Betsy's sister was terrified because she had never seen her father in such a rage. Betsy's mother also was holding him, worried that her husband would run on to the floor and do something he would always regret.

As usual, wives are right and this was no exception.

Betsy and her mother did hang on to Ed for what they thought was long enough for the officials to get off the floor and into the dressing room. When they let him go, Ed took off and ran around the police and everyone else and caught Murphy just as he was about to go into the officials' dressing room.

I never saw what happened, but I did hear about it.

In the Bulls' dressing room, Joe Lee, the ballboy, came up to me and said, "Know what happened out there?"

"What?"

"Somebody went berserk and attacked Murphy," said Lee. "He tried to pull the [NBA officials] patch off his jersey and they thought the guy was going to choke him until the cops pulled the guy off."

"Well, no matter how bad those guys are, fans shouldn't do that," I said. "That's a real shame. They ought to nail that nut."

Then I found out that the "nut" was my father-in-law.

Oh boy.

When we saw the newspaper the next day, there was a big picture of Ed being pulled away from Murphy by a bunch of ushers in Andy Frain uniforms. The caption under the photo said, "Johnny Kerr's father-in-law, Ed Nemecek, attacks official Don Murphy."

Ohhh boy.

Then we got a call from *Sports Illustrated*, and they wanted to do a big story on the whole thing.

Oh boy—again.

I told *Sports Illustrated*, "I don't know the guy. I don't know where he lives and I don't have anything to say."

My father-in-law was terribly embarrassed. My mother-in-law was mortified. *Sports Illustrated* called their house and she answered the phone saying, "I don't want to talk about it."

Then my mother-in-law did something that athletes and coaches have wanted to do for years but never had the guts to do—she slammed down the phone right in the ear of *Sports*

Illustrated.

The funny thing was that my father-in-law knew a lot of the officials and got along great with them. He would play cards with officials such as Mendy Rudolph and he'd have lunch with these guys. Mendy was a legendary official and he was absolutely floored when he heard about the incident.

"Not Ed Nemecek," he said. 'It couldn't be Ed."

Of course it couldn't—not if you knew my father-in-law—but it was what the pressure of pro basketball does to people.

And as for the officials—it's the old "Shoot the Messenger" syndrome.

Coaches and players spend countless hours talking about officials—who's good, who's bad, who's getting too old, who's too young. They talk about which officials hate what teams, or what players get breaks from certain officials. On and on it goes, hours at a time. It becomes a mania.

I know that I never could be an official. I could never call a fair game in Boston, because I would love a chance to nail the Celtics. The second one of those guys in green said one word to me, I'd blow the whistle and spend the next six years giving that guy technical fouls. I'd be thinking about how the Celtics always used to kick my team's butt back when Bill Russell was the center, and I'd think how the officials used to let K.C. Jones just beat the hell out of the guy he was guarding—baby, I'd want revenge.

Or there would be some guys I'd nail. When Moses Malone gets the ball, puts down his head and just plows right into someone as if he were a fullback trying to ram his way up the middle for a couple of yards, he can forget about picking up the foul on the defender, as is usually the case. I'd see Moses make that move and I know what I'd call—charging. Offensive foul. Moses, you've been getting away with that move for years, but not tonight, buddy. Not with Johnny Kerr wearing a whistle around his neck. Don't even say one word to me—you fouled and you know it, the other guy was just standing there.

This sort of sounds like fun. Give me two months and I can take out all these years of repressed hostility and straighten out the league at the same time. I wouldn't be an official as much as Charles Bronson in *Death Wish 47* or whatever, administering justice as I see fit.

Of course, this sort of thinking is exactly why I couldn't be an official and it's probably why it is best that former NBA players and coaches don't go into officiating. We'd bring too much baggage to the game.

I think it takes a very special guy to be an official.

First of all, you've got to like striped shirts and black shoes, because that's your wardrobe. You also need a sadistic—or is it masochistic—streak in your personality and take some perverse pleasure from being booed by 20,000 people almost every night of your life. I don't care what the officials say, they have to feel like they've been kicked around every night after they get off work.

I was just thinking that if I had been an official and my father-in-law had gone to the games, the poor guy would be in trouble every night because he'd be out there trying to fight all the players, coaches and fans who were on me.

That's why an official has to be a loner. His friends usually are other officials, who live the same warped existence that he does, and how healthy can that be? He never has a home game, and he can't take his family on the road to watch him work. What old man wants his kids to see him called an idiot? As it is, fathers get enough of that at home from their wife and kids.

That's why when I'm hosting a banquet and notice an official in the room, I'll say something like, "I see that Earl Strom is here with us tonight. Let's make him feel at home by giving him a nice round of boos."

It's always good for a laugh, but it's also true. Name one building in the world where people cheer after the officials are introduced.

Or suppose you're in a bar with a couple of other guys.

One is wearing a black shirt with a white collar. He has an Irish accent and he's having a few pops and talking about what a great bingo game they have set for next week at the parish hall and how the high school football team has a super tailback. You figure the guy is a priest, but he's got a fun streak and maybe you'll listen to the guy for a while.

Then another guy comes over and starts telling you about some fire they put out at an apartment building and you think, a fireman, this guy's okay. Who knows, maybe one day he'll be there for me.

Another guy shows up and you ask what he does.

"I'm an official," he says.

Suddenly, it's like one of those E.F. Hutton commercials—the whole place gets real quiet.

Then the guy explains that he's an NBA official.

Suddenly, everyone gets up and moves to the other side of the bar, leaving the official alone with his beer. It's like you just found out that the guy worked for the IRS.

Tax men and officials do have a lot in common—people see them and think what these guys have cost them—either in cash or in victories for their favorite team.

The next time anyone comes up to an official and says, "Nice game," will be the first.

Some fans come to the game for the sole purpose of berating the officials. These are people whose home lives are one long "Honey-do" weekend. You know, their wives tell them, "Honey, do this. . .Honey, do that. . .and Honey, when you're done you had better take care of the kids and buy a gift for my mother."

And all these guys have at home is a five-word vocabulary, "Right away, dear. . . Why yes, dear."

Then they come to the basketball game with their buddies and they all get a little oiled even before the game starts as they make a pit stop at the Do-Drop Inn. They jump on the officials at the opening tip and they don't let up until after the final buzzer when the refs are led off the floor by the security guards. Making matters worse is that this breed of fan pays attention when the officials are announced, he learns their names so he can get very personal.

Instead of yelling, "Hey, buddy, when did you retire?" They scream, "Hey, Jake, they got a rocking chair with your name on it at a rest home."

None of these lines are especially funny because most of these guys aren't humorous. They just attack. They specialize in using three different four-letter words about 100 different ways.

And the official is supposed to stand there and take it. To him, nothing is supposed to be personal. But how can they take it? How can anyone shut out the crowd, the coaches and the players?

How would you like to be an official and have to watch as the San Diego Chicken drags a stuffed ref onto the court and proceeds to kick it, stomp it and punch it while the crowd cheers?

You can see the officials standing there stoically, watching the Chicken do his act, and you know that those guys are thinking, "You feather-brained son-of-a-bitch, I'd like to ring your neck."

That night, you know the officials go to the Colonel's for dinner because eating Kentucky Fried Chicken is their only revenge. What I wonder is why more of these guys don't get ulcers. Perhaps they are closet wrestling fans and when no one is looking, they slip into an arena and throw tomatoes at King Kong Bundy. They have to go somewhere to yell at someone.

——————●

Some people like to make officiating into a science—you stand here, you watch for that, you don't let them do this. They make it sound like a paint-by-numbers set. You do A, then B, then C.

But basketball is a contradiction. It is a game governed by rules, but those who are in charge of enforcing the rules must view the game as art. A basketball game is a Picasso, not something you draw with a T square.

Remember this about officiating—there are very, very, very few rule infractions during the course of a game. But there are thousands of judgment calls that must be made.

Okay, you say that a 3-second call should be cut and dry. A guy is in the lane for three seconds or he isn't.

Well, it depends.

An official isn't out there holding a stopwatch. He doesn't even stand there staring at the player in the key and say, "One thousand one, one thousand two, one thousand three" in his head. If he did, he would be oblivious to everything else happening on the court and that would make him a lousy official.

Instead, the official sees a guy in the lane and thinks, "Jabbar has been in there long enough to build a house," and *wham*, the official calls Kareem Abdul-Jabbar for three seconds.

That's a judgment, not a fact. Maybe Jabbar was in the lane for five seconds instead of three when the whistle finally blew. Or else maybe he was in the lane for only two seconds this time, but during his team's last three possessions he had been in the key for a week. The reason the official calls three seconds is to keep players from clogging up the middle.

Then there's the illegal defense.

I defy anyone to coherently explain what is and what isn't an illegal defense, because I'm convinced that no one really knows. It's too complicated.

Most officials use this approach to the illegal defense—they know it when they see it, just don't ask them what they saw.

Many of the turnovers in basketball are called because "something doesn't look right." The flow of the game has been interrupted, so something illegal must have happened. Or two bodies collide and hit the ground. Neither official saw what happened, all they know is that two guys are on the floor, one with a broken jaw and another is rubbing his fist. Odds are that the guy with the sore fist punched the guy with the broken jaw, so they call it.

That decision is rather simple.

But what happens if both guys simply run into each other and then fall down? All the officials see are two flattened bodies. Sometimes, they blow the whistle and then try to figure out what happened. Or else, they don't do anything, just let the guys keep playing and hope that no one steps on the corpses.

That may be a bit of an overstatement, but not much.

One of the major problems facing officials is their size—they're too small and the players are too big.

It is a fact that while the players have grown over the last 25 years, the officials have stayed the same size.

So what?

So the officials are getting blocked out by the bigger bodies, that's what. The officials can't see over the players because the players are taller, and they can't see around the players, because the players are wider. Remember the 1987 playoffs between Detroit and Boston when Parish flattened Laimbeer and neither official saw it?

Here's two 6-foot-11 centers going at it at mid-court in front of about 17,000 fans and a national television audience and the officials tell us that they didn't see a thing.

You know what?

I believe the officials. They didn't see it because they were screened. There were too many other Winnebago-sized bodies between them and the action, so they missed it.

I'm not saying that an official should be at least 6-foot-6, I'm just suggesting that a guy that size would have an advantage.

One thing is certain, any official has to be in great physical condition. These guys will run between ten and fifteen miles a night. It's stop-and-go, twisting and turning and jumping. They have to do about everything the athletes do and they are on rigid conditioning programs. You see very few officials who look as though they swallowed a basketball. Some of these guys are in their fifties and they're in tremendous condition. Officials also suffer the same injuries as basketball players—bad knees, sprained ankles, etc.

Officials must laugh at their counterparts in baseball. To most umpires, every plate of food they see is home plate. They don't die from exhaustion, they die from over-consumption. You see the umpire at second base and you wonder why he's standing out there with a chest protector on, and then you realize that you're actually looking at the guy's stomach.

Basketball officials aren't superb athletes, but they are in superb shape. That's why I think that one answer to finding new officials would be to look for athletes in high school and college who aren't quite good enough to play basketball at the highest level, yet they love the game and know the rules. Then you can teach them how to become officials at an early age. Also, you'd end up with some taller officials because the guys playing the game now—even in high school and college—are much bigger than the average NBA official.

————●

I have to admit that the relationship between the fans and the officials isn't very interesting. What it comes down to is that fans think officials are morons and they say so. Meanwhile, officials think the fans are morons, only they aren't allowed to say a word.

But the interaction of the officials with the players and coaches is fascinating.

When I coached, there was an official named Joe Gushue, who was a carpenter in the off-season. It was very unfortunate for Joe that this got out, because I remember a game where a player dunked and broke a backboard and the next thing you know everyone was yelling at Gushue to go fix it.

Joe would mess up a call and I'd yell, "Gee, Joe, if you hammered nails the way you're calling this game you'd always have a broken thumb."

That was good for a technical.

Another way not to make friends and influence those with the whistles is to say, "You guys are so blind that you must have been the plane spotters at Pearl Harbor..."

Or else, asking a literate official, "Hey, Hugh, who wrote the *Iliad* and the *Odyssey*?"

"Homer," says the official.

"You got that part right," I'd say.

Once again, that's worth a technical, and I'm speaking from personal experience on these matters.

Coaches and players have to know the personalities of the officials.

One legendary ref is Sid Borgia, who was from the "Law Unto Themselves" school of officiating. That means he made up his own rules.

There was a game where a player obviously traveled with the ball and then he ran into a defender and stumbled out-of-bounds. So there were two turnovers—traveling and then stepping out-of-bounds.

Borgia gave the ball back to the player who had traveled.

"Hey, Sid," I yelled. "The guy walked."

He didn't say anything.

"Then the guy ended up out-of-bounds," I said. "How the hell can you give him the ball back?"

"He forced him to walk out-of-bounds," said Borgia.

What did that mean—he was forced out-of-bounds? He either walked or he didn't. There was nothing in the rulebook about this, Sid just made it up. He was like Wyatt Earp—the law was what he said it was.

One night I was getting particularly frustrated with Borgia. I never minded when he made up the rules so long as my team was getting the edge. But on this night, they were about ready to call in the coroner because we were just dead on the floor. Borgia came by and I yelled, "Sid, how do you spell your name— one I or two?"

"One I," he said.

"At least you got that right."

The one-eye line earned me a technical.

I respected Sid because he wouldn't be intimidated. As officials, he and Mendy Rudolph ran the NBA for years. Now, Earl Strom and Jake O'Donnell are at the head of the class—these guys are in charge. They usually keep their personalities under control. They aren't going to take any nonsense, but they also won't take it out on you because the eggs they had for breakfast were too soggy. Strom is a jewel and every team wants him when they play on the road because he refuses to be swayed by the crowd. If anything, Strom will turn on the home team if the crowd is especially hostile toward the officials. He'll make a tough call against the home team and then stand there at mid-court taking in all the boos and trying to stare down everyone in the stands.

Strom is a basketball fan. When there is an old-timers game, he shows up with his scrapbook and asks the former players to sign it. He is very friendly and relishes talking with just about anybody. He also is a tough guy who'll jump between a couple of 7-footers who have just squared off and are ready to kill each other. Earl can break up a fight faster than just about any official I've ever seen, and the reason is that the players respect him. Certainly a 6-foot, 175-pound Earl Strom wouldn't be able to stop a 7-footer physically—only a howitzer could do that. With officials such as Strom, O'Donnell and Jack Madden, the players and coaches know they may as well save their breath because these officials aren't interested in what they have to say. Their personalities are strong enough to put fear into the coaches and players.

There are other officials such as Joey Crawford, who is in great condition and really knows the rules. But Joey Crawford spends his life wearing this pained expression as if his underwear is always too tight. He hears everything everyone says about him and worries about it. Maybe that's why his face is always crinkled up and the back of his neck is crimson, causing some of us to say that Crawford is so hot under the collar you could fry an egg on his neck. No matter how hard Joey tries, he is destined to take something personally during the course of a game and then a quick technical will follow. Officials such as Crawford will say they whistle a fast technical because they want to stop things before they start. I'm not even sure what that means. How can you stop something when you're not even sure what it is? A lot of times, an official uses this rationalization to retaliate against people they don't like. These officials are too sensitive and need to lighten up.

Other officials are like putty. Putting these guys on an NBA floor is like sending Don Knotts to quiet down a riot at Attica. They spend the whole game getting verbally assaulted from both benches because they are just plain incompetent. They run up and down the floor, staring at one bench, then the other. They put the whistle to their mouths, threatening to blow a technical foul. These guys are the kind of fathers who are always telling their kids, "One more word, just say one more word and then you're in real trouble." Of course, the kid pops off again and the father can't do anything but say, "Don't you utter one more word...."

One of the common complaints you hear from basketball people is that the officials aren't consistent. At certain points in the game, you can clobber a guy upside the head with a 2-by-4 and there's no call. Later, you can just look hard at the guy, not even touch him, and the whistle blows. Officials naturally counter by saying that teams aren't consistent, either. One night they throw the ball away 10 times, then they do it 30 the next. Hey, we're all human, they say.

You know what?

They are. I'm reminded of this every time I meet an official away from the court. We usually have a great talk, swap stories and I forget how this guy maybe stuck it to the Bulls last month in Milwaukee. Look, I don't expect officials to be perfect. I don't know how they can completely separate themselves from the players, the coaches and the fans who are railing away at them all night. But they can try, and that's what the good ones do.

———●

The NBA does not release the names of the officials in advance. So you don't know from one night to the next who will call your game until they walk on the floor about 30 minutes before it starts.

This doesn't stop coaches from speculating about the officials. They'll say, "We just had Joey Crawford and Dick Bavetta last night, so we won't have them again. And we had Jack Madden and Hugh Evans the other day, so they probably won't be back.... Let's see, it's been a long time since we've seen Earl Strom. Yeah, I bet Strom shows up in the next couple of games."

On and on it goes and it means nothing.

So what if you know the officials, what can you do about it? The NBA office isn't going to be interested if a coach calls and says, "We don't want to play if Ronnie Nunn and Hue Hollins are working the game."

The NBA office isn't going to buy that.

It is the NBA that assigns the officials to the game and there seldom seems to be any process behind it. If anything, the NBA strives to keep things random. Officials don't work in the same pairs for more than a month or two, unlike baseball umpires who often are in the same crew of four for an entire season. Usually, they try to prevent officials from working a game involving the same team on consecutive nights, but that has occasionally happened. They also want to prevent the same official from calling too many games with one or two teams. In other words, they want to mix things up.

But that's about it.

In an important game, you'll probably see a veteran official— Strom, O'Donnell, Madden—but even that isn't assured.

So what's the pattern?

There is no pattern.

That's why I say coaches should block the officials out of their minds. Okay, that's what I say. What I know as a former coach is that will never happen. If anything, the situation is worse now than when I coached because computers have made record-keeping more sophisticated. Now coaches know exactly what their team's record is when a certain official calls the game. So a coach may walk out on the floor and see Ed Rush standing there and say, "Oh no, we're 1–8 with this guy. We've got no chance, he hates me."

Or he might see Bill Saar with a whistle and say, "We're 5–1 with Billy. I feel good about tonight."

Coaches try not to let the players know that they are worried about the officials. They don't want to have the players think the officials are out to get them or else the players will just quit in the middle of the game. Coaches will say things like, "We have Earl Strom working the game tonight. He calls it pretty loose so don't be afraid to go in there and bang around."

If they have an official who calls a lot of touch fouls, the coaches might say, "Be careful with Fred, we don't want to get into early foul trouble."

But coaches don't tailor their game plans to the officials. It isn't worth the trouble. Besides, players have their own styles and can't change for an official or anyone else.

What officials do is give the head coach and his assistant something to talk and complain about. Coaches are very aware that officials are human. In fact, they believe officials are *too* human and plagued with prejudices.

I've heard coaches say things such as, "Tony's working our game. We can forget it because he doesn't like my center. My guy will have four fouls on him before he works up a sweat."

Coaches have said that they'll lose a game because an official doesn't like one of their players, one of their assistant coaches, even their trainer!

Before a game, coaches are like the bulls right before they are let into the ring. They feel like they are in one of those little stalls and all they can do is wait for the main event. It's a helpless, claustrophobic feeling.

So what do the coaches talk about?

They ask each other, "Who's working the game tonight?"

One of the coaches will say, "I hope it's not that SOB Smith."

Then another coach will say, "That's all we need."

Then the coaches walk on the floor and see Smith standing there. The coach would like to bull his neck, rush out there and gore the poor guy with the whistle even before the game starts.

I'm not saying that any of this is rational, I'm just saying that is what coaches think and talk about. It seems they think they're playing against the officials, not the other team. I know because I had the same conversations before games.

When I coached the Bulls, we were playing the Golden State Warriors and right before the game the official called Warriors' coach Bill Sharman and myself over for a meeting.

"Look guys, I have to work this game by myself because the other official isn't here," he said. "I need your cooperation to make this work, so tell your players to take it easy and don't try to kill each other because we have only one official."

Sharman and I said we'd do all we could to make the official's life easier.

I got back to the huddle and told my players, "Listen up, guys, we've got only one official tonight and that means all he can do is watch the ball. So away from the ball, anything goes. You understand? On the weak side and on the boards, we can really be aggressive and go at it. The guy won't be able to see everything, right?"

I bet Sharman told his players the same thing because five minutes into the game, both teams were throwing body blocks at each other. As it turned out, the other official showed up in the second quarter and that completely changed the physical style of the game, and we ended up getting beat.

What I'm saying is that coaches are always looking for an edge, and they like to think that they can find one with the officials. Coaches also are convinced that officials intentionally set out to make their lives more difficult.

Ironically, the officials hold the same opinion. Before a game, they are saying the same things about the players and the coaches. As they are in the dressing room changing for the game, I know they are saying, "Jeez, we have (Knicks coach) Rick Pitino tonight. That little guy never shuts up, he never sits down. He runs up and down the sidelines, by the end of the game he's lost his voice and he's still screaming. All you hear is this rasp. He just wears my ass out."

Or else they'll say, "We've got (Cleveland coach) Lenny Wilkens. I like Lenny. He's low-keyed. He won't embarrass me."

Or "This is the third time I've had (Chicago coach) Doug Collins in the last two weeks. I don't know about you, but I'm just sick of seeing the guy. Every time you make a call against him, he acts like you just killed his mother.

Or "We've got Detroit and we know that (Bill) Laimbeer and (Rick) Mahorn are probably going to start something. We've got to watch those guys and nail them early if they step out of line. They just had a fight last week and we don't want to have World War III out there."

Sometimes, everyone involved in a game decides to enter into it with the best intentions.

The officials may say, "I know Pitino is emotional. I'm not going to let him get to me."

The coach may say, "I know this official has rabbit ears so I won't say much to him."

Right before the game, there is a meeting at half-court with the captains from the two teams. This is dumb and useless. What can they say, "Well guys, the basket is still ten feet off the ground?" Or else, "You've got a 20-second time out in each half." The rules are the same every night. They don't even toss a coin like they do in football. They don't exchange the lineup card like they do in baseball. They don't do anything. The players just say, "Yeah, yeah...let's go." They quickly shake hands and that's it.

Okay, these meetings also are harmless, but they just annoy me. Don't ask my why—I'm not rational, either.

So we've had the warm ups, the stupid half-court meeting and everyone has made promises to themselves that they'll be on their good behavior. It means nothing.

By the opening jump ball, the officials, the coaches and the players are all on the brink. Remember that every official's call is only 50 percent right. That means one team thinks it's correct and the other thinks it's not. So the first call goes against a coach—the same coach who vowed to be patient with the officials—and he screams. And the official—the same one who vowed to ignore the coach—is getting red under the collar and already thinking about calling a technical foul.

Once the game begins, some coaches have a running dialogue with officials from start to finish. The good officials ignore them. Hopefully, the coaches' voices blend into the crowd noise. But there are times when coaches go too far, when they take a couple of steps on to the court to argue a call, and that's when an official has every right to slap the coach with a technical.

Players also talk to the officials, but it's only a small fraction compared to the coaches. Usually, it's pretty mundane stuff:

"Hey, watch Ewing's elbows."

"How about getting Malone out of the lane?"

"Watch Michael, he's carrying the ball."

Of course, players are shocked any time they are whistled for a violation and some have worked up a collection of bemused, stunned and hurt expressions that they can summon at the appropriate moment.

What I like is the players who don't speak directly to the

ref. One player will say to another, "Do you see what Ewing's doing in there? Can you believe how he swings those elbows?"

Of course, the players make sure the official is standing right next to them when they hold this conversation.

One of my favorite players who used this technique was Walter Bellamy, a former Atlanta center. He'd say: "The foul is always on Walter. Why is the foul always on Walter? Walter was just standing there, doing nothing and they give Walter a cheap foul."

Norm Drucker was working a game when Walter had his crying towel out, "Poor Walter, he can't touch a guy without getting a foul. . . ."

Finally, Drucker tapped Bellamy on the shoulder and said, "Tell Walter that he just got a technical."

For the most part, officials don't like to talk to the players and it is not something the NBA encourages. The official is supposed to be the impartial authority, and joking with the players doesn't lend itself to that image. So most officials ignore the players, even when the player is standing right in their face, jabbering away. Some of the veteran officials such as Strom can talk to the players, but that's because they are NBA institutions. No one will ever question Earl Strom's authority just because he happens to laugh at something Magic Johnson said when the players were walking off the floor for a time out.

When officials do speak to players, it is in the form of a warning: "Corzine, get your body off of him."

"Oakley, watch the elbows."

"Guys, I want to see daylight in the middle."

When an official asks for daylight, he means that the players should stop grabbing and holding each other in the key. The official wants the players free to move in and out of the lane.

When it comes to officials, I have several pet peeves. Here they are.

Young Players Get The Worst Calls

I don't care what they say, officials are tougher on rookies. They always have been and I have a feeling that they always will be. Larry Bird, Magic Johnson, any of the stars or players with good defensive reputations can reach in for a steal and nothing happens. If a kid such as Johnny Newman or Scottie Pippen does, the whistle that follows is so shrill it's enough to shatter your eardrums. Young centers find themselves being bumped right off the court by Moses Malone, but when they push back, the whistle blows.

I'm not sure why this happens. Asking an official is a complete waste of time because he'll tell you that it never happens.

The two great lies are "The check is in the mail," and an official saying, "I call the game the same for everyone."

Sometimes, I believe the officials think that they are upholding the standards of the game. It's almost like the officials are telling rookies, "Don't reach on defense," when they call a foul on a young player. It's like the officials believe the rookie year is an apprenticeship. It's almost like boot camp or being a plebe at a military school. There is no justice and what the fresh meat thinks or says doesn't count.

Great Expectations For Great Players

Michael Jordan is going to get a certain number of breaks. So will Larry Bird, Magic Johnson, Kareem Abdul-Jabbar and the other stars.

This is another subject that officials won't discuss because they deny it exists. Yet if you watch enough NBA games, you'll realize that there is a privileged class of players.

The key word is expectations.

When an official sees Jordan drive through three guys and end up on the floor, he figures someone must have knocked Michael down or else why would he have fallen over? The great players have the knack of taking the ball inside and drawing contact. Are they charging or are they being fouled? That's a matter of opinion, but in most instances the player is drawing a foul because the defense is aware of him at all times and is geared to stopping him.

Every time Michael Jordan goes to the basket, he attracts a mob. Three guys are trying to block his shot and odds are that one of them will whack Michael. The great players are so smooth and so clever. You're not even sure what they did on a particular play, you just know that they scored. I figure if I can't see it from my broadcaster's chair on the sidelines, and then I have the benefit of watching a slow-motion television replay and I'm still not positive what happened, the officials have to be in a real bind, or is it blind?

That's where the expectations come in.

The officials become accustomed to seeing certain players perform certain moves. Why does Adrian Dantley always seem to get fouled when he drives to the basket?

Because he has a way of weaving through bigger defenders, giving them a fake and then having them jump into him. But sometimes Dantley does get stuck with the ball in all that tall timber, and he jumps right into the defender. He forces the contact and that should be an offensive call, yet the official's decision often will go in Dantley's favor.

Why?

Because the officials are used to watching Dantley draw fouls. He has been doing it for a million years, so if they aren't exactly sure what happened, that's what they call.

Rookies have a hard time because the officials don't know the script. By that, I mean the officials haven't seen the young guys play enough to know their moves, to figure out what they *expect* a young player to do on the court. After a few years it changes.

We've talked about players establishing positive reputations such as Michael Jordan and Adrian Dantley drawing fouls. Other players get a negative rap. Darryl Dawkins was known as a guy who fouled a lot and he was forever being called for fouls. Darryl would say he didn't touch the guy, yet there was a whistle. Actually, Dawkins did touch the man, but he probably didn't push or shove any harder than the other players on the court. But when a guy gets shoved by Dawkins, if he's smart he'll let out a groan as if he just took some buckshot in the stomach. This brings the official's attention to Dawkins, and the official thinks, "Darryl's at it again."

Boom!

Foul on Dawkins.

Players also have their tricks.

Bill Laimbeer gets an Academy Award every night. He's a man who is 6-foot-10, 250 pounds and he acts as if he got knocked over with a truck when a 6-footer such as Mark Price drives into him. Meanwhile, Laimbeer is dishing out all kinds of punishment, coming very close to starting a riot every night, yet he is absolutely flabbergasted when he is called for a foul.

Michael Jordan has a move I love.

He'll go to the basket, slicing between a couple of guys, and he'll shoot the ball with his right hand. At the same time, he'll slap his own thigh with his left hand.

The officials hear the slap.

Toot. . . toot.

Michael draws a foul. The officials don't know who did the slapping. . . they just heard a slap. So they usually call the foul on the man nearest to Michael. The guy starts to scream he didn't even touch Michael, and the official will say, "Don't tell me, I know what I saw. . . errr. . . what I heard!"

Traveling

One of the common complaints you hear from fans is that the officials allow the players to walk with the ball. I know that some of it is excessive, but it is not the problem that some fans insist.

That's because it is much harder to call traveling than you'd think. These players have such quick first steps and such long strides. . . when James Worthy decides to take a long step off of a running start, he seems to cover about ten feet, it's truly amazing. The officials don't let guys tuck the ball under their arms and run to the basket.

But the officials also use some very good discretion. If they can't tell that a player has traveled, they let it go. I think that's a good idea. It's like when a policeman sees a guy pull up to a stop sign. Maybe the guy came to a full stop or then again, maybe not. The policeman isn't sure. A good policeman doesn't sweat the small stuff, he just lets the guy go. It's the same with traveling. As it is, the game is interrupted enough with major rule violations, so why make the situation worse? Call the blatant travel, and that's fine with me.

Something else fans should know is that when there is a loose ball in the NBA, the players can dive on the floor for it and sort of roll around with the ball. That is not traveling. But if the player stands up and tries to dribble it, then he has walked. But what a player does while he is flat on his back with the ball is legal. This also is a good rule because it encourages players to throw themselves to the floor to get the loose ball, and that makes for better defense and a more intense game.

Dumb, Ticky-Tacky Fouls

There are too many of these.

Maybe I'm from the old "No fracture, No foul" school of pro basketball, but I still think that there are too many piddley fouls that do nothing but stop the game.

The one that drives me crazy is when a defensive player grabs a rebound and has control of the ball. Then he is bumped by another player, but not enough to lose possession of the ball. The official blows the whistle and calls the foul, and the ball goes back to the team that got the rebound in the first place.

All this does is interrupt the game and take away a fast break opportunity from the team that got the rebound. Just eliminate it. Let the guys play.

The same with all other fouls that really don't change the game. If a guy is dribbling the ball and he gets bumped, but not enough to cause him to lose the basketball, why call the foul?

Remember, fans aren't paying to watch these great athletes shoot foul shots.

The Perils Of The Road

The most talked about aspect of life in the NBA is the home court advantage, better known as the ultimate edge in pro basketball. In the NBA, the home team will win about two-thirds of the games during an average season—the highest home edge in any major sport.

If a team can win half of its road games, it's a happening on the order of the miracle of the loaves and fishes. A team that can go something like 19–22 on the road has a great start on a 50-victory season since it probably can go 31–10 at home. In the NBA, 50 victories out of 82 games is the magic number for teams that are in the elite class of the league.

I loved the movie *Hoosiers*, especially the scene where Gene Hackman takes his Hickory High School team to Butler University Field House for the Indiana State Tournament. Hickory is a very small school and Hackman's players had never seen a building as large as Butler. Hackman has his players measure the foul line—it's still 15 feet from the basket. Then he has them measure the height of the rim—still 10 feet from the floor. So there you are, the floor (and presumably the game) is the same as it is in little Hickory.

There just will be more people screaming—so what?

That seems to be what Hackman is saying, and it's a very good tactic for a coach to take when playing on the road.

But it also happens to be a fallacy.

It doesn't explain why the home team jumps higher, runs faster, pushes itself a little more when it is on it's home floor. I don't care if you're talking about CYO ball or the NBA, it happens. The fact is that players simply perform better at home.

Why?

They're human, remember?

To the coaches, the overriding last-minute factor is the officials. Remember how the coaches spend too much time thinking that, "this guy hates me, he'll stick it to my team at the worst possible moment"?

For the most part, the players don't have a long-term reaction to the officials. They are trained to "play through the calls," which is a nice way of saying, "ignore the guy with the whistle."

The fans are a different story. The players feel their energy, they crave the crowd's enthusiasm. I'm speaking from direct experience and I felt it when I played at Tilden Tech, at the University of Illinois, with Syracuse, with Baltimore and with Philadelphia. You know that the screams and cheers are for you. You know that they will jump all over the officials if they make a lousy call. Everything going through your head is positive— these people like me, these people are behind me, I am home and I am unbeatable at home. It's euphoria and it swells up in your body. Your heart starts pounding during the National Anthem, you start to sweat during the introductions and you feel a bit of chill (or is it a thrill) when your name is announced and you go out to mid-court to the cheers of the fans. It's a nice feeling—someone says your name and people applaud. By the opening jump ball, you are cranked and ready to leap through the roof.

As a coach, I never worried about motivating my team at home. All you had to do was remind the players what they had to do that night against that team. You say, "Come on, guys, let's play hard."

Then the players step on the floor and hear the cheers, and that's a better pep talk than anything a coach can give a team. It's also why a team such as the Lakers can get dumped "on the road" by the L.A. Clippers, even though both teams are in Los Angeles. It's why a great team such as Boston hasn't won a game in Cleveland for three years. The Cleveland fans turn out 20,000 strong and their team suddenly jumps higher, runs faster and plays better. There are a million examples of how the home court makes a team better, some experts have said it's worth 8–10 points. I don't know how you can put a number on it. I just know it exists.

There is the flip side to the home court advantage—the perils of the road.

A number of things are obvious—the team on the road is physically tired. It spends too much time in airports, in hotels, in restaurants. Really, it's too much time waiting for the game to start. Think about how draining it is to spend a long period of time in line. Waiting just saps you, and that's what happens to a basketball team. Also, the winter weather forces teams to take the first flight out to make sure they aren't delayed and won't miss a game. This means a lot of 5 a.m. wakeup calls, and not many of us who work the night shift—as basketball players do—function well if we are forced to get up at 5 a.m.

But there is more to the perils of the road than the travel.

It's an attitude.

Everything is positive for the home team—the crowd is behind them, the court is familiar, the players got a chance to sleep in their own beds.

Meanwhile, everything on the road can be a negative—the plane was late, the hotel rooms weren't ready and the players are tired. Then they come into a place such as Chicago where the place goes nuts every time Michael Jordan touches the ball. The players start to think—the crowd is against us, the officials will be against us, we've got no chance so why bust our butts.

So the coach of the home team is certain that he will get a full effort from his players; the coach of the road team has to worry if he'll receive the same from his guys. Mentally, the visiting team may have lost the game before it even steps on the floor.

On the road, the only reinforcement comes from within. There are 12 players, two assistant coaches, one head coach and a trainer—that's it—16 guys against the world. It's like you're a small family and you've circled the wagons and there are about a million indians out there preparing for the charge.

In Boston, the Celtics love to put things on the scoreboard such as, "The Celtics haven't lost a home game to the Bulls since Warren Harding was president." The Bulls engage in the same psychological warfare with messages like: "Chicago hasn't lost at home in six weeks."

Players will glance up at the scoreboard and they'll see something like that and say, "We really don't have a chance tonight, so why should I go out there and kill myself?"

Teams that come into Chicago will be told, "Don't let Michael Jordan get a dunk because it will bring the crowd into the game."

The players walk on the court thinking, "Don't let Michael dunk . . . don't let Michael dunk."

Then three minutes into the game, Michael gets out on the fast break and *wham*! he throws one down. Now the visiting team starts to think, "Michael's dunked, the crowd is going to act crazy, the game is over." That's why it is a serious mistake for a coach to tell his team not to let Michael dunk. In most games, Michael dunks because he is looking for every opportunity to slam.

Another thing some visiting coaches tell their team is, "Don't let them make a run at you."

That's a silly statement.

In every NBA game, both teams will mount some sort of run. By that, I'm talking about a stretch of the game where one team will outscore the other something like 15–2. An NBA game is a series of hills and valleys, of streaks—hot and cold.

The home team is certain to have one good run every night. Basketball is a momentum game, and when the fans are behind you and the adrenaline is pumping, a stretch of productive basketball is inevitable, and it often comes at the end of the game when the fans are on their feet begging and cheering for their players to give forth that little extra, to play through the fatigue.

Why do the fans in basketball have a more dramatic effect

on the game than they do in any other sport?

It is their proximity to the players. In baseball, the players are wearing baggy uniforms and hats, it is hard to recognize them. In football, they are in helmets and pads and you can't recognize anyone. The fans are loud in those sports. You can hear them, but you can't feel them as you do in basketball. That's because basketball fans are right on top of the floor. At the L.A. Forum, Jack Nicholson is about ten feet from the visiting bench. Fans can lean right in and hear what is going on during a time out in the huddle. Basketball players are running around in what amounts to their underwear—shorts and a T-shirt. You see their faces, their bruises, their freckles, their tattoos, their scars. You see them sweat, hear them swear, experience their joy and frustration. That's because so many basketball fans are sitting *right there.* Imagine having seats at a baseball game where the home plate umpire stands—that's how it is in basketball. A couple of times a game, a basketball player will land right in a fan's lap. That's why the fans inspire the home team—they are so close they can reach out and touch the players.

And they can do the same with the officials.

Think about that for a moment.

Imagine that you're a ref in Chicago and Michael Jordan drives to the basket. He goes up for a dunk and plows right into Robert Parish. You're not certain if Michael charged, or if Parish might have stepped in front of Michael at the last moment to force the contact.

In other words, it's a 50–50 call.

If you're in Chicago and you call a charging foul on Michael, the fans are going to scream bloody murder. As an official you may tell yourself that it won't matter; you can take heat from the crowd. Yet, you know it's coming.

Human nature would say—give Michael the break and call the foul on Parish. There will be 18,000 people saying you're right and only the 16 guys on the other bench saying you messed up.

If the same play occurred in Boston Garden, you might call the foul on Jordan.

This is where the crowd is a factor in terms of the officials. I don't think the fans will cause a ref to make ridiculous calls against the visiting team, but on those borderline ones it is much easier for the officials just to go with the flow than buck the tide and make the difficult decision.

It's a simple question—would you rather make 18,000 friends or 18,000 enemies? Most of us want to be liked and officials are no different.

There are no easy answers about what should be done to make officiating better. The NBA is going from two to three officials but I'm not sure that will make the game any better. I have a feeling we'll see more calls away from the ball and they will be those dreaded ticky-tacky fouls that serve no purpose other than to drag out the game and start a march to the foul line.

I'm amazed at what a good job the officials do, given the speed of basketball. Guys are going 100 miles an hour in one direction and three seconds later, it's 100 miles an hour the other way and the officials have to keep up with it. Officials keep mayhem from breaking out, and that's no easy task. If you don't think officials are necessary, drop in at the YMCA for a couple of hours and watch the games where the guys call their own fouls—after 15 minutes they are ready to kill each other—and these are lawyers and doctors on their lunch breaks.

There is no doubt that officials cost teams games. In a one point game, one call can make a difference. Of course, so do the fouls shots a guy missed early in the second quarter, but losing coaches tend to forget about their own sins and the mistakes of their players and focus on a decision made by the officials in the final seconds. In their heart, the only way the players and coaches can cope with officials is to subscribe to the theory that, "They all even out."

That means if the official cost you a game in December, a ref's call may give you a game in March.

Does that happen?

I don't know, but to keep your sanity you have to believe it.

Nonetheless, I'll leave you with one last story that tells you how players and coaches feel about officials.

I was with Syracuse and we had a game in St. Louis. Also staying at our hotel was Jim Duffy, one of the officials.

Duffy was one of my favorites. There was one game on national television where we had a big lead in the final minutes and I said, "Hey, Jim, put me at the foul line so my mother can see me on national television."

The next time down the floor, Duffy called a foul on the guy guarding me, and I went to the foul line.

"I didn't even touch Kerr," said the guy, and this was one of the few times when a player who used that line wasn't lying.

"Kerr shoots two," said Duffy.

"But he didn't even have the ball, how can he get two shots?" asked the player.

"I said Kerr shoots two," said Duffy.

As I went to the foul line, Duffy handed me the ball and said, "Okay, I got you to the line, now smile for mama."

The game was out of reach, so it didn't matter what Duffy called. The reason I'm telling this story is that it shows Duffy does have a sense of humor.

So now we were in St. Louis and Duffy also was staying at our hotel. Two of the St. Louis players—Bob Pettit and Clyde Lovellette—had stopped by my room. Clyde was a sheriff in the off-season and he always carried a pistol and a holster. He fancied himself a quick-draw artist.

"We're going to get Duffy," said Lovellette.

We knew that Duffy was staying on my floor and we waited for him. He showed up wearing a blue overcoat and you could tell he had downed a couple of beers.

He got to his room and he was digging in his pockets, looking for his key. That's when Lovellette popped out right in front of Duffy and yelled, "That's the last time you ever foul me out of a game!"

Clyde pulled out his pistol and *bang, bang, bang.*

He shot Duffy.

Duffy went down on his knees, holding his gut. He thought he was shot, even though there were blanks in the gun.

Bob Pettit and I were laughing so hard we rolled on the floor. There are a thousand times in the career of every player and coach when he'd like to shoot an official, and at least I got to see it happen once.

10 •————————————————

You Can Go Home Again

I was born in Chicago at a very young age....

That line is usually good for a laugh at a banquet. But it's sort of how I feel. It seems as if I've been reborn in Chicago several times in my life. I'm like a bounced check, I just keep coming back to where I started. That's because there is something special about it. Chicago is the second biggest city in the country, but the longer you live here, the smaller it gets. That's probably because I have everything here—my friends, my family, the Bulls. People remember me from my high school days at Tilden Tech or at the University of Illinois or coaching the Bulls.

I've run into people who say, "Hey, Big Red, I loved you when you played for the Bulls."

I wish I had, and it makes me feel great when people think I did, so I just say thanks.

Of course, I've had some old friends whom I haven't seen in years come up to me and say, "I remember you when you were on those great teams at Tilden. What have you been doing since then?"

"I'm in radio and television," I say.

"Game shows?" the guy asks.

"No," I say.

"The news?"

"No."

"Well, I only watch game shows and the news," he says. "I hope you're making out okay."

After a conversation like that, I think that maybe I should have told the guy that I played for the Bulls. Who knows, then maybe the guy would have said he remembered me.

What I like about Chicago is that people will give you an answer. You walk up to a guy in New York and ask, "What time is it?"

The guy says, "Hey, buddy, whadda I look like, a clock?"

Chicago is the kind of town where people tell you what time it is. I don't care how corny it sounds, when I was growing up I never imagined that I could coach and then later broadcast the games of Chicago's pro basketball team. I never imagined that I'd be the guy who has an office at Riverside Plaza and who owns a company called Kerr Financial Services, which deals with insurance and investments. Or stop at Red Kerr's when you are in Chicago for a great meal at a great restaurant.

I grew up with Democratic politics and I'm comfortable with it. When I was a kid and my mother was sick, I remember the Democratic precinct captain bringing over a couple of bags of groceries so we could have something to eat until she got better and was able to go back to work. I was raised knowing that Richard Daley was the boss; I was only five years old and I already knew I was a Democrat. What I like about Chicago is that it's more than my home. I understand it. I know how things work.

———————●

I grew up on the South Side, at 6418 May Street. My father was born in Glasgow, Scotland, and my mother, the former Florence Benson, is Swedish. My father first worked in the stockyards and then was with the Swift Company, where his job was to take meat in and out of the freezer. Once, when I was about three years old, my father took us to Jackson Park Beach and got a severe sunburn. There were blisters all over his body but he went to work, going back into those freezers. He ended up with pneumonia and died. That left my mother to raise my sister (Joan) and me. At the time of my father's death my sister was almost seven. My mother never married again. She never even dated another man. Her whole life was supporting her children. She said that she was still committed to my father, even though he had died. She worried that another man might take away time from her kids, or that he might want to intrude on our family.

She was a very strong-willed person, a woman whose advice to us always was, "Are you doing the right thing?" Or, "Would I be proud of you?" Obviously, she wanted us to make up our minds but she also wanted us to remember who we were and who raised us. We grew up with a sense of values. Things were clear-cut. We knew that there was a difference between right and wrong and we knew the meaning of sacrifice because my mother lived it.

We were Lutherans and I got an attendance pin for going to church something like 12 straight years without missing a Sunday—again, the influence of my mother.

My mother was very frugal. She was a secretary at the War Department and then became a secretary for one of the executives at Continental Can. We always scrimped and saved and there was a time in our lives when her two brothers, two sisters and a cousin lived in our house. So counting my sister, my mother and myself, there were eight of us. After work, she cooked the meals and one of our favorites was pork chops. The adults would each get two pork chops, my sister and I would each get one. I was always hungry and I'd ask her for a second pork chop. My mother would come up with a piece of bread smothered in gravy, and that's what I thought a second pork chop was. We never thought much about it because this was how most people in the neighborhood lived. There were a lot of people under one roof. Sociologists now call it extended families. We called it saving money. Most of the kids I grew up with had fathers who were either policemen or firemen. That was as good as it got on the South Side. There would be three generations of cops in some houses, from the grandfather to the grandson.

What I liked best about where we lived was that just a block from our house was Ogden Park, a great place where they had baseball diamonds, a running track, a lagoon where you could fish and a basketball court. The court was unique because it had out-of-bounds lines drawn on the sides of the walls. Remember the old force-out play in the NBA? If they had that at my court, guys would have ended up like pancakes. As it was, the baskets at the two ends of the court also were almost right against the walls, which made it an adventure when you drove. More than once I knew how wallpaper felt because they had to peel me off the wall after I made a lay-up.

But I didn't play that much basketball until high school. Before that, it was softball and soccer. The reason we played soccer was that this was an ethnic neighborhood and it's a game that the people brought from the old country. My father was a great soccer player back in Scotland. There was an old Scot named, appropriately enough, Scotty, who looked a lot like Andy Capp as he hung around Ogden Park and he had people playing the game.

Softball may have been my favorite. It was 16-inch ball, which you don't see anywhere but Chicago. The ball really is 16 inches and you play with ten men on a side. When I played, no one wore a glove. The ball was like a rock. When they lined that thing at your face, if you didn't get your hand up you'd find that your nose would be like a plate of lasagna. Now they let the players wear gloves. *Chicago Tribune* columnist Mike Royko (who was an outstanding softball pitcher when I played against him) shares my opinion of this alleged advancement—what we're seeing is another example of creeping wimpism. In other words, these guys playing the game now just don't have the same fondness for fractures that we did. Actually, by the fourth inning the ball would begin to soften up because it had been knocked around for an hour. By the seventh, it would almost be like a pillow because it had been pulverized for quite a while. When I was a teenager, these games were very serious. That's because they were money games—a dollar a man and we each also kicked in 15 cents for a ball, either a Wilson or a Clincher. A buck was a lot of cash for the guys in my neighborhood at that time. So we each kicked in a buck to the pot for the chance to win two. This led to teams importing ringers and trying to strangle umpires and having all kinds of good times. I can't overestimate the importance of living near Ogden Park. It gave my sister and me a place to go after school while my mother was still working. In the summers, my mother had a neighbor or relative stop by to give us lunch, then it was back to the park. It was a place where all the boys wore overalls, the kind where there is a little strap to hold a hammer and other tools. Back then those were the cheapest clothes you could buy. Now they are made by Levis and rich kids wear them.

The basketball I did play as a kid was for St. Brendan's Catholic Church on 67th and Racine. Even though I was a Lutheran and went to Perkins-Bass school, almost all my friends were Catholics and attened St. Brendan's. When I was in junior high, Stinky Fryer, Gene White and Don Goeppner recruited me to play for St. Brendan's in the CYO (Catholic Youth League) under an assumed name—Eddie Benson, who was a Catholic cousin of mine. I was about 6-foot and we got to the 1947 City Championship Game and won, but the coach from the other team protested. He knew who I was and he knew I wasn't Eddie Benson. It was a big deal; they took away my championship medal and all that. The kicker to this story is when I converted to Catholicism in 1981, they had a party for me and gave me a trophy that said, "1947 Ringer, 1981 Pro." They also found an old 1947 CYO City Championship medal and gave it to me.

———•———

There was a point in my life when all I seemed to do was grow.

I was 6-foot when I entered Tilden Tech, which was tall but not outrageous. Three years later I was 6-foot-8.

That was mind-boggling.

One of my teachers wanted me to have a medical exam because he thought I had a pituitary problem. Normal kids just didn't sprout up like I did. I felt fine. I was playing softball, soccer, having a great time. I didn't want to hear that there might be something wrong with me. I didn't want people to dwell on my height. Who wants to be the biggest guy in the class, to always have to sit in the back row or stand in the middle of the team picture?

I wore a size 16 shoe and there was only one place in Chicago to get shoes that big—O'Connor and Goldberg. And they had only one model of shoes and it came in two colors—brown and black.

My mother finally found this place called King Size in Brockton, Mass. Today they have a 50-page catalogue, but when I was a kid their idea of high fashion in size 16s was either a plain brown round-tip or a plain black round-tip. When you send for shoes by mail, you can't try them on and say, "They feel a little tight, you got another pair in the back room?" What you buy, you wear. If they're tight, you wear them until they loosen up or wear out. If they're loose, you put on an extra pair of socks.

I had an impossible time finding soccer shoes to fit me, and today I have all kinds of bunions and hammertoes that come from jamming my feet into shoes that were too small.

Clothes weren't much better.

There are a lot more "big and tall" shops now than there were when I was a kid. But those places often mean "fat." My pants inseam is 36 inches. I'd go into one of those stores and see pants with waist sizes of 50, even 54. You could have put Jackie Gleason and William Perry in there and still had room for me. But they also came with 33-inch inseams.

For years, I wore a 37-inch sleeve because that was the longest I could find. I just figured my sleeve was supposed to end about half-way down my forearm. Then one day I was measured by a tailor and found out that I wore a 40-inch sleeve.

Obviously, this growing kept my mother busy. I think it also confused her.

Why was her son growing like something you'd like to chop down with a machete?

My father was 5-foot-11¾ths and mother said he used to lie and say he was 6-foot, because he was 6-foot in his shoes. My mother was about 5-foot-7. I had an uncle who was 6-foot-4, but no one was anything like the 6-foot-9 that I became by the time I made the NBA. I still have no explanation for it and none of my children are taller than 6-foot-6.

When I was at Tilden, I probably was the world's tallest soccer goalie. I didn't think about that at the time, I just played. All my buddies were soccer players and so was I.

I didn't even think about basketball until my senior year.

Okay, this is a bit complicated. It seems that nothing in my life ever went directly from Point A to Point B to Point C. I always had side trips.

Anyway, Tilden was on a two semester system. For an

ordinary guy, it would have been the second semester of his junior year (January–June) when I went out for basketball.

But that actually was the first semester of my senior year. I was on a program to graduate in January.

So it was in January, 1949, the start of what was my senior year, when Tilden basketball coach Bill Postl collared me in the hallway. I was about 6-foot-8, 160 pounds.

"Come out for the team," he said.

"Oh, I don't know," I said. "I've seen those guys play. They all shoot left-handed and they can really dribble . . . ."

"Just come out," he said.

"I'm not good enough," I said.

"I'm the coach. I'll decide who is good enough. You come out and you'll thank me for it later."

So I'll do that right now—I thank Bill Postl for making me try out for basketball. If it weren't for him, I still might be the world's tallest soccer goalie. I also would be working in a factory, praying that the union could get me a raise and cut my hours.

Anyway, I made the team—even though I couldn't shoot left-handed.

Soccer had me in great shape and I could run and jump all day. That sport had developed the hand-eye coordination you need in basketball. I was lucky, basketball came easily to me.

We won the public league championship and then lost to St. Patrick's for the Chicago city championship by a point. That was the first time I ever played a game in Chicago Stadium.

The next year, we won 11 straight games to start the season and that was it for me. It was January and my eligibility had run out. By now, I was nearly 6-foot-9 and 185 pounds. I was getting scholarship offers from schools I'd never heard of, about 60 in all—North Carolina, Duquesne, a bunch of southern schools.

I'd get calls and letters from college coaches and they'd say, "Let us fly you down here for a visit."

Fly me down? Like on a plane? In the air?

I wasn't going to fly anywhere. I had never been on a plane, never wanted to be on a plane and never could figure out why planes didn't just fall down. We never even had a car. The highest I had ever been was on the elevated train. To take a girl to the senior prom, I had to borrow my uncle's pickup and there were all these tools banging around in the back as I drove, which didn't exactly make for romantic background music.

Colleges liked me because of my height; 6-foot-9 and able to run up and down the floor without tripping on the foul line. And 6-foot-9 made me a giant, especially in the early 1950s. So it seemed I kept running into people around town who'd hand me cards and say, "Fill this out and mail it to the school. Tell them you're interested in my alma mater." But the recruiting wasn't as intense as today. The only time I saw a coach was when I visited a campus. Most of the recruiting was done through the mail or when a local booster for a college saw me.

My life had changed. People from Tilden didn't go to college, they went to work. My courses were shop, woodworking, auto mechanics, mechanical drawing and foundry.

At Tilden in Shop I, you got to make a table. In Shop II, you painted it.

I figured I was going to get a job in a foundry or become the tallest elevator operator in Chicago. I couldn't become a police-man or fireman because I had flat feet. I never thought about college until college came to me.

Suddenly, I found out that the Big Ten schools didn't care how many chairs I could make, they wanted you to take real courses.

English!

They asked me how I did in English? I said I spoke it all right. That wasn't what they had in mind. They said...you know... English literature...Chaucer.

I said, I don't know anyone named Chaucer.

They said you better if you want to play ball in college.

Then I admitted that English was a foreign language at Tilden. They said take lessons. Cram. Boy, did I cram. I realize that it isn't saying much, but I never studied so hard in my life. I even took a book home from school.

———————●

I visited Indiana and Notre Dame, but the two colleges that interested me were Illinois and Bradley.

Bradley University at Peoria, Illinois recruited me very hard because two of my Tilden teammates—Don "Chick" Rose and George Macuga—were on basketball scholarships there. The

Bradley coach was Fordy Anderson and he really wanted me. It all sounded good to me. I liked those guys and they liked Bradley. So I figured if they thought Bradley was okay, it must be a good place.

Okay, it may not be the most systematic method of checking out a university, but I was just a high school kid who wanted to have a good time in college.

Bradley also had made me an offer.

One of their boosters pulled up in front of our house in a Cadillac. We lived on a cobblestone street and no one drove a Cadillac. So the mere fact that a Cadillac was parked in front of my house became a neighborhood event. Everyone was on the porch or looking through windows trying to see what was going on.

The booster told me that there was a lot of opportunities for a basketball player at Bradley. He said that I would have a house in Peoria for my family and $5,000 in the bank. He said that after I graduated, I could play for Caterpillar Diesel, which was an AAU team in Peoria that set its players up with well-paying jobs.

Then the guy pulled out his wallet and starting putting $100 bills on the table. My mind was like a cash register. I had never seen cash like that before. This was 1950 and recruiting scandals weren't the sports household stories that they are now.

The guy said, "What do you want to do?"

I said I wanted to talk to my mother. My mother and I went into the kitchen and shut the door, leaving him in the living room.

"Mom, it sounds great. They're gonna give us a house and all that money. . . ."

"Yes, but what happens after four years?" she asked.

"What do you mean?"

"We'll have to move to Peoria and after four years you'll get married and then maybe you'll want to live somewhere else," she said. "I'll be stuck in Peoria. I really don't want to move anywhere. I like it here. My job is here, my friends, everything. The decision is all yours. Don't take an offer to please me."

I ended up telling the guy I'd think about Bradley.

The University of Illinois at Champaign-Urbana was in the picture because it was the state university and I didn't have to take a plane to get there. I got a call from a guy named Irv

Bemoras, who had played at Marshall High. Irv's team had won the 1948 city championship and he was at Illinois and liked it, so I went down for a visit and just fell in love with the place. I liked Champaign and I accepted their scholarship.

Bradley found out about this and was not very happy. As I went to Illinois to start school, I ran into my old friends from Bradley—Don Rose and George Macuga.

"What are you guys doing here?" I asked them.

They said they were in Champaign to get me and take me back to Bradley.

"But I like it here," I said. "I don't want to go to Bradley."

"Look, just come with us," they said. "You don't have to stay. You can turn right around and come back."

That didn't make much sense to me. What was the point of me going with them to Peoria, and then going right back to Champaign?

"We get $100 apiece if we bring you with us," they said.

Meanwhile, Illinois had gotten word about the Bradley guys on campus. So Illinois assigned two of their own guys to follow me around until I officially enrolled at Champaign. I remember going to the movie with the Illinois guys and they each sat on one side of me. The guys from Bradley also were there, but the Illinois guys wouldn't let the Bradley guys get near me. Until I enrolled, wherever I went there was an Illinois guy watching me, and I never did go to Peoria with my friends.

It wasn't that hard for me to pass up the Bradley offer because we already had a house. My mother didn't want to move. As for the money, I guess I wasn't sure they would really give it to me.

When I visited Illinois, Red Pace was an NFL official and he also was with the athletic department. He gave me the keys to his big Chrysler and I got to drive it around town. Now, I thought that was great. I figured the car was mine, but after I enrolled Red came by and said, "Hey, I need my keys back."

So that was it. So much for getting a car.

While I was at Illinois, I always said that I only got exactly what everyone else on the team received—room, board and $600 a month for books.

Actually, I made about $60 a month working in the public relations office, helping the sports information director, Chuck Flynn. I know that some of the other players had a job where they were supposed to sweep up the stadium. It was legal because they had to punch a time card, but the players who lived in fraternity houses made the pledges ride their bikes over to the stadium to punch the players in and out.

I had a wonderful time at Illinois. I was in a fraternity, Phi Kappa Psi. I loved campus life and I loved basketball.

As for school . . . well, they were still talking about guys like Chaucer and I still was doing my best to remain a stranger to those people. We had an assistant basketball coach named Howie Braun and it was his job to tutor me. The night before an exam, he made me meet him in his office so that I'd be under his thumb and studying instead of sneaking off.

————●

Basketball is something that came a lot easier than Chaucer or chemistry. In the 1950s, freshmen could not play on the varsity so we had our own team.

I tell people that I scored 82 points in one freshman game against the Illinois varsity. What makes the story even better is that it's true. What people don't know is that we played about two hours longer than normal because Bob Hope was supposed to perform after our game and his plane was late, so they kept us on the floor playing until he showed up.

As a sophomore, I scored 17 points in my first college varsity game against Butler in the same field house where the championship game was played in the movie *Hoosiers*. I felt terrible. I remember sitting in the back of the bus thinking that I might never get to play again.

What happened was that Coach Harry Combes made me into a sixth man, and I led the team in scoring (13.7) as we won the Big Ten title in 1951–52.

Basketball went great and by my senior year, I was captain of the team. I finished as Illinois' all-time scorer and was the Big Ten's MVP. Things were working out. I knew that I was going to play pro ball. I knew I was going to get married. But lost in the middle of all that was school.

The spring quarter of my senior year, I just messed around and messed up a chance to get a degree. I took off to play in some post-season All-Star games. I got a chance to play for a team that would tour with the Globetrotters and we were going to make $100 a game for something like ten games. At the time, earning that $1,000 seemed a lot more important than taking a couple of courses.

So what happened is that I didn't get my degree, and that's something that has always bothered me. My mother never said anything, but I think she was disappointed that I spent four years at Illinois and didn't graduate. It wouldn't have made any difference in my life. I suppose it's no big deal, but I still wanted to do something about it, so I'm working with Illinois now to get those last credits so I can finish up.

The irony is that one of the courses I had to take was Psychology 101. I thought about the fact that my wife Betsy and I had five children of our own and we raised a total of seven. I've coached two expansion teams with some players who were a bit...ah...strange. I mean, if a shrink ever got those guys on the couch, he wouldn't let them up for ten years because they had so many problems. So I really don't think Psychology 101 had anything to teach me, but I took it anyway because I want the degree. Until I get my diploma, I guess I'll always look upon that part of my life as a place where I failed. It was something I started and didn't finish and even if I've been out of college for 35 years, I still would like to get it done.

———●

It's now time for a confession. When I went to Illinois, I didn't know much about women. I didn't even know that many women. Tilden Tech was an all-boys high school and we'd go to dances at places such as St. Killian's. The girls would be there in their skirts and bobby socks and we'd be sort of dressed up. It was like an old movie—the boys against one wall and the girls against the other, looking at each other. Then the music would start and none of the boys would move. Finally, the girls would start dancing with each other and we'd just stand there, holding up the wall and watching the girls.

Sometimes I'd spot a girl I liked and I'd say, "That one, the little redhead, she's my girl."

"You know her?" one of the guys would say.

"Ah...well...sorta." I'd say.

"What do you mean, sorta?"

"Well...you know...sorta." I'd say. It would be quiet for a while. Then I'd say, "Hey, I spotted her first."

Seeing a girl first was supposed to put some kind of claim on her. But it really didn't matter since we didn't have the guts to actually go talk to them.

I mentioned the high school prom before. I was all set to go by myself. I thought you went and met a girl there or something and my buddies were going so I planned to tag along. Then I found out from one of the guys that you needed a date and he fixed me up. I picked her up in Uncle Jack's truck with the sheet metal rolling around in back.

So that was high school. It was as if the guys were real and the girls were in another world. It reminded me of when I was a kid and we'd watch a Western and say, "the one there...that's my horse," knowing we'd never get to see that horse anywhere but safely on the screen. That was me and girls...they were very distant.

That changed at Illinois because that's where I met Betsy Nemecek.

I was at a place near the campus called Kam's, a local greasy spoon like Arnold's on "Happy Days." I was playing a card game called "Oh Hell," which is pretty much like Hearts, with three other people when Betsy came into the place. Betsy was the most beautiful girl I had ever seen. Two of the people playing were Betsy's roommate, Connie Juliuson, and Connie's boyfriend, Bill Blair. We got Betsy into the game and taught her how to play. When we were done playing cards, I asked Betsy if I could walk her and Connie back to their dorm.

I was a freshman at the time and Betsy was a sophomore. That didn't mean much to Betsy. As she has often told me, "I knew John before he was anybody." I was just a redshirted freshman, so that made no special impact on her.

But that day at Kam's when I first stood up, Betsy just stared.

"You kept getting up and getting up and getting up," Betsy told me years later. "I thought it would take forever for you to get out of the booth, you seemed to have your arms and legs all tangled up."

Until Betsy saw me, she said the tallest person she had met was 6-foot-6, so I made an impact on her. I was 6-foot-9 and she was 5-foot-6 and I can imagine what we looked like walking down the street. Betsy was in art school studying advertising design, and she wanted to illustrate children's books.

We really hit it off well and liked each other. Betsy was from Riverside, which is right outside of Chicago. She was a tomboy as a kid and used to play baseball and football with the boys in the neighborhood. Her father Ed was a big sports fan who would go to the Rose Bowl and events like that, so it was no problem that I was an athlete.

Of course, I did some dumb things. I never had a car—remember, I thought I would have one and then they made me give the keys back after I signed up for my courses—but Betsy used to have her father's car and I'd borrow it. She had a curfew at her Lincoln Avenue residence hall so I'd drop her off and keep the car with me at my fraternity house.

One morning I was supposed to get up and drive Betsy to class. One of our fraternity pledges tried to wake me up but I slept right through it. When I did get out of bed, I knew I was really late so I just ran outside and got in the car. It was raining that day and when I pulled up in front of her dorm, there was Betsy with about four of her friends, all wanting a ride so they could keep dry.

When they got in the car, they saw me in my robe and slippers. As I was driving, all I could do was say, "Dear God, please don't let the cops stop us because I have no idea how I can explain this."

Betsy and I went together for about a year and then I asked Betsy to wear my fraternity pin.

She turned me down.

I couldn't believe it.

"I thought we're getting along great," I told her.

"We are," Betsy said. "But I think the pin means more to me than just going steady."

So that was it. We dated for about two years before she finally took my pin, and when she did it was almost as if we got engaged.

It was during my junior year that I asked Betsy to marry me. I made a big production out of it, giving her a nice diamond ring and the whole routine. She was all excited, put the ring on and kept saying, "Johnny, I can't believe how big the diamond is."

I just smiled.

"How could you ever afford it?"

On and on it went, me acting like a hero until I had to tell her the truth. I said, "Betsy, what's the date?"

She looked at me suspiciously.

"The date?" I repeated.

"April 1st," she said, staring at the ring. "Johnny, you didn't." She was mad because she knew the ring was a fake and she didn't appreciate this kind of April Fool's joke.

When I did give her a ring—a real diamond ring, which obviously was much smaller than the first ring—Betsy never changed expression. All she did was put her hand out and say, "Johnny Kerr, I want to see the guarantee on this and I want it in writing."

I knew that she would ask for that, so I had a receipt from Leonard's Luggage and Jewelry Store showing that my monthly payments were $15.

So we dated through college and we were married right after I left Illinois. Betsy found out that I like more than basketball. Name a sport and I'll watch it. When we drove around Chicago on those soft summer nights, our background music was a White Sox game on the radio. We went to all the football games at Illinois. On weekends, we'd come home and I'd tell her that I had to play a 16-inch softball game with the loser buying a keg of beer for the winners. That was our Saturday afternoon. It was softball first and then we'd go out on a date at night.

I'm amazed she put up with me.

Betsy is a remarkable, independent, strong-willed woman. She could have had a career in commerical art, but when she married me, she gave that up to be a mother and a wife. She does some art work part-time, but her first obligation has been to her family.

I let her run the house. Being a basketball player meant that I often wasn't home for the holidays, birthdays, you name it. It seemed as if one of the kids was always getting the chicken pox when I was on the road. She graduated with an art degree from Illinois and I have asked her if she regretted not having a career, but she insists that this is the life she wanted.

On the day I accepted the job to coach the Phoenix Suns, I had a speaking engagement in Rockford that night. I told Betsy, "We're leaving for Phoenix so we've got to put the house up for sale." We talked a little about a price and that was it. I left it to her and drove down to Rockford to give the speech.

When I got home, there was a piece of paper on the kitchen table—a signed offer for our house. I said, "Betsy, we just sold our house!" I couldn't believe it happened so fast. She just did it. Some wives would have simply refused to deal with the realtors or make any business decisions.

She was in charge of the house and she took that seriously. She bought our place in the Chicago suburb of Riverwoods. It was a wonderful setup—two acres, something like 1,800 trees and a four-bedroom colonial with a horseshoe drive. The owner even kicked in his 1954 Ford.

The price was $42,500, which was far more than we wanted to pay in 1968. After looking at the house, Betsy and I discussed it over dinner that night.

"I like the place," said Betsy.

"It's awful expensive," I said.

"I do love the house," she said. "I think we should buy it."

We talked about it for a while and then I said, "Okay, I'll flip a coin. Heads we buy it, tails we don't."

The coin came up heads. We lived in the place for two years and then I left the Bulls for Phoenix. Betsy took over and sold the place—for $50,000, a $7,500 profit. Today the house is worth about $350,000.

Betsy bought and sold four houses in everywhere from Syracuse to Chicago. She supervised the addition we made on our current home in Riverside. She's an artist who can look at blueprints and sketches and know what they mean. To me, it's a bunch of lines on paper. She also can draw up her own plans for a house, a garden, you name it. You'd think she was the graduate of Tilden Tech, not me.

———●

Our first child, Jay (actually John) was born in 1957. That was when I was playing for Syracuse. I was there when she went into labor and I took her to the hospital. I was in the room with her for a while, holding her hand. She was in such pain and she was squeezing my hand so hard; I never believed that she had such strength. My face turned white and I felt dizzy, but I didn't know if it was from her almost squeezing the blood out of my hand, or the idea of being a father for the first time.

Then it dawned on me—I had a game in Philadelphia that night and if I didn't get to the airport soon, I was going to miss the last flight out.

It's funny—you'd think that I would have said, "The hell with it, I'm staying with my wife." Now players take three days off to be with their wives after the birth of a child. No one says anything, it's just what anyone would expect to happen.

But in the NBA in the 1950s and 1960s, you were scared to death to ask the coach or general manager for anything. The attitude was, "Is it you who is having the baby or your wife? Listen, everybody has a kid, no big deal. You can see it in a couple of days when we get off this trip." We were only making $10,000 or so and the last thing we wanted to do was get fined, and if we skipped a game management would act like the sky just fell. It was unthinkable. Today, it's unthinkable for a father not to be there when a child is born.

About an hour before Jay's birth, I left the hospital and got on an airplane for Philadelphia. When I reached the hotel in Philly, there was a message from my mother-in-law saying that we had a son. I was excited and I ran around telling the other guys on the team what had happened, but there was an emptiness. I couldn't see Betsy, I couldn't see Jay.

Instead, I went out and played center that night.

Betsy never said, "You've got to be here when our children are born." She never said anything except that basketball was my job and I had to go play. I felt guilty leaving and she'd tell me that I was a good father, not to worry. She'd joke that if I was in the operating room with her, I'd faint if I had to watch or else I'd run to the corner of the room and just hold up the wall, so I wouldn't be much good to anyone. But I know I bypassed a lot of the responsibilities. I was on the road when the kids got sick or were in a little trouble. Or when I was home, maybe I was mad at the coach or the general manager and I wasn't paying attention to what Betsy or the kids needed. Sometimes a professional athlete is just in his own world and that's not how it should be.

Our second son, Eddie, was born two years later in 1959. I was on the road with Syracuse and it was our friend, Chuck

Spuches, who took Betsy to the hospital to have Eddie. In fact, Chuck also took Betsy to the hospital for the birth of our fourth son, Bill.

As my children grew up, I picked up the name "Phantom Father," because I was on the road so much. That was my one regret about being in basketball, it did take away from my family too much.

It especially hurts because we lost our first son. I have so many memories of Jay, such as taking him to War Memorial Coliseum in Syracuse. We were playing the Knicks that night and it was a playoff game to be televised nationally. People made a big deal about the fact that the game's MVP would receive a watch. Jay heard about it and kept talking about the watch.

"You want Daddy to win the watch for you?" I asked him.

I had a good night, won the watch and after the game I was interviewed on the court by a television crew. Little Jay was running all over the floor, and the camera followed him while I talked. I wore No. 10 so I guess that means I was a 10 before Bo Derek. I had No. 10 on everything from my clothes to my suitcase. Betsy bought Jay a small bag and painted 10½ on it and he loved to carry it around the house. When I'd come off a road trip, Betsy and Jay would be waiting for me at the airport and Jay would have his 10½ bag with him. He was a real good kid. Even at three, I remember telling him to clean up all his toys and he picked them up and put them in his toybox. Then he'd pick up his little brother Eddie and put him on top of the toybox.

When we'd play baseball, Jay batted left-handed and was a true Kerr. He'd hit the ball and run to the wrong base. I'd chase him around our little make-shift infield—third to second to first to home plate—and I told him, "Jay, you just un-tied the score and you lost, 1–0."

One of my favorite stories about Jay was when I decided to make him some brownies. Betsy is a super cook, but I was going to play the role of Dad In The Kitchen and show everyone how it was done. I made Betsy take Jay out of the kitchen so I'd have room to work. After a while, Jay came back to see me and I yelled, "Hey, Betsy, get Jay outta here."

She walked into the kitchen and saw me with two bare hands in a bowl, stirring the brownie mix.

"Why don't you use a spoon?" Betsy asked me.

"Because the box says you're supposed to stir by hand," I said.

Suddenly I realized that I knew as much about baking brownies as Jay did about running the bases. Getting your hands all over the brownie mix was only a recipe for getting dirty hands.

Anyway, it became a big deal. Betsy brought her mother in to see me. Jay was laughing at me and he didn't know exactly why other than his dad had done something stupid and everyone else was laughing. They also declared my brownies a health hazard and decided it was best to pass on my baking.

It wasn't long after the 1959–60 season and we were in Chicago, visiting Betsy's parents, when something happened that forever changed our lives. Betsy was seven and a half months pregnant with our son, Matt. Jay caught a cold—or at least we thought it was a cold—and we didn't think much of it, but he did have a hard time shaking it. On Mother's Day in 1960 we were sitting downstairs and Jay was upstairs watching television.

I told Betsy, "He'll come down as soon as the commercials are over."

Betsy laughed and nodded because that was how Jay watched television—forget the programs, he wanted to see the commercials. When the commercials were over, he came downstairs and stopped at the foot of the stairs.

"Are your commercials over?" Betsy asked as she got up and walked over to Jay.

Jay just smiled.

Then he surprised everyone, especially himself, and vomited. Betsy and I still figured it was a cold or something he ate. She felt his head and Jay did have a fever, but it still didn't seem too severe. Betsy called a doctor who also was a friend of ours and described Jay's condition and the doctor prescribed some medicine to settle his stomach and bring down the fever.

Jay lay down on the sofa. His stomach was okay, but we couldn't get his temperature down. Betsy gave him some baby aspirin and he was quiet for a while.

Suddenly, he went into a convulsion.

Betsy called the doctor again. The doctor said, "Don't worry, three-year-olds sometimes have convulsions when they have a fever."

"But Jay never had one before," said Betsy.

The doctor told us to wait and watch Jay. We were staying

up with him. Betsy was getting tired so we convinced her to go to bed. My mother was there and I took her home. Betsy's aunt was watching Jay.

Betsy said that she remembered falling asleep and then she snapped awake a short time later. She said she didn't hear anything, it was like something just zapped her. She got out of bed and rushed into Jay's room just as he was going into a second convulsion.

Betsy picked up Jay and put him into a tub of water and it seemed like he stopped breathing. As it turned out, he was in a coma. Betsy called the doctor and said we were taking Jay to the hospital. When we got there, the nurses ran to Jay with an oxygen tank and Betsy held the mask on Jay's face, but now we were sure that he had stopped breathing and the oxygen wasn't helping. The nurses told us to leave the room and some doctors went in. They performed an open heart massage on Jay and then hooked him to a machine.

While we were outside the room, I heard someone say that Jay's heart had stopped. All I could think was, "Please God, let him breathe again."

When we were allowed back in to see Jay, the doctor told us that they would let the machine help him breathe for a while and then they'd turn it off and see if Jay would be able to breathe on his own. Betsy said that when the doctors told us that if Jay had lived he would probably be blind, deaf and paralyzed, she said, "I had a little talk with God and I prayed that Jay wouldn't be stuck in a little body that couldn't hear, or see, or feel or do anything that other children could."

Jay never breathed again. The cause of death was bacterial meningitis, something for which there is now a vaccine but none was available in 1960. It was a disease that would seem to come out of nowhere and attack a child and was often fatal. In Jay's case, about 24 hours after he told us that he didn't feel well, he was dead.

I cried right away when they told us Jay died. Betsy just held it all in. Words will never describe the sorrow that we felt, and to have a child die on Mother's Day while Betsy was seven and a half months pregnant. . . the sense of loss was overwhelming. I couldn't believe the strength Betsy showed. She went to Jay's wake the next day and she helped me pick out a grave site and a casket. I kept thinking about her being pregnant, praying that we wouldn't lose another baby. I was going to pieces and Betsy was a rock, and she made it through the wake and the funeral the next day.

One person came up to us and said, "God was good to you. He took away one child, but gave you another."

We knew the person meant well, but that was absolutely the last thing we wanted to hear. You don't replace children. Just hearing those words made us feel worse than we already did.

Right after the wake was over, we went home and she started to have labor pains and we went back to the hospital—this time for Betsy.

Matthew was born. He was named after the father I barely knew. Matt was only 4 pounds, 2 ounces. He dropped down to 3 pounds, 9 ounces and it was touch-and-go. Matt was in the hospital for a month and I kept praying that he would get bigger and stronger because we couldn't cope with another child dying.

Matt had to weigh five pounds before we could bring him home.

Within a few days, our family had drastically changed. Jay had died. Our second child, Eddie, was now the big brother at 14 months. Eddie was the one who sort of was lost as he was shunted from one relative to another while we were trying to hold ourselves together. I knew he sensed something was wrong because he started to suck his thumb. He was scared and wanted security, which was exactly how we felt. It was rough on everyone because we were living with Betsy's parents during this time. It was a summer visit to Chicago and then we planned to go back to Syracuse for the start of the next season.

I was very close to my in-laws Essie and Ed Nemecek. Ed owned a trucking company named Penrod Merchants, and in the off-season I'd drive a tractor-trailer. Ed would spend his vacations in Syracuse or wherever I was playing or coaching. He was fanatical about basketball and went to as many games as he could. Betsy was a tomboy, the son he never had. And to me, Ed was the father I never had. Even before Betsy and I were married, I had Ed stand next to me when the athletes and their fathers were honored at Illinois.

When Jay died, it was Ed who went to the cemetery and bought eight plots—his family and our family would all be buried in one place. Today, the house we live in is the same Riverside home that Ed Nemecek had. Betsy has expanded it, but the point is that their house always was our house.

So they were at our side when Jay died and my in-laws not only had to cope with the death of a grandson, they had to watch their daughter suffer. It had to be tearing them up, but they held us together.

Betsy said that she never had a chance to establish the usual mother-child bonding that occurs after birth because they immediately took Matt from her and put him in an incubator. Betsy was not even able to hold Matt until a few days later.

"In the mental state I was in, I kept thinking that I didn't want Matt, I wanted Jay back," said Betsy. "My mother sensed this and she gave Matt a lot of extra attention after we brought him home from the hospital. For a long time, I had trouble warming up to Matt, who had nothing to do with what happened to Jay. I love Matt so much, but I still feel guilty about how I felt right after he was born."

While Betsy didn't cry right after Jay died, I'd find her weeping at times years later and I'd know she was thinking about Jay. We still occasionally talk about Jay; not much in public, just Betsy and I.

———●

We now have five children—Eddie, Matt, Billy, our daughter Essie, and Jimmy. Betsy also had a miscarriage during the 1965–66 season.

I love our family and the fact that it's a big family. For a while, it was even bigger because we took in two of my sister-in-law's children.

In 1971, my brother-in-law Evan "Gabby" Ellis died. He had been a catcher in the St. Louis Cardinals' farm system but had to quit because of a shoulder problem. He became a football coach and social studies teacher at New Trier High in Winnetka where he was stricken with lung cancer.

We were living in Virgina Beach because I was vice-president of the Virginia Squires in the old American Basketball Association. About a month after Evan's death, his wife (Betsy's sister) Drusilla came to visit us.

Dru had five children—Laurie, Jodie and Drucie lived at home. Her oldest daughter, Betsy, was married. Her second oldest daughter, Mary Beth, lived in Colorado. Dru was drawing up a will and she asked Betsy and me if we would be the guardians for her children if anything happened to her.

It was just a natural thing—if anything ever happened to me, I would have expected Dru to help Betsy. Dru wasn't ill or anything, she was just putting her legal affairs in order.

We had this conversation during Christmas. Three months later, Dru was carrying the garbage out to the front of her house when she had a cerebral hemorrhage and died instantly.

When Dru died, she was still putting the final touches on her will and she had not signed any type of temporary document. So the State of Illinois became the executor of her estate and it was a legal mess.

We were still living in Virginia, but the state said that Dru's children could not leave Illinois until the estate was completely settled. So the three children moved in with my in-laws. This really upset us because we were designated as the guardians. The Nemeceks were older and did not need to start taking care of three more children, but the state handcuffed us for a long time. It took about a year for us to cut through the legal mess so Dru's children could move to Virginia.

We finally got the approval and my in-laws packed up the kids' things and shipped their furniture and clothes by a moving company to Virginia Beach. As the furniture was coming to Virginia, we were moving back to Chicago because I had been hired as business manager of the Bulls.

Anyway, that did make life much easier because everyone—our in-laws, Dru's children and us—would be in Chicago. Our family became our five children, Dru's two, a beagle, an Airedale and a St. Bernard. Two of Dru's kids—Jodie and Drusilla—were in high school and lived with us. A third, Laurie, had started college at Grand Valley College in Grand Rapids, Michigan. We weren't Laurie's guardian because she had just turned 18 when her mother died, but when Laurie came home from school she stayed with her grandmother and sometimes us.

Laurie was a good student in pre-law and she was doing well on her own.

One day a police car pulled into our driveway, lights flashing, the whole bit. I had a friend with the sheriff's department, Ray Olsen, and he liked to come to my house with his car lights flashing and the siren blaring so the whole neighborhood would think I was going to be hauled off. What Ray usually wanted was to talk for a while, or maybe go somewhere for a couple of beers.

That's exactly what I was thinking when I saw the police car.

"Hey, Ray, is that you?" I yelled when I opened the door.

A policeman got out of the car and he wasn't Ray. He had a very grim look on his face . . . all business.

"Are you John Kerr?" the policeman asked me.

I thought Ray was up to something. Maybe this was a practical joke and he was going to have his buddy arrest me and then escort me to a bar for a drink.

"Okay, tell Ray I know he's up to something," I said.

The policeman stared at me very hard.

"Are you John Kerr?" he asked again.

"Yes," I said, still waiting for the other shoe to drop.

"Do you have a niece named Laurie Ellis?" he asked.

Right then, I knew something was very, very wrong.

"That's right," I said.

"There's been a homicide."

I felt my heart sink so low that it dropped right through my shoes. I kept thinking . . . homicide? Did the guy really say, "There's been a homicide?" Why would someone kill Laurie? What do you say in a situation like this?

Betsy's mother was staying with us while she recovered from surgery. I mentioned that she was very close to Laurie and all I could think about was how we could possibly tell her that her granddaughter had been killed. If I told the women that, she might have a heart attack. We really didn't know what had happened. The policeman had no answers, he was told there was a homicide and that's what he told us.

I went across the street to get a neighbor who was a doctor and I brought him to the house. The doctor was right there when we woke Essie up and told her about Laurie. The doctor immediately put her under sedation and she handled it as well as anyone in her situation could.

Betsy and I caught a flight to Grand Rapids to see the police and make the funeral arrangements. The detectives asked us a lot of questions, trying to find a motive for the killing. We didn't know much about Laurie's life on campus and we didn't know her friends at Grand Valley. In Chicago, it would have been different, but we weren't much help.

To this day, the murder is still unsolved. She was stabbed repeatedly in her own apartment, and as far as we know, the police have never had a serious lead. Whenever I hear of one of those serial killers being captured, I think that this was the guy who might have done it. If the killer had been someone she had known, it is more likely that he would have been caught by the police. At least that's what we've been led to believe.

Laurie's death hit her sisters very hard. These kids had watched their father, a big ex-Marine, former pro baseball player and football coach, fade away from cancer in 1971. A year later, they saw their mother die suddenly, almost as if someone snapped their fingers and took the life out of her. Now their sister was murdered in 1975.

Also, their grandfather, Betsy's father, died in 1974. He had triple-bypass surgery and was supposed to be recovering very well. One night he was listening to a Bulls game on the radio and was screaming for Chet Walker to make a shot when he suffered a heart attack that killed him. It seemed as if we were going to a funeral a year in the early 1970s.

After Betsy's father died, we were thinking about selling the Nemecek's home in Riverside and getting a big house where we all could live. We didn't want Betsy's mother to be by herself, but the kids hated the idea of her selling that house. They kept telling us that they wanted to live in their grandparents' home in Riverside. My father-in-law once told me, "If you ever need this house, it's yours. It's all paid for and it's big enough to take care of everybody."

We bought it from Betsy's mother and moved in, which made Betsy's mother and the kids very happy. Betsy then supervised an extension for the house so it really could handle the eight of us.

Betsy and I have loved having a big family. I look at all my kids and now my three grandchildren and I think that they're the greatest miracle in the world. Even when Dru's children were living with us and I had no idea how I should treat them—all I knew was that I couldn't get tough with them when they were bad and give them a whack as if they were my kids—it was good because it seemed that with so many kids, everyone took care of each other. All the kids have turned out great. One of my sons—Billy, his wife Tammie and our grandson John G. Kerr II—now live with us while they save up to buy their own home. My daughter, Essic, and her husband Neil Harrington are at our house a lot with our grandchildren, Neil Harrington IV and Brittany Dru. Our other granddaughters come from Dru's children—Drucie has little Lindsey, Jodie has Laurie, and Betsy has Becky. My sister Joan and her husband Joe had five children—Jody, Judy, Janet, Jacque and Jimmy Joe. On holidays our house is filled with laughter. We have a lot of people, a lot of generations of this family around. Betsy and I've been married since 1954 and I have the greatest job in the world doing the Bulls' games.

So when people tell me, "You know, you're a lucky guy." I tell them, "You know what? You're right."

————●

The fact that I ended up as a basketball player was luck. If Bill Postl hadn't dragged me out of the hallway at Tilden and into the gym, then I probably never would have played 12 years in the NBA. Even the circumstances surrounding the start of my pro career were a little strange.

I was drafted by the same guy who invented the 24-second clock. I always wondered if that was because he could only bear to watch me play for 24 seconds. His name was Danny Biasone, and he was the owner of the Syracuse Nationals. He was at the East-West College All-Star Game in New York, sitting in the stands with Jack Andrews of the *Syracuse Post-Standard*.

"Hey, Jack, I know who we'll draft," Biasone said.

"You do?" asked Andrews.

"That's right."

"But the game hasn't even started," said Andrews. "Okay, who is it?"

"That big red-haired kid down there," said Biasone.

"But you haven't seen him play," said Andrews.

"I like the way he looks in warmups," said Biasone. "I like his hook shot."

And Biasone did make me the sixth pick in the 1954 draft. Here was the situation. You had Danny Biasone, a man who made his money from owning a bowling alley in Syracuse, telling a sportswriter that his first round draft pick was based on how the kid looked in warmups! And making the story even better was that the sportswriter thought it was a little strange, but no big deal. He just wrote it. Imagine Jerry Krause trying to pawn something like that off on the Chicago media today.

Obviously, the NBA was a different game in 1954 than it is now. But I had no idea what the NBA was like when I came out of Illinois because I had never seen a pro game. The only NBA player I really had heard of was George Mikan. I couldn't name all the cities in the eight-team league and I wasn't sure where to find Syracuse. No one from Syracuse even called me and there was no draft-day party on ESPN. I read that I was property of the Syracuse Nationals in the newspaper. There were eight teams and I was the No. 6 pick, meaning I was the sixth best player in the country in 1954. Today, that would make me a lottery pick and all the basketball fans would know my name before I even got to the NBA. But back then, there were no pre-draft interviews with various NBA teams for college players. I don't even recall reading a mock draft.

Anyway, I was Syracuse-bound and that was fine. I was just happy someone wanted to pay me to play basketball.

Now we come to the part where I say, "Boy do I wish I knew then what I know now." That's because now I run my own investment and insurance company—Kerr Financial Services. If I don't know the answer to a question about finances, I know lawyers, accountants and other experts who can give me the answer. Our company handles investments for several NBA players, corporation executives and guys with regular jobs. One of the areas I feel strongest about is helping NBA players once they are released, because they have to change their insurance and medical policies and other investments. It is a crucial time that often determines the financial future of an athlete and his family.

Okay, that's what I do now.

Back then, I took hook shots and hit the boards. Money was something other people had. I thought it would be nice to have some, but I had no idea how to get it.

What I was about to do was negotiate my first contract. Actually, that's about the same as saying a bank teller negotiated with Jesse James.

When Syracuse General Manager Leo Ferris finally called me, he said they would fly me to Syracuse so I could sign my contract. I had no idea what to ask for. I didn't even know what NBA players made. Today, players have agents, accountants or lawyers. Some guys have agents, accountants *and* lawyers, and that's before they even play their first NBA game. Everyone knows what everyone else in the NBA makes. Usually, a guy drafted sixth can look at last year's draft, see what the player received and get maybe a 10 percent raise. A guy drafted sixth usually is worth a five-year, $4 million deal.

For advice, I asked my college roommate and he said, "Try to get a signing bonus out of them."

As I was going to Syracuse, I was thinking about how much I should ask for. The more I thought about it, the better $10,000 sounded. Ferris picked me up at the Syracuse airport and we went to the team's offices to talk contract.

"John, we'll give you $5,000," they said and they made it sound as if they'd just opened the vault.

I still liked the sound of $10,000, but at this point I was scared to death to ask for that much.

"I really don't know if $5,000 is what I should sign for," I said. "I don't think I can live on $5,000. I'm getting married and I need more than that."

"Well, we can't pay you as much as our veteran players like Dolph Schayes," they said.

"I still don't think $5,000 is enough," I said.

"Why don't you call someone you trust for advice," they said. "Call someone you respect the most."

That sounded like a good idea. I went into another room where they had a phone and I called Harry Combes, who was the coach at Illinois.

"Coach, I'm in Syracuse and we're doing my contract and they've offered me $5,000," I said. "I want more, but I really don't know what to do."

"John, you were drafted by Syracuse so you really don't have anywhere else to go," said Combes. "So if they offered you $5,000 and you want to play professional basketball, that's what you'll have to do."

"Thanks for your advice," I said and as I heard the coach

hanging up the phone, I heard another click on the line. Then I hung up and went back into the other room.

"Did you talk to the coach?" Ferris asked me. "How did everything go?"

Ferris had this faint smile on his face like he knew damn well that I did talk to the coach and he knew exactly what the coach said. That's because the click on the phone belonged to him. I wasn't thrilled about them listening in, but I also knew that they had me.

"I'll take the $5,000, but I want a $500 signing bonus," I said.

"Why a bonus?" they asked.

"Because my roommate told me to get one," I said. It was kind of a strange thing to say, but I figured that I may as well tell the truth. We talked for a while and they gave me the $5,500.

Betsy and I were married on Sept. 25, 1954, and I had to be in training camp on October 1, so we just drove from Chicago to Syracuse after the wedding. Syracuse had a very good team in 1953–54. The Nats were 42–30 and they lost in the NBA finals to George Mikan and the Minneapolis Lakers. The amazing thing is that they did it without a legitimate center. They ran an offense called the "Syracuse Weave," which was a motion offense but no one played the low post as a center would. If they had a center, it was 6-foot-6 Earl Lloyd, one of the first blacks to play in the NBA. So there was an obvious need for a guy with my size.

We trained at Manlius Military Academy, which was about 15 miles outside Syracuse. They would pay three of the players a nickel a mile to drive the rest of the team to practice and back. That meant three guys with cars each had three passengers. I picked up that mileage every day, which was worth $1.50 a day. I thought that was a big deal. Betsy and I had bought a 1954 Chevy convertible and it was the first car I really owned. I loved that car. It was turquoise with stripes on the side and lush, white seats. It was a classic and Betsy used to say that she wanted to be buried in that car.

To make room for me on the roster, they cut Ebberle Neal, who was 6-foot-11 out of Wofford College in South Carolina. He had played very little the year before, so there wasn't much change in terms of the chemistry of the team. The same guys who had played so well the year before were back with the exeception of me taking Neal's place.

Early in the season, I played very little, maybe 15 minutes a game. I was alternating with Earl Lloyd. It got to the point where it was ridiculous, because Earl and I kept switching off and neither one of us could get enough time on the floor to get a good feel for the game and be effective. One of us would come in, tap the other guy on the back and say, "Sorry, but I'm in for you," and the other guy would go to the bench.

One day I just had had it. Our coach was Al Cervi. His nickname was Digger and he made being scrappy an art form. The guy would challenge you to play him 1-on-1 after practice. If you beat him, then he'd want to play another game . . . and another game . . . and another game . . . until he won. Remember that you were already tired because you had been practicing. The veterans would tell me, "Hey Rook, just let Cervi win the first game then you can come in and take a shower."

Sixteen games into the season, I went to Cervi and said, "Look, I need a chance to play. You have Lloyd and me running in and out, doing the Shuffle Boogie out there. Neither of us is helping you. Give me a shot so I can show that I'll help you." That was it. No threats or anything, but I was pretty firm. Cervi started me that night in Rochester, which was our big rival because both teams were in upstate New York. I had 23 points and 19 rebounds and we won. Earl Lloyd got a lot of time at forward and we showed Cervi that we could play together.

I was the starting center for the rest of the season and I felt very comfortable playing pro ball. I was lucky because transitions—high school to the Big Ten and then the Big Ten to the NBA—didn't bother me that much. It was just basketball and I went out there and played without thinking about it. Of course, the pro game wasn't as sophisticated as it is now. When a player comes out of college, he is often facing a tough man-to-man defense with all those double-teaming principles for the first time. The defenses are far more complex now than when I played. Back then, everyone just played a straight man-to-man defense.

The games were physically rougher in the 1950s. Whenever we played Boston, there was a fight. If a player drove down the middle—especially a guard—you didn't let the guy take a lay-up, you flattened him. You didn't even think twice—the guard drives, you kill. Now, they play Star Wars basketball. A guy goes up for the dunk, the defender goes up for the block and they are a foot above the rim. It is a much purer form of basketball. We never thought about the blocked shot, we just went for the body block instead.

Most of our travel was by trains. It would take us seven and a half hours to go from Syracuse to New York City and we hadn't even left the state. For a basketball player, the sleepers on a train were like a toybox. They were made for people about 5-foot-8 and the only way we'd fit was to curl up in the fetal position. When we'd wake up, we'd be so stiff and sore we'd feel like someone had thrown us out of the train in the middle of the night. We were tired after a game but we didn't want to jam our bodies like pretzels into those sleepers. The coach had a rule that no one could have more than two cans of beer on the train. My room-mate, Billy Kenville, found out that Fosters put out a beer in a quart can, so he'd get two of each of those for us and we'd sit around drinking, trying to knock ourselves out. That's where a lot of our $5-a-day meal money went—the beer bill.

One of the most memorable trips was to Fort Wayne. We'd ride the train all night and stop in Waterloo, Indiana, to let off some passengers. It would be about five in the morning and the players also would get off the train. The town looked like the set from the Spencer Tracy movie *Bad Day at Black Rock.* We'd walk to this greasy spoon named the Green Parrot, where we'd get something to eat. That joint usually had three or four James Dean-looking guys in leather jackets drinking coffee, and you knew that they had been up all night. Usually one of the guys would give us a ride from Waterloo to the Van Ormond Hotel in Fort Wayne and we'd pay the guy a sawbuck. That was our way of getting breakfast. Those kids knew the train schedule, and knew we were coming, and they'd wait for us so they could pick up the extra cash.

Not wanting to risk sounding like an old fart and rather than beat to death an obvious point, I'll just say that I'm not especially sympathetic when players today complain about their travel and hotel conditions. Most of the hotels then had beds with footboards, just what a 6-foot-9 guy needs.

Nor did we have the trainers they have today. The Bulls' trainer is Mark Pfeil, one of the best in his field, and he puts the team through stretching drills and makes sure that injuries are kept to a minimum. We didn't even have a trainer on the road. If something was wrong with us, we had to see if the trainer for the other team had time to examine us. Sometimes they'd hire a trainer by the day in the town where we were playing. We'd take a look at some of those guys and decide it was better if they didn't touch us. We didn't lift weights. In the off-season, we needed jobs to supplement our income so there were no organized conditioning programs. To stay in shape, I went down to the YMCA and played handball. That is why a lot of players from my era have bad knees, hips, feet, you name it. The medical care just wasn't very good.

During my rookie season, we won the regular season championship and faced Fort Wayne in the NBA playoff finals. We played our first two games in Syracuse and won them both. The next three games were supposed to be played in Fort Wayne, but we couldn't get into the building because it was rented to the American Bowling Congress. That's right—the NBA finals were bumped out of Fort Wayne by a bowling tournament. And that tells you a lot about the position of NBA basketball in the 1955 sports universe. Our games were farmed out to Indianapolis, and we lost all three. That meant we were down 3–2 in the seven-game series with the last two games on our home floor in Syracuse. Thank God that our owner Danny Biasone also owned a bowling alley so we didn't have to worry about the American Bowling Congress.

We won both games at Syracuse. The finals came down to one play. We were in front 92–91 with eight seconds left and Fort Wayne had the ball. I knew they were going to pass the ball to my guy, Larry Foust, who was 6-foot-11, 265 pounds. Foust was their leading scorer and he was one of those guys who cause coaches to yell, "Hey, Kerr, *hold your ground,* that guy is shoving you all over the floor."

Fort Wayne brought the ball in bounds and it went to a guard named Andy Phillips. He threw it to George Yardley in the corner, who passed the ball back to Phillips. Meanwhile, Foust was posting me under the basket. They just were clearing out that side of the floor so they could give Foust some room once he got the ball. Phillips was dribbling and suddenly he was double-teamed by our guards—George King and Paul Seymour—and King stole the ball, time ran out and that was it.

You'd never believe how relieved I was that the ball never went in to Foust.

That was it, we were the NBA champions and I was only a rookie. But we never did get a ring, just a plaque from the Syracuse Optimist Club that read, "Congratulations, World Champions."

I thought this was the beginning of a dynasty or something and Syracuse would always be playing for the championship. What I didn't know was that a couple of guys named Russell and Chamberlain were about to come into the league, and in the next 11 years I played, I never made it to the finals again. That's because we could never get past Russell and Boston in the Eastern Conference. We'd play them tough, but not quite good enough to win.

When people do remember me as a player, it usually is because of The Streak. It began on October 31, 1954, and it ended on November 4, 1965. In between, I played 844 consecutive regular season games, an NBA record until Randy Smith broke it when he played in 906 straight, his streak ending in 1983.

For the most part, I didn't think much about The Streak. I went out and played every day just like a guy gets up every morning and goes to work. I won a lot of perfect attendance awards in school, so I guess I didn't know any better. I became aware of my streak when Dolph Schayes was in the process of setting his consecutive-game record, which ended at 706 in 1961. Dolph and I were teammates in Syracuse. One year, he broke his right wrist in the playoffs against Boston. I figured he was finished, especially since Dolph was right-handed. But he played the next night, shot the ball left-handed for the rest of the playoffs and averaged 15 points. That was truly amazing. Dolph's streak ended when he collided with Al Attles and broke a cheekbone.

I just kept playing, and as I got closer to Dolph's record, it was something that the writers mentioned and I became aware of it. I was proud of The Streak. I wanted to keep it going and so did Betsy. One time I sprained my ankle very seriously. I was at home and it started acting up in the middle of the night. I got up, got a pail and went outside. I scooped up a bucket of snow and stuck my foot in it.

Obviously there were nights when I didn't feel like playing. I'd shave about four in the afternoon, go to the arena and I still didn't feel like going out there because usually something was hurting me. I'd think, "It would be great to take a night off." But when I'd get to the dressing room, I'd see the guys, I'd smell the analgesic and then I'd get taped up. When I'd go out for warmups, I'd start to feel a little better. But what really got me going was hearing the "Star Spangled Banner," and hearing my name announced for the introductions. My heart would pound. I was like an addict who needed a fix. I felt I just *had* to play and I couldn't wait for the ref to throw the ball up and the game to start.

To keep The Streak alive, I missed births, graduations and a lot of other things with my family. Betsy became like a doctor, taking care of me so that I could play every night. The only person who fully understands what a player goes through in a situation like this is the player's wife.

My legs were a problem. Toward the end of my career, they were tired and they'd tell me so.

Before some games, I'd be alone in the dressing room and I'd have a conversation with my legs. To be exact, I'd lie to them.

"Legs, we've been together for a long time," I'd say. "You know what, I'm going to quit all this stuff. I'm going to stop all this foolishness. I'll retire, just quit. You get it? But all I want from you is one more game. That's all I'm asking."

Naturally, there always was one more game. And some of the guys overheard me talking to my legs and they'd rag me about it. After a while, I suddenly realized that I had played for a long time. I was being called "a veteran," in the newspapers. I was "ageless," the "old pro" and the "wily veteran." That always seemed weird. But I didn't think about it much, I just kept playing.

When I broke Dolph Schaye's record of 706 games, we were in Philadelphia and the Sixers gave me 707 Kennedy half-dollars. I wish I had them now because they'd be worth a lot more than fifty cents each, but my kids used to take them to school for lunch money. Also when I set the record, I got a telegram from a friend that said, "Congratulations, John, you're only 1,200 games behind Lou Gehrig."

The Streak lasted through nine years in Syracuse, through two more years in Philadelphia and into the 1965–66 season with the Baltimore Bullets. I was 33 in my last year when the Bullets traded for me to be a back-up to Walt Bellamy. But then they traded Bellamy to New York for about half of the Knicks team— Bad News Barnes, Johnny Egan and Johnny Green—and that meant I was a starting center again. Bob Ferry was my back-up and Paul Seymour was the coach. The Streak was over 800 games and I was starting to think about 1,000 games. One night we were playing Boston and Paul Seymour didn't start me. As the game went on, Seymour never called my name. Ferry and Barnes were getting all the minutes in the pivot. In the fourth quarter, some of the fans yelled at Seymour to put me in because they knew about The Streak, but he never did. At that point in the season, I was averaging 28 minutes a game.

That's how it ended. Paul Seymour just decided not to use me. This was the same Paul Seymour with whom I played in Syracuse on a world championship team. We lost 129–118 to Boston, so it wasn't like I would have interrupted a good flow in the game if I had played.

After the game, Seymour just said to me, "John, it had to end sometime." He then told the reporters, "The Streak had to end sometime." He also said that he didn't want to use me in the last minute just for the sake of keeping The Streak alive, and he said it was "best that it ended," whatever that meant. I don't think it was best for me.

The kicker was that I started the next game, so it wasn't as if Seymour thought I was ready for a rocking chair. I don't know if Seymour was mad at me for some reason I never knew about, or if he wanted to show me that he was boss by not playing me...I'm not sure and he never really said.

After the game, I was upset but I didn't want to rip Seymour to the press. I didn't think that would do much good, so I just told the writers that now I had to start another streak. I mentioned that the two guys who played ahead of me—Barnes and Ferry—combined for 41 points and they did it against Bill Russell. What was I supposed to say—The Streak died at 844 games. Actually, it was 917 games when you throw in the playoffs.

Betsy was in Chicago and when she picked up the newspaper the next morning and didn't see my name in the Baltimore box-score, she called me.

"Honey, are you all right?" Betsy asked me.

"I'm fine," I said.

"That son-of-a-bitch," said Betsy.

I didn't have to ask her who she was talking about. Betsy had done a lot to keep me playing—all the rubdowns and everything else—and she had a lot of pride in The Streak.

A couple of days later, Betsy met us at the airport and I could tell that she was still hot. She started heading toward the team and I knew she wanted to talk to Seymour. I cut her off and told her, "Betsy, forget it. Don't do anything."

What Betsy wanted to do was punch Seymour in the mouth.

The record was mine for 17 years until Smith, a 6-foot-4 guard, broke it. That really didn't bother me. When Randy did set the record, he was asked if he'd ever met me. He said that he had not, but suddenly our two names had become linked together. I always liked that. And when Randy did break my record, a lot of people interviewed me about my streak, and I got a kick out of the attention.

I did miss a couple of more games that season because of a sore back. I also knew that this was my last year. My legs didn't want to hear any more lies. When I talked to them, they talked right back because they hurt like hell. To this day, I still have terrible feet—bunions on top of corns, hammertoes, and two toes that haven't touched the ground in 50 years. My epitaph should read: "I told you that my feet were killing me."

At the end my body just said, "No mas."

And now I know what "No mas" really means—my feet hurt. I'd be in bed at night and suddenly my legs would just start quivering and jerking—and that was their way of talking back to me. Instead of trying to block shots, I'd just stand in the key when someone drove, hoping they would run into me so I could draw an offensive foul. One night I got the ball at the top of the key, made my move to the hoop but before I could get off a shot, I was called for three seconds. That told me I was really slowing down.

It was possible that I could have played one more year as a back-up center, but the Bulls coaching job was open and I really wanted to live in Chicago. The ironic thing was that Paul Seymour announced that he was quitting as coach in Baltimore, and the Bullets wanted me to coach their team, but I couldn't picture myself doing that. I couldn't tell the same guys I used to drink with what to do. It would be very hard for them to see me as a teammate one year and then as the coach the next.

My last NBA game was in St. Louis when Baltimore got knocked out of the playoffs. I stayed in the dressing room for a long time, slowly taking off my uniform. I remember sitting there in my stocking feet. The lights were dimming and in the distance I could hear the popping sound made by guys stepping on paper cups. I could hear them taking down the folding chairs and sweeping up the trash. Then I walked out into the empty Keil Auditorium and watched a couple of guys dismantle the floor. I was thinking that there would be no more cheers, no more friends on the team, no more running out on the floor when my name was announced. There were tears streaming down my face because I loved every minute of being a pro basketball player and it was over.

I never made more than $30,000. I never won a scoring or a rebounding title. With Russell and Chamberlain in the league, I couldn't get my team into the NBA finals. I played in three All-Star games and I averaged 14 points and 11 rebounds for my career. I was proud of the fact that I was there every night when the coach needed me. It was a helluva job—you get to sleep in most mornings and then you go to the gym and shoot baskets or play in scrimmages. I probably took eight million hook shots in practice and when you play basketball for as long as I did, the game isn't second nature, it's first nature. The guys were very close, closer than the players are now. It was common for a number of us to go out after a road game, have a few beers and then re-play the whole game in the bar. After home games, one of us would invite the others over to his house, we'd have pizza and beer and talk basketball. I miss that stuff as much as the games. It's just like I miss the jokes—waiting until my old roommate Al Bianchi got into his best suit and then pouring a little salt on his shoulders to make him think he had dandruff. Once in the middle of a game, I went down on my hands and knees as if I was looking for a contact lens. I didn't even wear contacts. I knew it was a good way to get my picture in the paper—big guy on the floor looking for a little lens with nine other players and two officials also crawling around. Sure enough, it worked, as I saw when the paper arrived.

The strange thing about being a player is that I was finished at 34, and that's ancient by NBA standards. In business, you're a "young man" at 34, not a "wily veteran." In my financial business, a smart guy in his early 30s is considered a whiz kid. No one says he's doing yeoman work. Of course, I got a couple of breaks; being able to coach and broadcasting the Bulls games.

———●

By now you have the idea that I love my family, the city of Chicago and the Bulls.

I still can't believe that someone actually pays me to watch Michael Jordan and the Bulls. But I also think that doing the Bulls games on radio and television has sort of kept me in a state of suspended adolescence.

I've spent my life—and made a living—playing games. Whether it was 16-inch softball at Ogden Park, Big Ten basketball at Champaign-Urbana or in the NBA; thanks to sports I never had to grow up, and there are a lot of good things that can be said for that.

I still feel like a player or a coach. I take the team bus to and from the games. I go down to the dressing room. I talk to the players and coaches, hear the rumors and go to practice with the team. I sit at mid-court for every game and I feel my heart start to pump a little bit right before I go on the air just as it did when I would get ready for the opening jump ball. The only difference between my life now and then is that I don't get to go on the floor and play, but watching and talking about it is the next best thing.

I backed into broadcasting just like I stumbled into basketball. It was someone else's idea. Instead of a high school coach seeing a big kid lumbering around the hallway and pointing him toward the gym, the Phoenix Suns found themselves wondering what to do with the coach they had just fired. The coach was me and the year was 1970. As you know, I had been replaced after the Suns started the year with a 15–23 record. The Phoenix play-by-play man was Bob Vache and the color guy was Hot Rod Hundley.

Vache was killed one night when the car he was driving hit a pole. Suddenly, the Suns needed another announcer right in the middle of the season. They made Hot Rod Hundley do the play-by-play and they brought me in to do the color. The only radio work I had done up to this point was one NBA All-Star game in Boston when I was a "guest" commentator, just as television now uses many current players and coaches for one night shots during the playoffs.

Hot Rod Hundley was the perfect guy for me to start with in broadcasting. He grew up in West Virginia and attended West Virginia University. During his sophomore year, he had a chance to become the school's single-season all-time scorer with one more basket, but Hod Rod decided he'd rather take a hook shot from half-court than drive for a good shot.

The writers asked him why he just heaved the ball from 50 feet.

"If I got the record now, what would I have to shoot for as a junior and senior?" he said.

Actually, if Hot Rod were going to break the record, his style would be to do it on an outrageous shot from half-court. He loved to be flashy, but he also was extremely talented, good enough to be the No. 1 pick in the 1958 NBA draft. He later wrote a book called *Clown*, which is how he viewed himself. Hot Rod always said that he started in the NBA as a player making ten grand, and he went out six years later making about ten grand, and in the process he was traded for about 52 other players. Hot Rod was the kind of guy who liked dribbling through his legs and passing the ball behind his back and he never, ever missed a party or a game of pool. He reminded me of the man who joins the army as a buck private and ten years later he's still a buck private. That may not sound like much progress, but the guy had the time of his life for those ten years.

So I was teamed with Hundley and they billed us as The "Red-Hot" Show.

Hot Rod always tried to set me up:

"Okay, Red, here we are in Milwaukee and the Bucks have the ball out of bounds in front of the Phoenix bench. The Suns are down by a point with three seconds left. Now tell us what can the Suns do to win this game?"

"Rod, if I knew that, I'd still be coaching," I'd say.

Another time the Suns were playing Los Angeles and Hot Rod asked me about Laker guard Jerry West: "They call him Zeke from Cabin Creek. Tell me, Red, about Cabin Creek, West Virginia."

"Well, Rod, Cabin Creek is so small that the Baskin Robbins there has only one flavor of ice cream—vanilla," I said.

What did I know about Cabin Creek? I'd never been there. But Hot Rod said we should have a good time and not worry about anything—that was his motto about life—and that's exactly what we did.

Bob Allison was the sports editor of the *Phoenix Gazette* and I thought he was right on the money when he wrote, "Hundley and Kerr may not be as professional as most, but they are as refreshing as a head-on collision."

———●

After the end of that season, I wanted to get away. I really wasn't being paid much to broadcast and it still hurt to be fired as coach. So I spent a year as vice-president of the Virginia Squires before coming back to Chicago as the Bulls' business manager in 1973. I worked for the Bulls for two years until I got swept out with several other front office people in 1975.

I had no idea at the time, but getting fired from the Bulls' front office was the best thing that ever happened to me.

Phil Nolan was the general manager of WIND radio and he asked me if I would do a little half-time radio show, just as a way of giving play-by-play man Jimmy Durham a break. It sounded great to me because I was still going to the games. I really wasn't doing anything but watching because I still liked to see the Bulls play. Nolan offered me $35 a game and we named the half-time show "Kerr's Korner." They gave me a good seat at the press table next to Jimmy Durham, and Jimmy and I just hit it off.

Even though I wasn't on the air during the game, Jimmy would lean over and ask me a question and then he'd hand me a microphone so I could answer. That was how it was for several games, then one day Jimmy said to the engineer, "Can we rig up a mike for Red?"

That really got me started and I've been doing the Bulls on either radio or television since 1975. The amazing thing was that Jimmy Durham just went out of his way to put me on the air with him. The hardest thing for most guys to do is to share air time. Most guys are in love with the sound of their own voice and all they want to do is talk and talk and talk. They'd rather have their tongues cut out than give the mike to someone else for 30 seconds. Jimmy is the opposite. He put the mike in front of me. He asked the engineer to set me up. It's truly amazing, something you just don't find in this business.

Now Jimmy and I simulcast the Bulls games—all 82 on radio and about 70 a year on cable television. We get letters from fans all over the country who see us on the satellite, because Michael Jordan has made the Bulls a hot item for basketball fans everywhere. Michael even bought his parents a satellite dish so they can watch the games from their home in Charlotte.

When I am broadcasting a game, sometimes I picture a guy I believe is the average Bulls fan. The guy has a tough job—either a lot of physical labor or he is in a pressure-cooker at the office. He's got worries—a mortgage that's steep, a mother-in-law who is mean, kids who won't listen to him, a car with a bad muffler. I admire this guy just for going out there every day, punching in and punching out, giving a good eight hours of sweat and work and keeping his complaints to a minimum. Then he comes home from work and he's beat. He strips off his clothes and sits down in his favorite living room chair wearing his underwear and a T-shirt. He's got a beer in one hand, a copy of the sports section in the other hand and maybe a Marine Corps tatoo on his shoulder. The television is on, his wife is in the kitchen making dinner and the guy is thinking, "I hope the Bulls don't stink up the joint and I hope Michael jams on somebody."

What this guy wants is a break. He wants to be entertained and he wants the Bulls to win, because when they win, he feels a little better.

That's why I like to keep the broadcast very light. I watch some college games and the commentators are X-ing and O-ing you to death. They're talking collapsing zones, defensive rotation, box-and-ones, triangles-and-twos, you name it. They take their title as analyst literally—all that's missing is a pipe and German accent. These guys want to be the Freuds of the hardwood. And I can hear the guy in his livingroom saying, "Hey, Madge, this bozo on the television, he drives me nuts. I don't know what the hell he's talking about."

If there is any advice I have for broadcasters, it's keep the game moving. Don't show off.

For example, when an official calls an illegal defense—something even an official can't explain—I say it's an illegal defense and leave it at that. There is no reason to go into a long, pointless dissertation because no one wants to hear it. Someone was standing in the wrong place at the wrong time. The guy sitting in front of his television set will buy that.

I think most Bulls fans feel the same way about the team as I do. We don't always like what the Bulls are doing and sometimes we just ache because we know that they made a move that was just plain dumb and is going to cost them a game.

It's almost as if the Bulls are one of our children.

We can sit there and say, "Don't do that."

Then they'll do that, and it will be wrong and all we can do is shake our heads because we saw it coming.

Or we'll be watching Michael with the ball going down court and we know the dunk is coming and before Michael even has started his jump, we're on our feet screaming.

Or we'll see Michael drive to the basket, get knocked down and he'll be on the court for a moment, holding his leg and our hearts will seem to skip a few beats until he gets up.

What I am saying is that I'm not a cheerleader and neither are the fans. Rather, we are involved. We care about the team and if you push us hard enough, we'll probably admit that we bleed red and black. We care about the team. If the Bulls lose, our lives aren't any worse for it. But if they win, we do feel better at least for a few hours.

11 •————————————————————

A Next
Year Worth
Waiting For

Ever since I coached the Bulls, I've been waiting for a next year like 1989, a year when I could say that the Bulls are getting ready to start playing for an NBA title and not be worried about a couple of guys in white coats with a butterfly net coming after me.

That's what last season told us about the Bulls—they're getting close.

Maybe the Bulls won't win a championship in 1990 or 1991, but they are now at the stage where they can seriously begin talking about it. Given the age of the team—the fact that Michael Jordan is just 27 yet he's the third *oldest* starter—why not say that the Bulls are heading into a five year stretch when they can go after a title every season?

That's how basketball fans everywhere—not just in Chicago—view the Bulls. In the playoffs, they were the NBA's Cinderella team and Michael charmed the entire country. In a survey of stores in the Los Angeles area, Bulls' T-shirts were outselling Lakers' shirts by a 3-to-1 margin during the playoffs. That's because the Bulls were under the big eye of CBS as they beat Cleveland in the first round, beat New York in the second round and made it rough for Detroit in the Eastern Conference finals. CBS couldn't get enough of Michael and the Bulls as their ratings went through the ceiling. The Bulls did it while they were real underdogs, they did it without the home court advantage and they did it with the most exciting player the country has ever seen. It was Come Fly With Me time with Michael Jordan guiding the magic carpet in the playoffs. We can and will talk about Michael's double-pumping shot at the buzzer in Cleveland in Game 5. We will discuss Michael slicing through the entire Detroit defense and banking in a twisting, mind-boggling, wildly improbable shot for anyone but *him* in Game 3 against Detroit. We can and will talk about the heroics, but right now I want to talk about progress.

In the last three years, the Bulls advanced from the first to the second to the third round of the playoffs. Each year was better than the last come playoff time, and that's really the only time that counts. The idea of the NBA is to be great at the end. Training camp gets you ready for the regular season, but the regular season gets you ready for the playoffs.

For a variety of reasons, the Bulls really weren't ready for the regular season. Doug Collins could have used at least another six weeks of training camp, given all the changes in personnel and adjustments in strategy that had to be made.

But come playoff time, the Bulls were prepared. This was a year when the Bulls started to take on that toughness and grit that a team needs to advance in the playoffs. It was a year when the Bulls learned that Horace Grant could play and that Scottie Pippen could play and play in big games. Those two guys have made Jerry Krause's 1987 draft perhaps the best in Bulls' history, aside from Rod Thorn's choice of Michael in 1984. It also was a year when the Bulls found the position for Michael Jordan that is best for the team. Michael Jordan anywhere on the court is a great player. Michael Jordan at point guard made the Bulls one of the four best teams in the NBA by the end of the 1988–89 season. And it was a year when they discovered the value of the 3-point shot courtesy of Craig Hodges and a year when they learned what it meant to have a serious scoring threat in the middle thanks to Bill Cartwright.

All of that sounds and is great right now, but a year ago was a different story. The team that came together for training camp in October of 1988 was a team that had won 50 games, a team that had gone past the first round of the playoffs for the first time in 12 years. It also was a team that made one of the most controversial trades in the history of the franchise when Charles Oakley and a draft pick (Rod Strickland) went to New York for Cartwright and the draft rights to Will Perdue. I love Charles Oakley. He got more rebounds from 1986–88 than any man in basketball. But Charles Oakley *wasn't* a center and Bill Cartwright wasn't just a center, but a *legitimate* one. That was something that escaped those people who really ripped the deal when it was made and when the Bulls struggled during the regular season. Notice I didn't say that Cartwright is a great center, but Cartwright is much better than anything the Bulls have had this decade. The only Chicago center whose talent could compare to Cartwright's is Artis Gilmore, but Cartwright obviously meant more to the Bulls than Gilmore did.

As the 1988–89 season began, Doug Collins and his staff faced several challenges:

1. Collins had never coached a low-post center like Cartwright. He had to devise plays for Cartwright to get the ball and create room for him under the basket so that Cartwright could do something with the ball after he got it. When Dave Corzine was the center, it was simple. Corzine would get the ball at the high post, about 18 feet from the basket. He either shot it or passed it. He seldom went inside and played with his back to the basket, which is exactly what Cartwright does.

2. Michael and the rest of the team had never played with a low-post center. They had to learn how to get the ball to him and more importantly, find out where and when Bill wanted the ball.

3. With Cartwright near the basket, that sometimes clogged up the middle because of the defensive attention he drew. So that meant when Michael went to the basket, he often found Cartwright and Cartwright's man in the way, and that was a frustrating situation early in the season. With Corzine, that never was a problem for Michael because Corzine played so far from the basket.

4. Pippen and Grant had to learn what it meant to start in the NBA and had to deal with the pressure that comes from being expected to deliver every night. They had great rookie seasons, but they came off the bench. If they played well, everyone said, "Isn't it great how the kids came through." If they had a hard time, we said, "Well, they're still rookies and rookies need time to develop." As last season began, Pippen and Grant were no longer rookies and they were supposed to produce like veterans, even though they were still young players, guys in their second seasons.

5. Pippen got hurt. During the summer of 1988, the coaches wanted Scottie to work on his ballhandling. He tended to dribble too high and that made it easy for the smaller guards to come up and steal the ball from him. But Pippen needed back surgery in the summer, so his basketball summer school was out. And so was training camp and so was the early season and so were some of the best laid plans of Jerry Krause and Doug Collins.

Something that most people don't realize is that the Bulls went to war at the start of the 1988–89 season with a totally different front line from the one that ended the 1987–88 season.

That starting front court was Oakley and Pippen at the forwards, Corzine at center. The new front court was Grant, Sellers (for the injured Pippen) and Cartwright. For much of the season, Collins had to feel like a kid who had to write a paper and the teacher kept sending it back to him, telling Doug, "That's nice, but why don't you do it over?" This was a season when the coaching staff needed a big eraser and lots of ideas.

For a while, it was really crazy. The Bulls had to learn how to play *without* Pippen, then when Scottie came back eight games into the season, they had to remember how they played *with* him. But Scottie really wasn't in shape, because the back operation meant he missed training camp and he was playing himself back into condition during the regular season, which meant that both he and the team were out of synch.

In the middle of all this was Cartwright—the Bulls were learning him and he was learning the Bulls. For a while, it was pretty grim and the Bulls were taking a lot of heat about the Oakley trade. Then Cartwright pulled a calf muscle, and Corzine moved back into the lineup at his old starting center spot. The Bulls went 4-1 with Corzine in the lineup and people were saying the Bulls should just forget about Cartwright. You could tell that even the players were asking themselves, "Are we better off without Bill and with Corzine at center?" The confidence of the team was so fragile, the on-the-court leadership so shaky that everyone was looking for both a scapegoat and a savior. They needed someone to blame for the hard times, then someone to lead them into prime time. Many of the players were looking outside and pointing fingers instead of looking in the mirror for an answer.

To Doug Collins' credit, he never wavered on Cartwright. He resisted what would have been a grandstand move, to bench Bill in favor of Corzine when Cartwright came back from his injury. That was because Doug saw that the problem went deeper than Cartwright. One of the reasons Cartwright wasn't producing was that he wasn't getting the ball when and where he needed it, and that was because the Bulls were in trouble at yet another spot—point guard.

Sam Vincent had finished the 1987–88 season looking as if he would be the Bulls' best point guard since Norm Van Lier. But he just couldn't give the Bulls what they needed in terms of getting the most out of Cartwright.

Here was what happened:

Sam Vincent is not a good outside shooter in a slow, walk-the-ball-up-the-court game. But when you have a low-post center such as Cartwright, the game sometimes crawls as the guard waits for the center to set up near the basket and prepare to receive the pass.

Vincent would throw the ball to Cartwright, and Vincent's man would immediately leave Sam and then double-team Cartwright. That meant Bill would throw the ball back to Sam, who should take the shot. At first, Sam did shoot, but it didn't go in. Then he lost confidence in his shooting and just stood out there with the ball. He was in a real turmoil. The coaches wanted Sam to get the ball to Cartwright, but the defense was dropping off of Sam and taking away the pass inside. Compounding the problem was that Sam wasn't shooting well. In the end, the defense wasn't paying Sam any attention and the Bulls ended up playing 4-on-5 as Vincent wasn't a factor.

In Sam's defense, it should be said that Cartwright is not a great receiver. He isn't athletic like Akeem Olajuwon, where a guard just throws the ball up there and Akeem jumps over everyone and catches it. Bill is a very mechanical player and doesn't have great hands. A guard has to be very precise when it comes to passing him the ball. But when Cartwright did get the ball so many good things happened—he scored, he was fouled or he scored and then was fouled for a 3-point play.

Also, the fast break was a mess. There seemed to be a hesitation when a Chicago player got a rebound. Do I throw it to Vincent? To Michael? To Pippen? There were times when it seemed that three guys were waiting in the back court to receive an outlet pass and no one was running up the court to start the fast break. That also worried Doug.

So by early March, the Bulls were in trouble. They had lost three in a row and four out of six. The record was still respectable—34-24, but you knew that things were going to get a lot worse because the team was heading into a big-time funk. The basketball dog days were really taking a toll, wearing the team down. The best thing a coach can do in this situation is to make a change because change tends to snap a team back to attention.

———————●

Under these dire circumstances, some coaches try short-term gimmicks. Doug Collins made a move that would have long-range ramifications for the Bulls. It began with a closed door meeting between Doug Collins and Michael. It came after the Bulls lost 104-95 in Boston, a game that Michael sat out because of a groin pull. That game also broke a streak of 235 consecutive games played by Michael. It was a tough time. Michael was depressed about his groin pull, about the losing, about how things were going with the Bulls. Collins was pretty much in the same state of mind. At that point, both Michael and Doug knew that something had to be done—and the point was the answer.

"You don't tell a player such as Michael Jordan that you want him to change positions, you talk to him about it, you ask him what he thinks," Doug told me. "Michael and I both knew that something had to happen. He wasn't happy with how things were going and neither was I. We both spoke our minds and we were very candid with each other. We got a lot off of our chests. We knew the team couldn't go on as we were and we both were aware that we had to do something about the point guard situation."

That was when Doug suggested that Michael move to the point. It was something he had experimented with in training camp, and it was a move I liked right from Michael's first dribble for a very simple reason—if Magic Johnson can be a great point guard, why not Michael Jordan? What is the real difference between those guys? As players and athletes, they should wear a letter S on their jerseys. Everyone knows they can do anything on the court, but more importantly, what they really want to do is win. Personal achievements mean nothing to these guys, championship rings do.

So Doug put the ball—and the Bulls—in Michael's hands, the same way the Lakers give control to Magic Johnson. I often mention that Magic and Michael have the same initials—M.J.— and I believed that Michael could play the point like a Magic Jordan.

Michael had been saying for years that scoring titles didn't mean anything to him. He was upset when people didn't talk about him in the same breath as Magic and Larry Bird, they didn't say that Michael Jordan made his team better. They just said that Michael was a great player, perhaps the best 1-on-1 player ever. Michael insisted he wanted to be more than that and the move to point guard gave him a chance to show it.

"I've always said that Michael is a true champion," said Collins. "That means he is a player who considers winning to be paramount. Michael knew that I wouldn't have gone to him unless I was convinced Michael Jordan as our point guard was best not just for the Bulls, but for him. I think after playing for me for three years, he developed some confidence in me and my judgment. We've been through a lot together. I know that in my first year, I had to prove myself to Michael, to show him that I was more than just a former player, that I really could coach. Maybe in my first year, Michael would not have agreed to the move because he wouldn't have known where I was coming from. But over the years we've learned to trust each other."

Here is what Michael at the point did for the Bulls:

1. He ended the confusion on the fast break. When a player got a rebound, the first pass immediately went to Michael and everyone else ran up the court filling the lanes.

2. Michael Jordan in an open-court, fast break situation is the ultimate basketball weapon. He can score on anyone, and the man seems to have eyes in the back of his head because he can pass the ball to anyone, anywhere. Also, Michael was looking to pass the ball, looking to reward his teammates for running up the court. Michael Jordan at the point got the Bulls running again, especially Grant and Pippen, who thrive in the uptempo game and who love to finish a play with a slam dunk. Michael's ballhandling and passing put them in position to do just that.

3. Cartwright found himself open under the basket. You can be sure that Michael's man wasn't going to leave him to double-team Cartwright. Dropping off Michael Jordan is a good way to drop right into the coach's doghouse. So Cartwright found himself in a lot of 1-on-1 situations under the basket, situations where he is virtually unstoppable, and suddenly people could see why the Bulls wanted him.

4. Michael is a very good outside shooter. If the defense takes even a half-step off Michael, he can pull the trigger on the 20-footer. He gave them the outside scoring threat from the point that they had been lacking.

5. Point guard also saved Michael's body. When he was playing shooting guard, he would run back and forth along the baseline and around picks trying to get open. Sometimes, he was like a pinball as the defense tried to bounce him around. Officials allow far more contact away from the ball than they do when the player has the ball. Too often, Michael couldn't get open until the shot clock was down to six seconds and then he had to quickly get off a shot. At the point, he was less likely to be double-teamed because he was 35 feet from the basket, and the defense couldn't beat on him because he had the ball and the officials were likely to call a foul.

From a personal standpoint, I love watching Michael play point guard. He is so creative, so able to push the ball up the court and get the other guys involved in the offense, yet Michael still averaged 31 points a game. Also, Michael's passion for the game returned. He was presented with a new challenge and he seized it with both hands. He was asked to expand what he does, to actually show that he could do for the Bulls what Magic Johnson does for the Lakers and that inspired him.

The Bulls won 10 of their first 13 games with Michael at point guard. Michael played 23 games at the point and he *averaged* a triple-double—31.7 points, 10.8 assists and 10.8 rebounds. He

had 15 triple-doubles, including seven in a row. Some basketball people like to mention that Oscar Robertson averaged a
triple-double for an entire season early in his career. That's true,
but I played against Oscar, and this is not to deny his greatness,
but Oscar didn't have to face the same double-and-triple-teaming
defenses as Michael does every night. When Oscar and I played,
the defenses were strictly man-to-man.

————————●

   As the playoffs began, all was not well with the Bulls . . .
again. Actually, the trouble was that the Bulls had not been well.
Craig Hodges and John Paxson were out with sprained ankles,
Scottie Pippen had a sore shoulder, Cartwright was suspended
for a game for a fight with Isiah Thomas and Horace Grant had
sprained his wrist. The Bulls limped to the end of the regular
season, losing eight of their last ten games. In the final regular
season game, the Bulls lost 90–84 at Chicago Stadium to a
Cleveland team that was without three starters—Mark Price,
Larry Nance and Brad Daugherty.
   Cleveland would be their first-round playoff opponent, and
some Chicago writers said the Bulls would be swept, or at least
be lucky to win a game. In the 1988 playoffs, the Bulls beat the
Cavs in a best-of-five series, but the Bulls had the home court
advantage. This time, that belonged to the Cavaliers. But in the
week between the end of the regular season and the start of the
playoffs, the Bulls had time to rest, heal and prepare. Best of
all, Hodges was healthy and ready to play.
   Hodges' return was both a lift and a relief to the Bulls. He
is the one guard who seems best suited to playing next to Michael
Jordan, especially the Jordan who was doing his Magic act at
the point.
   Over the years, so many Bulls' back court plans just fell apart.
In 1984–85, it was Quintin Dailey who was supposed to play next
to Michael, but Dailey had drug problems. Then it was supposed
to be Ennis Whatley, but he just had problems—period—such as
playing the game. Then came 1985–86 when Kyle Macy and John
Paxson were supposed to alternate at the guard spot next to
Michael and supply the 3-point shot, but Michael broke his foot.
On and on it went. Sedale Threatt took a shot and missed. So

did Rory Sparrow and Sam Vincent.

Then Jerry Krause made one of those small, shrewd mid-season deals that really helped the Bulls when he got Hodges from Phoenix for Ed Nealy and a second-round pick. In that trade, absolutely nothing was lost and a starting guard was gained.

The Bulls had always liked Hodges, a Chicago kid from Rich East High School, a kid who always said that his one dream was to play for the Bulls. He would go to Chicago Stadium to watch the Bulls of Norm Van Lier and Bob Love. When he was in the NBA with Milwaukee and Phoenix, Hodges talked about how he'd like to play next to Michael Jordan. He talked about seeing Michael drive to the basket, drawing the defense and then throwing a pass out to Hodges for the 3-pointer. And Hodges is at home shooting from long distance. He holds the NBA's single season 3-point record for shooting 49 percent in 1987–88. So Hodges had an idea of how best to play with Michael and the Bulls even before he came to Chicago.

While most of the credit for the trade should go to Krause, assistant coach Tex Winter also put in a lot of good words for Hodges. Winter had been the coach at Northwestern and had recruited Hodges when he was a star at Rich East High School under Steve Fisher—and yes, that's the same Steve Fisher who coached Michigan to the NCAA title. When Winter went from Northwestern to Long Beach State, he took Hodges with him.

So Winter and Hodges were together again in Chicago, and all Hodges did was swish his first nine 3-pointers with the Bulls. Hodges had been in the NBA for seven seasons and was 28 years old. He was as ready as he ever would be to play for the Bulls. And the team really clicked with him, especially on the West Coast trip in the middle of March when the Bulls won five in a row. There were no doubts, Hodges could flat-out shoot and his 3-pointers were opening things up for Michael outside, for Cartwright inside, for everyone, everywhere. If the defense sagged back and ignored Hodges, he hurt them three ways—as in a 3-pointer.

The team with Michael at the point and Hodges at the shooting guard was becoming a good one, and that was the team that took the court against Cleveland in the playoffs.

————————●

At the start of the playoffs, Doug Collins was at his best. He publicly played the underdog theme for all it was worth, putting the pressure on Cleveland. Why not? Cleveland had won 57 regular season games, the Bulls 47. Cleveland had won all six regular season games between the two teams. But in the dressing room, Collins talked about how he was convinced the Bulls could beat the Cavs, how Hodges coming back made them a better team, how everyone was 0–0 in the playoffs and it really was a new season so it didn't matter if the Bulls were 0–82 against Cleveland. Collins never said it but it was understood that any team with Michael Jordan was a good bet to win a short playoff series.

Michael also sensed that he needed to do something, so he predicted that the Bulls would win in four games. It wasn't like Michael to shoot off his mouth, but he knew that his team needed to really believe they could upset Cleveland. Other players picked up on the theme. Brad Sellers said that everyone should wear black shoes and everyone from the players to the coaching staff to Jimmy Durham and I did. That was a nice touch from Sellers, an almost forgotten guy on the team, a guy who had been booed by the fans for much of his career. Instead of moping, he was trying to play a role and showing that the guys on the bench wanted to be a part of this thing, too. Michael shaved his head and several other players followed. Doug gave the players a pop quiz on the bus where they had to identify the vocal and hand signals used by Cleveland when the Cavs called out their various offensive plays, and the players scored extremely high.

What happened was that the Bulls were coming together. Collins talked about how you really didn't know what kind of a person you were until you faced adversity and this series with Cleveland would tell the Bulls a lot about themselves. Doug was issuing a challenge and he devised a very aggressive and gutsy game plan. The Bulls would go into Cleveland and fire away from the 3-point range. It was a charge-the-hill-and-plant-the-flag style of attack. Meanwhile, the Cavs were without Mark Price (groin pull), the pint-sized point guard who has killed the Bulls over the years, and Doug thought if the Bulls could jump on Cleveland early and take the crowd out of the game, they had a chance.

That's exactly what happened. Hodges and Pippen were hot from the 3-point range, Michael was great as always and the Bulls won 95–88 in a game that wasn't nearly as close as the final score.

This game set the tone for the entire playoffs. If the Bulls had lost the opener, forget it. They were at the stage where they could go either way, where their confidence needed a boost. They *thought* they could win the opener at Cleveland, but they needed a great first game in order to *know*. After the game, they *knew* they were going to beat Cleveland and go on to the second round.

Certainly the series wasn't over. Cleveland is a great team with a super coach in Lenny Wilkens and a lot of character. In fact, Wilkens and Collins became very close during the season. Doug said that he and Lenny talked for a long time during the bleak days for the Bulls in December. "I remember Lenny telling me that I had established myself as a coach in this league and that I was a good coach," said Doug. "Lenny also told me that I can't heal the sick or pull off miracles. All I could do was coach the people I had. Lenny didn't have to take the time to listen to me and to give me some advice, but he did. The entire Cavaliers organization is class from top to bottom."

And that class showed as the Cavs won Game 2 on their home court. The Bulls took Game 3 at Chicago Stadium, setting up Game 4, Bulls ahead 2–1 and Michael ready to become the Great Karnac as his words "the Bulls in four games," really did look prophetic. The Stadium was rocking. The feeling was that this was the night, the Bulls would wrap it up in four. Bring on the Knicks. There would be 30 lead changes in the game. Michael would score 50 points, but 50 wasn't enough and the fact that he didn't score 52 made him "feel as sick as I have about a basketball game in a long, long time."

You watch Michael Jordan and you expect him to make free throws at the end of a game. You just do because he always does. Sure, Michael misses. He shot 85 percent, meaning he was something like 9-for-11 most nights. But the two that were off usually were in the second quarter. The shots that really mattered, the ones that you remember at the end of the game, well, they're just automatic with Michael. Either Jimmy Durham or I will say, "We need these free throws from Michael," and then we'd get the free throws from Michael. Not once in five years could Durham or I recall Michael blowing an important foul shot.

But this night was different. He missed one with 47 seconds left, he missed another one with eight seconds to go. Then the Bulls had the ball with two seconds left and the score tied. Doug set up a nice play for Michael to take the last shot. Michael caught a long pass and took a fall-away 12-footer on the baseline. As the buzzer sounded, Michael's shot banged against the rim. The Cavs then won the game in overtime, reminding all of us that there was a reason they had the NBA's second best record in the regular season.

Michael was torn apart after the game. He felt that he had let the team, the whole town of Chicago down.

"I put my credibility on the line and I didn't come through," he said. "I was crushed. I'm telling you, tears came to my eyes when I thought about those foul shots. You could pin the whole thing on me because I didn't produce. I made the prediction that we'd win in four games because I wanted to be sure my team-mates were motivated, that they believed we could win like I did. I knew my words would get back to Cleveland, but that was a chance I had to take. Before you can do something, you have to believe you can do it."

So Michael believed the Bulls would win in four games and he had a chance to make it happen, but he didn't.

Okay, I had a hard time holding anything against Michael during that 50-point night. He wasn't the only guy to blow a foul shot, but what I was really interested to see was how Michael and the Bulls would react for Game 5 in Cleveland.

At Richfield Coliseum, the Cavs were 37–4, the third best home record in NBA history. They had won 22 in a row on their court and this was the essence of the home court advantage—to have the last and deciding game of a playoff series played in your arena in front of your fans. The Bulls would know how the early Christians felt when they were thrown into a lion's den.

The day before the game, Doug didn't have a practice, just a team meeting. He talked for about half an hour, asking his team to visualize how they would beat Cleveland the next after-noon. Michael never said what he thought about, but I have a feeling he saw himself taking the last shot and making it.

That's how Michael's mind works.

That's also what happened.

This would be one of the most exciting basketball games I'd ever seen, one where there would be nine lead changes in the last three minutes. It also would be yet another chapter in the legend of Michael Jordan.

It was Michael's 12-footer on the wing with six seconds left that put the Bulls ahead 99–98. Because of what was to come, people tend to forget that this was a great shot, one where Michael had to put on some extra arch just to get it over Larry Nance, a premier 6-foot-10 shot-blocker.

Then Cleveland got the ball. Hodges blew a defensive assignment, allowing Craig Ehlo to catch a pass for a wide-open lay-up putting the Cavs in front 100–99 with three seconds left.

Collins called a time out. As the Bulls were walking to the huddle, Michael saw that Hodges' chin was so low that he almost tripped on it.

"Michael winked at me and said, 'Don't worry, I'll make the shot,'" said Hodges. "Then he smiled. I said, 'Do it, man.'"

Meanwhile, I said to Jimmy Durham, "If they don't give the ball to Michael on this play, I'll kill myself!"

As you can tell, I was cool, calm and collected.

Okay, I wasn't but thank God because Michael was. And thank God that the Bulls did get the ball to Michael even though the Cavs double-teamed him with Nance and Ehlo.

Right now, I want to say something about Brad Sellers. When people think of Sellers in the playoffs, they may remember that he had the idea for black shoes for the team or that he played very well when he filled in for the injured Scottie Pippen in the final game against Detroit. But it was Sellers who had the Cleveland series on his shoulders because he was taking the ball out-of-bounds, trying to get the ball to Michael when the whole world knew that was where the ball was going. Sellers only had five seconds, which can be the fastest five seconds of your life when you're in that situation. I would not have wanted to be Brad Sellers if the five seconds had gone by and he was still holding the ball. He probably would have wanted to eat it.

Anyway, I saw Brad look at not one but two other Bulls players who were open. He could have made the easy pass to either of those guys and no one would have said a word. He was there to get the ball in bounds and when he did he would have been off the hook. But Sellers really was there to get the ball to Michael and he waited until the last second when Michael finally broke free and then made the good pass.

You won't find a guy showing more composure than Sellers did in that sequence.

Now, it was up to Michael.

Most guys in this situation would have been running away from the ball after what had happened in Game 4. Who wants to blow two shots in a row at the buzzer?

But great players relish taking the ball in these situations. They can't think of anyone but them taking the last shot.

Michael even had a plan about what he wanted to do. "I was going to take a jump shot. I didn't want to drive and take a chance at getting fouled and end up at the line again."

So Michael drove to the foul line. He went up for the jumper and Ehlo went right up with him. Then Ehlo came down and Michael was still up there, hovering, double-pumping, getting everything just right before he released his jumper.

Naturally, it went in. I say naturally, because that is what we have come to expect from Michael.

When he scored, Michael leaped and threw his fist in the air.

"I yelled, 'Take that,' " he said. "All game, the fans had been on me. They had been telling me to practice my foul shots and they were saying that they were going to get me a tee-time. I just wanted to shut them up."

Shutting them up was an understatement. When the ball left Michael's hand, the noise was deafening. When it went in, the place was like Madame Claude's Wax Museum. Whatever is quieter than the sound of silence was what you heard on that Sunday in Richfield, Ohio.

Brad Daugherty would later call the shot, "Unfathomable, simply unfathomable." Remember that Daugherty and Michael were teammates at North Carolina for two years.

Then it was Larry Nance who just said, "Michael Jordan... superstar. That's my only comment."

That was all that needed to be said.

———●

Three days after The Shot, as Michael's jumper had come to

be known, the Bulls were opening a seven-game series with New York. Now, the team really did believe in itself and it was a kind of scary confidence for the opponents—the Bulls thought they were *destined* to do something very special.

From a practical basketball standpoint, I liked the Bulls' chances because I had yet to see a team that could press Michael Jordan. In the regular season, the Bulls went 3–2 against New York with the home team winning each game, but the Bulls were 2–0 after Michael moved to point guard. What I saw was Michael dribbling through the Knicks' press with Pippen and Grant on the wings. I saw a lot of easy lay-ups, and I also saw Hodges wide open to fire away from the 3-point range. Finally, I had a feeling that Bill Cartwright would hold his own against Pat Ewing. And the Bulls saw things the same way and that's exactly how the series went.

Just as was the case in the Cleveland series, the key was the opener, a victory on the road for the Bulls. This time, it was 120–109 as Michael had nine of his 34 points in overtime. He also had 10 rebounds, 10 assists for a triple-double. Ewing had 22 points, 10 rebounds while Cartwright had 18 points and 14 boards. Poor Charles Oakley seemed lost out there as he had only three points and two rebounds.

New York took Game 2, then the Bulls returned to Chicago Stadium and rolled to a 23-point victory in Game 3, a Saturday game where Michael pulled a groin muscle in the second half. He aggravated the same injury he had suffered earlier in the season.

Before Game 4, Knicks' Coach Rick Pitino said he wondered if Michael was "faking" an injury. He later said the Bulls "got what they deserved" if Michael was hurt because Doug had let Michael play too long (39 minutes) in the Bulls' 111–88 victory in Game 3. Making matters worse, Pitino said all these things to the guys with tape recorders and notepads in their hands, and all of it immediately got back to Collins and Michael.

Doug was outraged. "People think that Michael is superman, that he doesn't get hurt, that he isn't frustrated, that he doesn't ache like the rest of us. A pulled groin is painful and Michael is in a lot of pain. I can't believe that anyone would question Michael's heart."

Immediately after Game 3, Michael was treated by trainer

Mark Pfeil and spent the night hooked up to Pfeil's Micro-current Electric Nerve Stimulator. Everyone knew that Michael would play in Game 4. As Oakley has said, "Michael doesn't know he's hurt until they put him in a cast." Nonetheless, there was real concern about how well Michael could play.

   . . . Forty-seven points later, we knew that Michael could play just fine. Rick Pitino knew what the foot he put in his own mouth tasted like as the Bulls were up 3–1 in the best-of-seven series after the 106–93 victory.

As Michael said, "I never considered Rick Pitino a doctor and he's certainly not my doctor."

Mark Pfeil was his trainer and Michael said that, "anywhere I ever play, I want Mark to go with me."

It should be stated that Michael was in pain. At times in the game, he was clearly limping. It sounds crazy to say this, but even though he had 47 points (18 in the fourth quarter) Michael wasn't able to make some of his moves because his leg was bothering him.

James Jordan has told me several times that his son is at his best when he's hurting the most. I've found that to be true and I've thought about why it happens. I believe it is because Michael understands the difference between pain and injury. When he's injured, he raises his concentration level. Instead of becoming a distraction, the pain caused Michael to focus more clearly on the job at hand. He reminds me of one of those guys in the Far East who can walk bare-footed on hot coals or sleep on a bed of nails. They simply obliterate the pain. I have never seen an athlete play through injuries as Michael has, and I'm saying this from the position of a guy who played 844 consecutive NBA games and played with a lot of injuries. Michael simply refuses to let pain undermine him.

After Michael's Show in Game 4, it no longer was a question of will the Bulls beat the Knicks, but when? It happened in Game 6 at Chicago Stadium, a game where the Bulls had a four-point lead with six seconds left, only to see Trent Tucker drill a 3-pointer and then get fouled by Craig Hodges. Tucker made the free throw to tie the score at 111–111 and Doug said, "Craig Hodges is going to kill me yet."

But there were six seconds left, and just as he did in Game 5 at Cleveland, Michael told Hodges not to worry, he would take care of things. Once again, Michael got the ball and drove to the foul line, only this time he was clobbered and the shot didn't go in. But Michael got off the floor, made the two foul shots with four seconds left and the Bulls pulled out a 113–111 victory. Michael went 8-for-8 from the line in the last 78 seconds. I kept saying "Michael needs to make these free throws," and he just kept making them. He ended up with 40 points and the Bulls were in the Eastern Conference finals against Detroit.

After the game, James Jordan told me, "Michael said he wasn't going to miss any more free throws in the fourth quarter."

I said, "I wish you had told me that *before* the game because I was having a heart attack just watching Michael."

A lot of what I remember about the playoffs centers around Michael, but without a center, the Bulls never would have had a crack at the Pistons, which is why Bill Cartwright deserves a lot of credit.

————●

The game that you see in the playoffs is different from the one that is played during the regular season. There is more contact, more accent on being able to beat the hell out of the other guy and holding your ground under the boards. You had better have a good half-court offense or you're going home early, I don't care how fast you are, how much you press or how many different players you use. For references, check the New York Knicks, who pressed their way to 52 wins and then ended up junking their press when the Bulls put the breaks on them in the playoffs. Chicago was ready for the playoffs, New York wasn't. I'm not saying that the fact that the Bulls beat the Knicks in the playoffs means that Cartwright is better than Oakley because you can't compare those guys—one is a center, the other is a power forward. They have different jobs and different talents.

But the Cartwright deal did exactly what it was supposed to for the Bulls:

1. It gave the Bulls a serious low-post player, a guy who could score and draw fouls under the basket. You know that I am a big Dave Corzine fan, but it only took one guy to guard Corzine, since he is a jump-shooting center. Cartwright has several moves near the basket and it usually took two guys to stop him. Guess what? Someone else besides Michael was drawing a double-team. Someone besides Michael was a serious, consistent scoring threat and that was something Oakley could never do for the Bulls.

2. Trading Oakley cleared the decks for Horace Grant to play power forward. Sometimes you just have to make room for a kid if you think he can play and it was time for Grant to play.

3. Suddenly, the Bulls had more depth at center as they had both Corzine and Cartwright. They also have Perdue, who I think has a chance to become a decent big man in the NBA, but it won't happen right away. The Bulls couldn't play Perdue as much as they would have liked because they needed Cartwright on the floor as much as possible to speed the period of adjustment between him and his new team. Perdue must do a lot of work in the off-season. A young player who sat as much as he did during the year has to play as much as possible during the summer. He also needs to build up his stamina because playing center in the NBA will be the most physically demanding thing Perdue has ever tried.

If Perdue is smart, he will watch how Cartwright conducts himself off the court. Bill is a true professional, a man of immense class and just a good person, a sincere family man. You'd never know it from seeing Cartwright play. He seldom smiles and he has the sort of facial expression that makes you say "That's a rough customer out there." He is also an awkward player who has accidentally elbowed some people during his career, but Bill Cartwright is not the ogre that some people in the NBA have made him out to be.

What tells you a lot about Bill is all the garbage he had to put up with in New York. They called him "Medical Bill," because he missed two seasons with a broken foot. He also was "Invisi-Bill" or "Billy Idle." He was an easy target because of his looks, because he sometimes seemed clumsy and because his corkscrew style of shooting seemed so strange. On the court, Bill is no beauty contest winner. As Doug Collins said, "It's easy to malign Bill," and the New York press did.

Nor is Bill the type of person who will scream at writers. He just took the cheap shots—silently—and he waited for a chance to make people gag on their words, which is exactly what happened in the playoffs.

In the opening round, he faced an All-Star center in Brad

Daugherty and held the Cavs' big man to 11 points and 36 percent shooting from the field. In the second round, he went against
another All-Star in Patrick Ewing, a man he backed up in New
York, and more than held his own. What Cartwright did against
Ewing was occupy the big man. Because Bill has a true center's
game—the turnaround jumper, the hook shot and some power
moves to the basket—Ewing had to stay with Cartwright. That
kept Ewing from roving and blocking shots. If Ewing can leave
the opposing center, he will set up a one-man zone in the key
and suddenly you won't be able to drive against the Knicks. The
stats showed that Ewing averaged 20 points, but he shot only
46 percent in the playoffs because Cartwright put his body on
Patrick and kept it there, making Ewing earn every basket. For
his part, Cartwright averaged a highly respectable 14.5 points,
7 rebounds and shot 58 percent.

In other words, Cartwright gave the Bulls precisely what they
wanted when they made the trade—a center who could compete
against the league's best big men. After the playoffs, Cartwright
also had every reason to try and rub it into the Knicks, but that's
not Bill's style.

"People acted like I had this big vendetta against the
Knicks," said Cartwright. "But what I really feel is grateful to
Jerry Krause, Doug Collins and the Bulls' coaches for getting
me. They took a gamble when they traded for a 31-year-old center
and they stayed with me early in the season when things weren't
going well. So when people ask me how I feel the answer is that
I'm happy to be in Chicago."

Cartwright is a man very conscious of his image in the community, his image with his teammates. He wants to do *the right
thing.* In New York, the writers were just begging him to lash
back at his critics, to take a cheap shot at Oakley, who was really
struggling. Instead, Cartwright retained his dignity. On the
court, he has very little grace. Off the court, he is a gentle, graceful man whose character enabled him to step up his game in the
playoffs.

At the other end of the trade was Oakley, who had a
miserable time with New York in the playoffs. By now, it should
be obvious that the Bulls would not have won any more games
with Corzine as their center and Oakley at power forward than
they did with Cartwright in the middle and Horace Grant at

Oakley's old spot. Where the Bulls did miss Oakley was in the dressing room. I'm talking about the area of intangibles. Charles was a good friend to Michael away from basketball and he was Michael's body guard on the court. Charles got along well with everyone on the team and the young players especially were close to him. He cuffed them around as if they were his cubs. Charles was a team leader with the Bulls, a guy who always played hard. He complained about not getting enough shots and liked to talk back to Doug, but I think it's Charles' nature to talk back and to speak out when something is on his mind.

That is a big difference between Cartwright and Oakley—Bill had the ability to bite his tongue and bide his time. Charles was too emotional for that.

When the deal was first made, the consensus among most NBA writers was that the Knicks had pulled another Brinks robbery. And when the Knicks got off to a fast start, much of the credit went to Oakley. But I really wonder how much Charles helped New York and I'm convinced the Knicks would have won 50 games without him. They were a young, talented team ready to take that next step up as Mark Jackson, Gerald Wilkins, Johnny Newman and Ewing mature.

It seemed that Charles didn't fit into their pressing style. He spent a lot of time taking the ball out-of-bounds and sort of running all over the court instead of being positioned under the basket where his rebounding would do the most good. Charles is best in a slow, half-court game which is where the Knicks were at their worst last season.

By the end of the year, Charles started moaning about his lack of shots. . . again. If you take out the stat sheet, it shows that he averaged nearly the same number of points (12.9 to 12.4) and took about the same number of shots per game (10.1 to 9.7) with New York as he did the year before with the Bulls. The big difference was in rebounding. Charles was better in Chicago—13.0 to 10.5 per game.

To me, the bottom line on the trade is this—maybe it helped the Knicks but I doubt that it did very much for Charles. What the deal did was definitely make Cartwright and the Bulls better.

When the Bulls ran into Detroit in the Eastern Conference finals, they ran out of bodies. The Pistons come at you in waves, and a couple of guys on their bench are better than their starters. I would pray that Detroit Coach Chuck Daly would leave Mark Aguirre out there, because I hated to see Mark sit down and Dennis Rodman come into the game. Back-up power forward John Salley played better than starter Rick Mahorn. Detroit's third guard, Vinnie Johnson, goes into his Microwave routine and he's playing on another planet. Back-up center James Edwards was scoring more than starter Bill Laimbeer.

The Pistons are just loaded. Detroit had more talent, more depth and more experience than the Bulls. Early on, Michael & Co. were able to overcome that by sheer desire. As they had in the first two playoff series, the Bulls won the opener on the road and they did it on pure emotion. They won Game 3 at Chicago Stadium 99–97 despite the fact that the Pistons had an 86–72 lead with 7:30 left. They won on Michael's mind-boggling running jumper over Rodman and Isiah Thomas with three seconds left, giving Jordan 46 points.

Afterwards, Michael accurately called it, "a stolen basketball game."

But that would be the end of the thievery. Detroit buckled down and played as well as it could, winning the last three games to advance to the finals and then winning the NBA title. I just wish that Scottie Pippen hadn't been knocked out cold by a Bill Laimbeer elbow only one minute into Game 6. Detroit had the people to overcome the loss of a starting forward, the Bulls didn't.

I've asked myself if Laimbeer's elbow was intentional. Doug Collins thought it was. From looking at the replay, it seems that Laimbeer made a move to get Scottie off him. Did he want to knock Pippen out? Who knows? I just find it ironic that here was Laimbeer, who was ejected for a flagrant foul in Game 3, in the middle of yet another incident. I'm not saying that the Bulls would have won the series if Pippen had stayed healthy because the Pistons are a helluva team. But the stuff Laimbeer and these guys have been doing for years just eats at me.

I know that Commissioner David Stern isn't waiting breathlessly to hear what I think needs to be done. But it's time for the league to hand out some severe suspensions. If it's your first incident, one game. Your second, two games. Anything after that, five or more games. Forget fining these guys. They can write a $5,000 check like you or I pay the water bill. Suspensions are what hurts a player and a team the most, and the league should have guts enough to suspend a player in the middle of the playoffs if he is a Laimbeer-type with a history of fighting.

———●———

This was a tremendous year for Michael, who was even greater than ever. The move to point guard can have a profound effect on his career.

"I have a label that I don't make my teammates better, that I'm just a scorer," said Michael, who reached the 10,000-point level faster than any man in NBA history except Wilt Chamberlain.

But Michael wants to do more and playing point guard lets him do it. By the end of the playoffs, that label had changed.

"I like challenges and I like doing something new," Michael told me late in the season. "Being the point guard is what I need to do for this team. It's where I can show the most leadership, where I can get everyone involved because I can control things—ball distribution, pace of the game, things like that. I'm convinced that I can play that position for the rest of my career, although I'll have to work a lot on my ballhandling in the off season. Look, anybody can go out there and run the offense, make the obvious pass on the first option of a play. But to be a good point guard, you have to be aware of so much, like where everyone is on the court, I mean your teammates and the defense. You have to watch the clock, make sure guys are in position to catch and pass. For example, I never played with a center like Bill Cartwright before. It took me a long time to figure out what he likes and what he doesn't like on the court.

"Then there is the question of when it is best for you to take your own shot. It has given me a greater appreciation of what Magic Johnson does and believe me, I'm no Magic."

Then Michael smiled at me and said, "I'm going to learn how to play the position or die trying."

I don't think we'll have to worry about having to call in the last rites for Michael. If anything, his personality is bigger than ever. His face is on Wheaties boxes and now you see grown men lined up to get Michael to autograph their boxes of cereal. The Spike Lee commercials for Nike where he does the Mars Blackman routine just enhanced Michael's image. So did the Wilson commercials where they say, "Wilson was once the official ball of the NBA. Now it's the official ball of Michael Jordan."

On and on it goes.

Michael and I do have one thing in common as we both recently went into the restaurant business. But there is a difference. At Red Kerr's, I'm there to greet and mingle with the customers. At Michael's place, there is a huge glass-enclosed room in front where you can watch him eat. I guess the crowds have gotten so bad for Michael that the only way he can go out to eat is to buy his own restaurant.

This also was a big year for Michael because his son was born. Before one Bulls game, Michael and I were the only ones in the dressing room and he talked about Jeffrey Michael Jordan:

"We had a game the night Juanita [his fiancée Juanita Vanoy] went into the hospital, we had a game and I didn't think I'd make it for the delivery. I was with Juanita all day in the labor room, then I left and went to the arena for the game. I was hoping the doctors could make the baby just wait a few hours so I could get back from the game in time. Then the game went into overtime and I kept thinking, 'I'm gonna miss it. I bet he's born already.' We won the game, I dressed as fast as I could and got back to the hospital at 10:40. My son was born at 10:49 p.m.

"I was elated to be there on time and to see it. I know this will sound crazy, but I thought if I ever had a chance to come back in a second life, I'd like to be a woman. I used to think I'd like to experience what they go through in becoming a mother, but after watching my son being born, I think I'll skip it because the mother goes through more pain than I'd like.

"I am just amazed to have a son. I love just to watch him. He started crawling, but he was crawling backwards first. For years, I've gotten a kick out of making other people's kids smile, but to get a smile from your own child, it really makes me teary-eyed. I'm just so proud of him. I like bringing him to the games so he can hear the crowd. I just like knowing that when I'm playing, my son is there. It doesn't matter if he's too young to know what is going on. Actually, I don't know if he's going to be a basketball player or not. If it was totally up to me, I'd just hand him a golf club and tell him to have a good time.

"We named him Jeffrey Michael. He is going to have enough pressure growing up as my son without being named Michael Jeffrey Jordan Jr. I wanted him to have my name, but not the pressure, so Michael is his middle name. His mother and I want to make things as easy as possible for him. At the moment, Juanita and I aren't living together. She has her own place downtown and we have a good relationship. Perhaps we will get married one day. We have a commitment to each other to make sure that Jeffrey is taken care of and raised right. If he's happy, then we'll be happy."

————●

Along with the changes in Michael's life, a lot of good things happened to the Bulls.

In some ways, Doug Collins really grew as a coach. This was his most difficult season because of all the changes and adjustments he had to make. He took a lot of heat early when the team was hurt and ragged, then he caught it again late in the year when everyone was hurt again for the final ten games of the regular season.

But what he did was get the Bulls to learn how to play with a center, he found the best position for Michael and he helped Scottie Pippen and Horace Grant become starters in the league. He created a role for Craig Hodges and made a commitment to taking the 3-point shots, not just in desperation but as part of the offense.

That's a lot of changes to make in one year and it wouldn't have happened if the coaching staff wasn't on top of everything. When the playoffs began, it all came together and the Bulls were able to put together their best run since 1974–75.

Assistant Phil Jackson did a great job with the defense, Johnny Bach and Tex Winter helped Doug in several ways. As for Doug, he was his usual nervous self. During games, you'll often see him on one knee looking at index cards. Those cards contain plays that he and the assistant coaches believe will work best against that night's opponent. But sometimes, Doug got so *into* the game that he couldn't remember what pocket he put the cards in, so he sort of frisked himself looking for them.

I don't think I've ever been around a guy who feels every play and every game so deeply. I remember being on a plane coming back from New York in the playoffs and a stewardess recognized Doug and said, "I remember you from about three months ago. You were asleep the last time I saw you."

I said that also was the last time Doug got any sleep. It was good for a laugh, but it wasn't far from the truth. Doug will never be a Cool Hand Collins, but he really does need to relax for his own health. And his emotionalism may have been a factor in his firing.

The 1989 draft was one of the biggest in Bulls' history, with the team owning three first round picks—No. 6, No. 18 and No. 20. You can thank Jerry Krause for two of those choices. He got the No. 6 pick from New Jersey in the Orlando Woolridge deal, and this probably will be the last time the Bulls have a lottery selection in the Michael Jordan era.

On the eve of the draft, he talked Seattle into trading the 18th pick in the draft for Brad Sellers. It's a good deal for both parties. Sellers obviously needs a change of scene and he just wasn't going to play much with the Bulls. Sellers believes he can contribute if he gets some minutes, and now he can prove it with the Sonics. The Bulls got another first-round pick in a draft that I considered fairly deep in terms of players who may not become stars, but who can be productive in the NBA.

A final trade sent Dave Corzine to Orlando. I was sorry to see Dave go, but he just wasn't going to play much this season. With the Magic, he'll start. Krause got not one, but two second-round draft picks from Orlando, and those will be almost the same as late first-round picks; the Magic are destined to finish low in the standings, which means they'll draft high in June.

With the No. 6 pick, the Bulls wanted a big man to back up Horace Grant at power forward and they had the choice of two players—Stacey King or Randy White. Krause loved them both, but he went with King who is 6-foot-11 as compared to White at 6-foot-8.

Remember the importance of a low-post game in the playoffs and how Cartwright was the only Bull who could handle that job? Now they have another guy in King, a 26-point-average scorer from Oklahoma with a sensational turnaround jumper. He gives the Bulls something else they really need—a serious shot blocker. King can play either power forward or back-up center, although the Bulls hope that Perdue will progress enough to relieve Cartwright.

At No. 18, the Bulls went with Iowa's B.J. Armstrong, a 19-point-average scorer who led the Big Ten in assists. B.J. has the 20-foot range on his jumper, yet he handles the ball like a point guard. He is a guy who can fill in for Michael at the point, or run the team if Michael wants to play some shooting guard. Like King, Armstrong gives the Bulls some versatility off the bench and he should make an immediate impact on the team.

The No. 20 pick was a Krause small-college special—Jeff Sanders from Georgia Southern. That's Jeff Sanders as in 6-foot-9, 230 pounds of power forward with a nice shooting touch from 15 feet. He is also a good high-post passer. One guy wrote that he didn't know if Georgia Southern was a university or a train line, but Krause is convinced that Sanders is one of those talents who will be worth a lot in a few years. He'll replace Sellers and is definitely worth a gamble. Hey, we know what kind of player Sellers is and we know that he was limited on the Bulls. Let's see if Sanders can do more.

Going into the draft, the Bulls wanted two big guys and a good little guy. That is exactly what they got, although I think that it may take a full season for these guys to blend in with the team and a new coach.

Doug's firing caught me totally by surprise, just as it did Doug. I saw him at Michael Jordan's golf tournament on July 5, 1989. Doug was there with his attorney, John Langel. We talked about the draft and Doug said how excited he was about getting the young players and how he couldn't wait until training camp started. Then I said, "Hey, Doug, when are you going to come down to my new restaurant?"

Doug said, "Let's do it tomorrow, Red. Tomorrow at 3 p.m. I have a meeting with the front office in the morning."

Tomorrow came and it was at that meeting that the Bulls told Doug that he was no longer the coach. About 11 a.m., I got a call from Bulls' public relations man Tim Hallam and Tim said, "Johnny, are you sitting down?"

I said, "Sure, why?"

"Doug just got fired," said Hallam.

"Tim, come off it," I said. "You know that Doug is coming

over to the restaurant this afternoon. I've got a photographer all lined up to shoot his picture and everything."

"Johnny, I have this statement to read," said Tim, who then indeed read a statement from Bulls' owner Jerry Reinsdorf and general manager Jerry Krause:

"The Chicago Bulls today terminated the contract of Coach Doug Collins. Chairman of the Board Jerry Reinsdorf and Vice-President Jerry Krause said, 'We know it will be an unpopular decision, but it is in the best interest of all parties. We appreciate the effort Doug has given us in the last three years. However, through the years philosophical differences between the management and Doug over the direction the club was going grew to the point where a move was required. We wish Doug all the best in his future endeavors.' "

It was about that time that I dropped the phone and got a really terrible feeling in my stomach. I knew Tim was serious, I knew that Doug was hurting and I knew that the front office was, too. This was a tough time for everybody. It reminded me of occasions when I've had some very close friends sit in my living room and say, "We're getting a divorce." You don't take sides, you just feel bad for the husband *and* wife.

In their statement, the Bulls also said they planned to offer a contract to their first choice to take over for Doug in the near future, and that turned out to be assistant Phil Jackson.

The Bulls were right, this was an unpopular decision. But something that should be considered is that there are no bad guys or villians in this story—Reinsdorf and Krause have spent the money and made the moves to turn this team around. Doug coached his heart out and every year the Bulls improved in the playoffs. Phil Jackson is a good person and is as ready as he'll ever be to be a head coach in the NBA. None of these people wanted to do anything to mess up what is a good situation, and what the Bulls did in replacing Doug with Phil Jackson is what they believe will make that good situation even better. What I am saying is that everybody had the right intentions.

So did it have to happen like this?

The phrase that sticks out is "philosophical differences" between management and Doug. Notice no one said a word about Michael Jordan's role in this. That's because Michael had no role. He and Doug got along well and were good for each other. Doug's biggest problem is Doug, something I've mentioned throughout the book. I've discussed Doug's relentlessness, his perfectionism, his driving personality that kept him up nights, caused him to skip meals and pushed him to the brink of total exhaustion. Over the three years, instead of lightening up, he began coaching with an even heavier hand. He pushed himself too hard, and demanded too much from everyone—himself and the players. The Bulls had concerns about Doug's health and the health of the franchise, because if Doug faltered, so would the Bulls.

Rather than wait too long to make a move, the Bulls felt that they should make it now—give Phil Jackson a training camp and a chance to establish his style as the head coach. To me, that's the right approach—if you have to change coaches, do it in the off-season so the new guy can organize and prepare from day one.

What happened to Doug is the same thing that happens to a lot of young coaches—they want everything *now*. The Bulls were concerned that Doug was sacrificing too much of tomorrow to win today's game. They wanted him to play the rookies more and Michael Jordan a little less.

Something else young coaches often don't understand is the chain of command. It is the general manager's job to get the players and the coach's job to coach them. Sounds simple, but egos can get in the way. Yes, the coach should have a say in roster moves, but in the end it's the head of the general manager that will roll if the draft picks and trades don't work out.

Before he was hired by Jerry Krause, Doug's only coaching experience was as an assistant at Arizona State. In a college program, the coach is the king, the Emperor of the North. What he says, goes. The NBA doesn't work that way. That is a lesson every coach must learn. Doug is a very confident, high profile guy. He was the youngest coach in the NBA when hired by the Bulls, and probably had more to learn than he was willing to admit. I think that the conflict between Doug and the front office was almost like Truman and MacArthur—you had two very strong-willed people. MacArthur was the general, but Truman was president. As Truman said, the buck stopped at his desk so the final decisions were his. So it was with the Bulls. Collins was this team's MacArthur, driving them beyond most expectations. But Jerry Krause and Jerry Reinsdorf are Truman. The future of the Bulls rests on their desks. Like Truman, they pulled the trigger and drew a lot of heat, but it is a move they felt had to be made.

I said earlier that Doug Collins has a chance to be a great coach and I still think so. I hope he thinks about his three years in Chicago and remembers the many things he did that were good and learns from the few things that didn't work out. They say a man really doesn't learn what it means to be a coach until he's been fired. I can say that as a coach who was fired not once, but twice. It does change your perspective and it can teach you a lot about yourself and the business if you let it. In the meantime, Doug will be paid for the last year on his contract with the Bulls. He'll be courted by network and cable television stations and he'll probably be back in the NBA in the near future. Coaches who win 55 percent of their games don't stay out of work for long.

Now the Bulls belong to Phil Jackson, who played for those great New York Knicks teams of Bill Bradley, Willis Reed, Walt Frazier, Earl Monroe and Red Holzman. Jerry Reinsdorf was an admirer of those Knicks teams in which Jackson was a 6-foot-8, backup forward. After 13 years as an NBA player then five years as a coach in the Continental Basketball Association (believe me, that's doing your time in purgatory and paying some heavy dues) followed by two years as a Bulls assistant, Phil Jackson was going to be someone's head coach very soon even if the Bulls hadn't promoted him. Phil has a couple of advantages over the Doug Collins who took over the Bulls in 1986. Phil has sat through meetings with Reinsdorf and Krause. He knows them and they know him. He should be very aware of how that chain of command works. He knows the Bulls and knows exactly what management has in mind. He also was the guy in charge of the Bulls' defense, which has been among the NBA's best the last two years. He has established relationships with the front office, the players and the writers. As a former member of the Knicks, he should know about pressure. Even though he grew up in Montana and went to school in North Dakota, he played basketball in New York, which is pretty good training for coaching in Chicago.

But one thing Phil will need is patience from everyone—the fans, the media, etc. With three rookies, there will be a breaking-in period. The Bulls say they want to cut Michael's minutes because he has spent more time on the court in the last three years than any other NBA player. Doug said the same thing, but had trouble sticking to it. He'd take Michael out, watch a lead slip away and then put Michael back in earlier than planned. If Phil can find a way to save Michael Jordan, that will be a big help to the Bulls come playoff time. It may take a full season for Jackson to get the rookies experienced and to develop a role for Michael, be it as a point guard, a shooting guard or a little of both. So we need to keep our expectations for this team under control, yet we should be excited. Jackson has the credentials of a good coach, the Bulls have raised their talent level and they have gained some serious playoff experience.

All of this means that I can't wait for next year. I can't wait to see how Michael comes back from a summer during which I know he will develop his dribbling skills. I can't wait to see Grant and Pippen after they've had a year of starting behind them. I can't wait to watch how Hodges and Cartwright are further incorporated into the offense and I can't wait to see how some of the Bulls' new players develop. That's because I think about being the first coach of the Bulls and being around for the worst of times. Now I'm ready to see what's ahead and I have a feeling it will be the Bulls at their best.

I get emotionally involved in the game just as a fan would. I say the same things that the fans say—I'm talking about the guy watching from the last row or the guys at the bar watching the game on the television set.

I was here when this franchise was born. And one of the reasons I so desperately wanted to be the Bulls' first coach was that I wanted to make sure the franchise came into the world in the right way, so that I could come back ten or twenty years later and still watch an NBA game in Chicago, even if I had to buy a ticket. Now I get to see all the games, and I feel like a father whose son has grown up, and that kid has turned out even better than the father ever dreamed.